Tualatin High
Media Center

Arthur Conan Doyle

Arthur Conan Doyle

Don Richard Cox

Tualatin High
Media Center

Frederick Ungar Publishing Co.
New York

Dedicated To My Mother
Eva Margaret Means Cox

Library of Congress Cataloging in Publication Data
Cox, Don Richard.
   Arthur Conan Doyle.

   (Literature and life series)
   Bibliography: p.
   Includes index.
   1. Doyle, Arthur Conan, Sir, 1859–1930. 2. Authors, English—19th century—Biography. 3. Authors, English—20th century—Biography. I. Title. II. Series.
   PR4623.C68 1985   823'.8 [B]   84–28050
   ISBN 0–8044–2146–3

Printed and bound in Great Britain by
Biddles Ltd, Guildford and King's Lynn

Contents

Chronology

1859 Born in Edinburgh, Scotland, to Charles and Mary Doyle.

1868–75 Attends Hodder and Stonyhurst, Catholic public schools established and maintained by the Jesuits.

1874 Sees London for the first time when he visits his uncle Richard "Dicky" Doyle, illustrator for *Punch*.

1876 Enters University of Edinburgh to study medicine.

1879 Publishes his first story, "The Mystery of Sasassa Valley," in *Chambers Journal*.

1880 Interrupts his medical studies with a trip to the Arctic as surgeon on a whaling ship.

1881 Returns to school, finishes his medical degree, and travels to Africa as a ship's surgeon.

1882 Begins medical practice in Southsea, accompanied by his younger brother Innes.

1885 Marries Louise Hawkins, the sister of one of his patients.

1887 Publishes *A Study in Scarlet*, the first Sherlock Holmes story, in *Beeton's Christmas Annual*.

1890 Publishes *The Sign of Four*.

1891 Publishes *The White Company*. Begins series of Holmes stories in *The Strand Magazine*.

1893 Tires of Sherlock Holmes. Publishes "The Adventure of the Final Problem," "killing off" the detective.

1895 Travels to Egypt for the winter because of Louise's consumption. Becomes involved in Sudanese war.

1897 Meets Jean Leckie and a close friendship develops.

1899 Boer War begins. Doyle volunteers for combat duty but is rejected because of age.

1900 Serves in South Africa as a medical officer, working in typhoid-ridden Bloemfontein. Publishes *The Great Boer War*.

1901 Begins the serialization of *The Hound of the Baskervilles* in *The Strand*.

1902 Publishes *The War in South Africa—Its Cause and Conduct*. Knighted for his writings defending Britain's role in the Boer War.

1903 Publishes "The Adventure of the Empty House," in which Holmes returns alive from the incident at Reichenbach Falls.

1906 Louise Doyle ("Touie") dies after many years of illness.

1907 Begins his public defense of George Edalji. Marries Jean Leckie.

1912 Publishes *The Lost World*. Begins defense of Oscar Slater.

1914 World War I begins. Doyle visits battlefronts as a correspondent.

1915 Publishes *The Valley of Fear*.

1916 Receives spirit message that completely converts him to spiritualism.

1916–20 Publishes *The British Campaign in France and Flanders*, a six-volume history of the war.

1920 Lectures on spiritualism in Australia. Meets Harry Houdini, beginning an unusual friendship.

1922 Lectures in the United States on spiritualism. Publishes *The Case for Spirit Photography* and *The Coming of the Fairies*, creating a storm of controversy.

1925 Opens his "Psychic Bookshop, Library and Museum" in London.

1926 Publishes *The History of Spiritualism*.

1927 Publishes "The Adventure of Shoscombe Old Place," his last Sherlock Holmes story.

1929 Publishes *The Maracot Deep*, his last novel. Becomes embroiled in ever more bitter arguments over spiritualism.

1930 Dies at Windlesham, his estate, surrounded by his family.

1

Doyle's Life

When Sir Arthur Conan Doyle was buried in 1930, his grave marker bore the following inscription:

STEEL TRUE

BLADE STRAIGHT

ARTHUR CONAN DOYLE

KNIGHT

PATRIOT, PHYSICIAN, & MAN OF LETTERS

If an epitaph is to summarize in some small way the life of the soul it memorializes, then Conan Doyle's epitaph does a perfect job. It metaphorically captures the essence of an extremely courageous man of the highest moral character and principles; he was in all respects an Arthurian gentleman—a true knight.

Arthur Conan Doyle, whose life and work in many ways typified the spirit of Victorian England, was born in Edinburgh in 1859, a year we now associate with the peak of the Victorian era. Wrapped in a glow of optimism, the British Empire at this point of "High Victorianism" seemed to be capable of achieving anything it attempted. It was a prosperous, confident time, a time that prompted the historian G. M. Young later to write, "Of all the decades in our history, a wise man would choose the eighteen-fifties to be young in."[1] Doyle was of course very young in this decade, but he did grow up quite nearly at the center of this era of nationalistic fervor. Although he lived well into an age that was more practical and pragmatic than the years of queen and country in which he spent his youth, he never lost the chivalric idealism that imbued

England in the middle of the nineteenth century.

Doyle's granduncle and godfather, Michael Conan, apparently assisted in the choosing of the name Arthur, and Michael Conan's surname was added to that of the baby who would later make Conan Doyle a name famous around the world. Born into a Roman Catholic family, Arthur Conan Doyle spent a quiet childhood, attending in England the Jesuit schools Hodder and Stonyhurst, and taking occasional vacations to London to visit his famous uncle Richard ("Dicky") Doyle, an illustrator for *Punch* magazine. While at Stonyhurst young Arthur grew even closer to his mother Mary Doyle (Doyle called her "The Ma'am"), and kept in constant touch through detailed letters, a habit he continued throughout her life as he frequently sought her guidance and counsel.

Interested in sports as a youth, the Conan Doyle who returned to Edinburgh to begin university study in 1877 was an active and athletic young man, more distinguished by his performances on the cricket field than those in the classroom. Despite his fairly average academic record, however, Doyle, after careful consultation with his family, decided to study medicine. His fascination with the outdoors—with sport and adventure—as well as his attraction to literature seemed to consume him as much as his interest in medicine. It is difficult to say he made the wrong choice of a career, yet one cannot find that he ever displayed—either in his training or his subsequent practice—any real enthusiasm for this profession. A letter written while he was still a medical student, in fact, suggests that Doyle considered supplementing his income with literary endeavors while he built a reputation in medicine. This was the plan of action he finally did follow out of necessity, of course, but his renown as a man of letters far outstripped his reputation as a physician, ultimately making his medical practice a passing sideline. Indicative of Doyle's diverging interests was his acceptance in 1880 of a position as a ship's surgeon on a whaler bound for the Arctic. Such an adventure undertaken before he had finished his degree or even taken his examinations suggests the restlessness Doyle was feeling in his medical studies. For seven months Conan Doyle was an active participant in a world filled with harpooners, whale boats, and ice floes—and he loved it. This nautical life was so overpowering, in fact, that after a short interlude back at Edinburgh, during which he passed his examinations, he again signed on as a ship's doctor, this time setting sail for Africa.

Returning from this sojourn at sea Doyle was ostensibly ready to begin his career in earnest. There was one final diversion, however, in the person of a Dr. Budd, who had been a medical student with him at Edinburgh. Budd, a flamboyant young man who had built a practice at Plymouth with a combination of bravado and outrageous behavior, invited Doyle to become his assistant. Doyle was both fascinated and horrified by Budd's unusual practice of insulting and abusing his patients. He remained Budd's assistant for only a short time before deciding that he could not live with Budd's abrasive manner. After a dispute he left for Portsmouth to begin his own practice; the bizarre episode with Budd he later transformed into *The Stark Munro Letters*, a thinly disguised fictionalized biography.

Portsmouth was a turning point for Conan Doyle. There he rented a somewhat shabby house in a quiet neighborhood, furnished as best he could the rooms people might see (leaving bare the others), hung up his brass plate, and waited to begin his medical career—and waited. Anyone who has ever sat alone in a quiet house can imagine what some of Conan Doyle's thoughts must have been in the first days at Portsmouth. He was young, educated, strong, eager—and alone and apparently unwanted as a physician. He was joined by his younger brother Innes, who served as a kind of receptionist, ushering in those infrequent patients seeking assistance. In the quiet days and nights that followed, Doyle turned to literature, no doubt seeking to find in that world of the imagination something that would fill the very large void in his real world.

He had done some writing before and actually had published two short stories while he was still a student in Edinburgh. Now, without the pressures of medical school or the pressure of a bustling career, Doyle could devote a good deal of energy to his writing. One early story, "J. Habakuk Jephson's Statement" (1884), has a curious history. Published anonymously, it was a fictionalized "eyewitness account" explaining the mysterious "ghost ship" *Mary Celeste*, found floating abandoned near Portugal in 1872. Ostensibly written by Habakuk Jephson, a survivor of the tragedy, the story was accepted by some readers as the truth, demonstrating that even at this early stage Doyle was able to create fictional characters and situations so real that their existence was believed to be factual. The realism of stories such as this, however, did not mean Doyle was a financial success as a writer. He was finally forced to rent some of the vacant rooms in his house to supplement his income.

But better times were to come in Portsmouth. In 1885 he met and married Louise Hawkins, the sister of one of his patients. Then in 1886 he finished what must be considered the single most important book of his career (because it established the beginning of his career)–*A Study in Scarlet*. But even this novel introducing Sherlock Holmes to the world was not an instant success, and it was turned down by a number of publishers before appearing in *Beeton's Christmas Annual* in December 1887. He sold the book for twenty-five pounds. Doyle then turned to work on *Micah Clarke* (1889), an historical novel emblematic of the type of fiction he seemed to prefer writing, finished it and began research on *The White Company* (1891), a novel of the fourteenth century.

It was the publication of the second Holmes novel, *The Sign of Four*, in 1890 that established clearly the direction his life as an author would take. Doyle would continue to write historical fiction, supernatural fiction, and adventure stories, but what the public wanted was Holmes and Watson. In 1891 *The Strand Magazine* published "A Scandal in Bohemia," the first of the tales that were later anthologized as *The Adventures of Sherlock Holmes*. Illustrated by Sidney Paget, whose drawings caught so deftly the precise image of Holmes and Watson, the stories were to become progressively more popular. And the more popular the Holmes stories became the more money *The Strand* offered Doyle to write new ones. As the sums in the contracts spiraled ever higher, the more difficult it became for him to turn them down. He wrote the first six stories for two hundred pounds; the next six were sold for three hundred pounds; the next twelve he agreed to write for one thousand pounds. And so it went for the next thirty-five years, through fifty-six short stories and four novels. The circulation of *The Strand* rose to half a million, and Dr. Arthur Conan Doyle did not need to practice medicine anymore.

During the next few years after Holmes became a household word Doyle moved about freely, living in Switzerland to alleviate his wife's tuberculosis, traveling to the United States for a lecture tour in 1894, visiting Egypt in 1896, and finally returning to England in 1896 to settle in a somewhat permanent fashion.

In the ten years since the publication of *A Study in Scarlet* he had become a celebrity. He now had two children and a solid income as a writer. He had also become publicly involved in the cause of spiritualism, a subject that would absorb more and more of his time—and his income—

for the next thirty years. Furthermore, by 1897 he had also met and fallen in love with Jean Leckie, the woman who was to become his second wife ten years later. His attachment to Jean—one cannot truly call it an affair—is one of the more curious aspects of Conan Doyle's life. Doyle, the consummate gentleman, would never bring disgrace or dishonor to his marriage or his wife Louise, and so, although he was in love with Jean Leckie, he refused to divorce Louise. Instead, he and Jean agreed to live apart as platonic lovers as long as Louise lived. This was an arrangement known about and condoned by Doyle's mother and in time by his sisters and children as well. Louise Doyle's health was such that she remained a semi-invalid the last ten years of her life while Sir Arthur kept this secret from her. Some may find it ironic, given Conan Doyle's refined sense of chivalry, that he genuinely seems to have felt no guilt at all about this romance. It is perhaps because Doyle, unlike other Victorians who also had "secret lives" and secret loves, steadfastly refused to consummate his romance that he avoided the guilt and frustration that wracked some of his contemporaries. In his mind, and apparently in the minds of all those who were party to his romance, his actions were completely honorable. Given the impeccable character of Doyle, one has to believe they were.

As the century closed, the autumn of 1899 brought war in South Africa. The Boer War (1899–1902) was fought to determine the control of the Transvaal and the Orange River Colony. Inhabited by Dutch settlers, these territories were held by the Boers, but loosely claimed by the British. Still, it was the Boers who provoked the confrontations by harassing British colonials in the area, then issuing an ultimatum and insisting that all British claims be withdrawn. An angered England responded, and a war many British believed would be short and simple began.

For Doyle, the patriot who had grown up with stories

of the Napoleonic wars and the Crimean War, this was a golden moment. This war would be fought for and by "The Empire," and Conan Doyle, as his history of the event repeatedly illustrates, was fascinated by the fact that soldiers from so many different social classes, military units, and parts of the world were fighting side by side for the same queen. He could not sit on the sidelines; he volunteered for duty before the year was out. It was a selfless, courageous decision on his part. He was forty years old, and he was leaving behind his children and his ill wife. There was always the chance that he, like many other British soldiers, would not survive the hazards of the campaign. In a letter Doyle wrote to his mother thanking her for understanding his decision to volunteer he revealed a part of his character. "What I feel," he wrote, "is that I have perhaps the strongest influence over young men, especially young athletic sporting men, of any one in England (bar Kipling). That being so it is really important that I should give them a lead. It is not merely my 40-year old self–though I am as fit as ever I was, but it is the influence I have over these youngsters. . . . If all is well I shall see a bit of history in the making[;] if men are wanted I shall help to make it." On the dangers of the war Doyle noted: "I have gone carefully into my money affairs and there is ample to keep you *all* going if I were not here. I shall draw a careful will. If it were not so I should not feel justified. All our Xmases are dark this year, but they will be lighter in the future if we all do our duty to the highest."[2]

Doyle was to serve as a medical officer (he volunteered for combat duty first and was rejected because of his age), but this was not a particularly "safe" assignment, because typhoid outbreaks claimed as many casualties as Boer guns. Despite the exhausting hours and the lack of staff in his field hospital, Doyle threw himself into the experience with characteristic intensity. It would not be fair to him to say he enjoyed the war, but the hardships of Africa, like the hardships of the Arctic he had previously experienced, presented the emotional and physical challenge on which Doyle thrived. He would never regret his participation, and when he returned to England he carried on the fight at his desk, writing a massive history and analysis of the struggle, *The Great Boer War* (1900), and then writing and overseeing the publication of a shorter volume defending and explaining Britain's part in the war, *The War in South Africa, Its Cause and Conduct* (1902), that was translated into many languages and sold worldwide. It was for these books and his patriotic support of his country in the South African struggle that Sir Arthur Conan Doyle was knighted by Edward VII in 1902. It was characteristic of Doyle that he hesitated over accepting the award because he felt he had done only what any loyal citizen should have done.

The end of the Boer War brought with it not just peace, but the return of Sherlock Holmes. In 1899, an American, William Gillette, had gone on tour with a play entitled *Sherlock Holmes*, collaborating on its dramatization with Doyle. The success of this tour brought a renewed flurry of interest in the detective that Doyle had "killed off" in "The Final Problem" in 1893. There has been a great deal of discussion on Doyle's attitude about Holmes. Some who knew him contended he despised his creation; others have stated that it was only the pressure of coming up with new and clever stories that Doyle disliked. Clearly Holmes was the vehicle that had given Doyle the literary prominence he now held. Partly because of the constant inquiry about the fate of Holmes, partly because of the renewed commercial possibilities (although Doyle did not now have the same need for money he had in 1887), partly because he must have felt—at midlife, with his African war behind him—he had reached a certain watershed or turning point in his life, he then returned to the fixed points in his changing world—Holmes and Watson. He wrote what many consider his very best story, *The Hound of the Baskervilles* (1902), being careful to set the story in a time frame before the detective's plunge into the Reichenbach Falls so that Holmes was still safely dead and apparently beyond resurrection.

The reaction to the new Sherlock Holmes novel was quite predictable; *The Hound of the Baskervilles* was a smashing success and the inevitable clamor for more went up. Doyle responded by agreeing to create a new series of stories for *The Strand* in 1903. To do so he felt he needed Holmes alive again, so he explained away his supposed death and was able to extend Holmes's "life" well into the twentieth century. Of course the price for each Holmes story had gone up. He sold the American rights for five thousand dollars a story, earning in the United States alone as much per story as he received for the entire last twelve he had written.

This new century first brought Doyle political aspirations. He made a bid to be elected to Parliament in 1900 and was defeated. He tried again in 1906 and was again defeated. Deciding that a formal political career was not in his future, Conan Doyle then became involved in the causes of several individuals who had apparently suffered legal injustices. One of the penalties of being the creator of Sherlock Holmes was that people often wrote Doyle asking for help in solving their own mysteries. Several of these calls for help were answered by Doyle, who could not look the other way when wrong was being done. The more famous of these episodes cost him a great deal of time and money. Unfortunately his work did not always even win him the gratitude of those he helped.

There was, for example, the case of George Edalji, the son of an east Indian minister. Edalji was accused and convicted of cruelly slaughtering and mutilating farm animals on mysterious midnight wanderings through the countryside. Doyle approached the case as Holmes would have done, collecting and evaluating evidence the police had missed. Although Doyle was not able to overturn Edalji's conviction, his persistence in this matter actually resulted in the creation of a new division within the courts–the Court of Criminal Appeal–intended to prevent similar injustices from occurring in the future.

In the case of Oscar Slater, Conan Doyle's efforts were ultimately successful, but the struggle for vindication lasted twenty years. In 1908, Slater, an unemployed gambler with a sketchy criminal record, was accused of a diamond theft and brutal murder. Identified by witnesses after his apprehension, Slater was convicted and sentenced to life imprisonment. As he did in the Edalji case, Doyle published extended analyses of the evidence involved in this crime and argued for a review. Years slipped by, World War I intervened, and it seemed as though Doyle's crusade was in fact hopeless. In 1927, however, Doyle's exhaustive efforts paid off. Slater was released from prison, a special act of Parliament was passed to grant a retrial, and the retrial finally cleared Slater of suspicion. Conan Doyle was once again a hero, refusing to give in to injustice as long as he felt he had truth on his side.

In Doyle's personal life the new century also brought several changes. His wife Louise died in 1906. Slightly over a year later, to the surprise of absolutely no one who knew him, he married Jean Leckie. They honeymooned in the Mediterranean and the Middle East and their next few years together were quiet ones. In 1909 he wrote and produced a play based on his book *The Tragedy of the Korosko* (1898). It was not terribly successful, but another effort, *The Speckled Band* (based, of course, on that Holmes story), was very popular, proving once again that Holmes would always be his lucky charm. Jean also brought a certain luck to Conan Doyle by giving him three new children—two boys and a girl—in rapid succession. This second family was a genuine source of delight and fascination to him; one book, *Three of Them* (1923), was generated directly by his conversations with these children.

In 1912 Doyle published what is probably his best known story that does not involve Sherlock Holmes—*The Lost World*. For it Doyle also created what would become his second most popular hero, Professor Challenger, a loud, fiery scientist who is the antithesis of Holmes in nearly every respect. Challenger's trip into the Amazon jungle, where he discovers dinosaurs who have been living for centuries unknown to civilized man, caught the imagination of readers, perhaps because in 1912 there were still vast unexplored regions in the world that very well might be inhabited by such creatures. Challenger, like Holmes, returned in several scientifically oriented adventure stories, but his popularity never really came close to equalling that of Holmes and Watson. Another landmark work at this time was Doyle's short story "Danger!" In this piece of fiction Doyle envisioned what would happen if a fleet of enemy submarines surrounded Great Britain and cut off all shipping. The startling efficiency of this fictional attack that forces Britain to surrender in a matter of weeks was proof, Doyle felt, of the island's basic vulnerability to German U-boats. His foresight was unfortunately proved to be valid a few years later during World War I when German submarines were able to strike with all the precision Doyle had predicted.

Conan Doyle's public campaign for better submarine defense (and a call for a tunnel to be dug under the English Channel) reflected his conviction that the British fighting machine was not as innovative as it should be. Doyle certainly was charmed by the pomp and splendor of the military, but his experiences with Boer commandos in

South Africa had convinced him that some of that pomp had outlived its usefulness. He repeatedly urged his government to experiment with new equipment and concepts, and, as was the case with his predictions about submarines, history has proved that Doyle was usually right.

In 1914 he visited the United States and Canada, stopping at places as disparate as Niagara Falls and Sing Sing prison. Treated royally wherever he went, Conan Doyle returned to England just a few weeks before the outbreak of World War I. The Great War, as it was known to him in that time before anyone could imagine there would ever be another, in most respects marked the end of Conan Doyle's fiction-writing career. There was his final Sherlock Holmes novel, *The Valley of Fear* (1915), and a few more Holmes stories in *The Strand*, but most of his work for the years following World War I (a considerable body of material) was nonfiction prose. He wrote several books about World War I, including his six-volume history *The British Campaign in France and Flanders* (1916–19). He spent most of the last fifteen years of his life, however, writing and speaking on spiritualism, the cause that filled his life totally, closing out all other interests.

The spiritualist movement of the early twentieth century was a phenomenon that has largely ceased to exist in the form Doyle knew it. There are people today, of course, who are advocates of spiritualism; that is, they believe that the spirits of the dead can be contacted and messages from the "other side" can be transmitted from these dead souls. In Doyle's time, however, these spirits not only spoke to assembled seances, they blew trumpets, banged tambourines, and generated "ectoplasm," an oozy rubberlike material which was the substance that apparently composed their essence. "Spirit photography," capturing the images or coronas of these spirits on film, was also very popular. Although there were ardent spiritualists in the nineteenth century (and in fact they have existed throughout history), it was in the years immediately following World War I that the movement truly caught fire. Popular interest in this communication with the dead seemed to decline sharply with the depression of the thirties, perhaps because the economic crisis caused people to focus on the problems of this world rather than the next one, or perhaps because the often promised "breakthrough" that spiritualists continually forecast never occurred.

There is evidence that Doyle was interested in the spiritualist phenomenon for much of his life, even as far back as his days at Portsmouth. Like many others, moreover, he lost friends and relatives in the war and this seemed to intensify his interest. Sometime in 1916 he received what he felt was absolute proof of the validity of spiritualism in the form of a message from Jean's dead brother Malcolm, and he began making public lectures on the subject soon afterwards. Doyle's efforts on behalf of the spiritualist cause lent a credibility of sorts to the movement, but probably damaged his own reputation in the process. There were a number of frauds and tricksters pretending to be mediums, and, as one might expect, these people were all too ready to stage phony "reunions" with lost loved ones for the grieving and gullible.

Doyle deplored the frauds as much as anyone, but the frequent exposure of faked seances did not shake his faith one bit. First of all, he himself had received a number of spirit messages containing information he insisted only the dead could have known; he was convinced these contacts were genuine. Second, he argued, quite logically, that the exposure of a phony medium, or a thousand phony mediums, did not make the messages received by genuine mediums any less real. Finally, when some of the respected and supposedly genuine mediums were caught performing hoaxes, Doyle simply contended that they had been driven to fraud because their genuine contacts with the dead were not established as easily and repeatedly as the public demanded. Again, he argued, catching a trusted medium cheating did not mean that all of that medium's contacts were fraudulent. In some ways Conan Doyle's attitudes about spiritualism were the opposite of what many might have expected from the creator of the great rational thinker Sherlock Holmes. Holmes might have disbelieved in spirits until he discovered sufficient proof that they did exist; Conan Doyle, however, seemed to want to believe in the presence of spirits, and would challenge anyone to come up with definitive proof they did *not* exist.

He found no more skeptical observer of spiritualism than Harry Houdini, the famous American magician. Doyle met Houdini in England in 1920, and their friendship continued until Houdini's death in 1926. In some ways the men were exact opposites. Sir Arthur Conan Doyle was large, distinguished, a very traditional English gentleman whose achievements had been recognized by royalty; Harry Houdini (whose real name was Ehrich Weiss) was a short, stocky, flamboyant showman who had made his reputation on the vaudeville stage. Houdini, of course, knew all of the tricks mediums used to fake seances, and his position on the issue was that he had never seen the performance of a medium he could not duplicate himself with his own "magic." Still, Houdini approached spiritualism with an open mind, and even though he exposed dozens of fake mediums who had preyed upon the gullible, Houdini, like Doyle, did not feel that their existence precluded the possibility that some true psychics existed. In any case, Houdini was impressed by Conan Doyle's integrity and sincerity and treated him with respect, even though his admiration for Doyle was severely strained by Doyle's childlike faith in the supernatural. Doyle, for example, believed Houdini actually possessed supernatural powers, perhaps even the power to dematerialize, and insisted that these powers explained Houdini's success as a magician. Houdini's denials, strangely enough, did not alter Conan Doyle's opinions much, because Doyle believed it was quite possible that Houdini was unaware of his own capabilities.

It was this kind of blind acceptance when dealing with the unexplained that caused Doyle to be derided in the press when his published statements seemed particularly naive. Doyle's book *The Coming of the Fairies* (1922), for example, which presented what he felt was solid proof of the existence of fairies and elves, brought a solid round of condemnation. Such rejection from a public that had so often praised and even demanded his work must have had at least a chastening effect on Doyle. It was not as devastating for him as it might have been for others, however, because he was convinced that he had the truth on his side. Many times before, his had been the lone voice raised on behalf of a particular cause, whether it was a belief in the power of submarines as strategic weapons or the innocence of George Edalji. He was quite used to embarking on quests that seemed futile and battling alone against the establishment. He had complete faith that on the issue of spiritualism, as had happened so many times before, he would ultimately be proved correct.

In 1920 he and his wife (who was now a practicing medium herself) took their spiritualist crusade to Australia. He followed this up in 1922 with a trip to the United States where he presented more lectures on spiritualism; these were mostly well received, although there was the expected skeptical reaction in the newspapers. While in the United States he met again with Houdini, and Jean conducted a seance that supposedly produced a written message from Houdini's dead mother. Houdini totally rejected the message (although not in the presence of the Doyles), because the message was in English, a language his Jewish mother never learned. A more successful experience for Doyle on this visit was the screening of a new movie, *The Lost World*, starring Wallace Beery and based on Doyle's Professor Challenger novel. It is not clear why Doyle could accept the animated dinosaur models he saw in the film as camera tricks and also believe that the many "spirit photographs" he had been shown were genuine.

His first spiritualist tour of the United States was so successful Conan Doyle made a second crusade in 1923. When he returned to England afterward he began work on his two-volume *History of Spiritualism* (1926), and wrote his last Holmes stories for *The Strand*. These stories were not as well received as his earlier pieces had been, partly because of their own weaknesses, and partly because Doyle himself was no longer as respected as he once had been. Some articles in the press were quite scornful of all his work; he did not seem to be winning this battle as he had the others. He announced the permanent retirement of Holmes and plunged back into the spiritualist cause, opening his own spiritualist bookstore in 1925. He served as the Acting President of the International Spiritualist Congress in Paris in 1925 and traveled to Africa to present lectures on the subject in 1928. All of this activity was taking its toll on him physically. His spirit remained strong, but his giant frame began to weaken and he himself admitted he was beginning to be worn down by his work. A fire at his home in 1929 seriously damaged the building, but Doyle and his family were unhurt; the loss was another setback for him, however. A final speaking tour in 1929 took him to Scandinavia and he returned exhausted, heavily dependent on bottled oxygen.

These last few months of his life were not happy ones for Conan Doyle, and were marred by disputes probably generated in part by his failing health and invalid condition. He angrily resigned from the London Spiritualist

Alliance, and then, in a bitter dispute, also resigned from the Society for Psychic Research. His actions brought a good deal of attention from the press and it seemed his reputation was going to continue its decline. Finally, on the morning of July 7, 1930, an ailing Conan Doyle asked to be moved from his sickbed to his armchair. More oxygen was sent for but it arrived too late. The tired but resolute knight died in his armchair, his loyal family seated about him.

2

Historical Fiction

Historical fiction is not as popular a genre today as it once was. In the nineteenth century all the major novelists–Dickens, Thackeray, Eliot, Hardy, and of course Scott, to name a few–wrote historical fiction and considered it the proper work of any serious novelist. Today historical fiction is seldom written by most serious artists, and exists primarily in the "romance," a kind of fiction churned out by teams of writers for adolescent audiences. Seriously crafted historical fiction, such as Norman Mailer's *Ancient Evenings* or Umberto Eco's *The Name of the Rose*, is a rarity in today's literary marketplace.

Such was not the case in Conan Doyle's time. He spent a good deal of his career researching and writing serious historical fiction. And the work involved in research should not be minimized. Doyle would frequently spend months with dozens of history books absorbing both the atmosphere and detail necessary for making his fiction accurate as well as interesting. The finished products read so smoothly it is easy to overlook the sheer amount of factual data Doyle has slipped into his fiction, or to forget that these details are things about which he has only read and not experienced firsthand.

Before *A Study in Scarlet* was actually published, while it was still making the rounds of publishers in fact, Doyle began work on his first "serious" literature, a historical novel called *Micah Clarke*. *Micah Clarke* (1889) is subtitled *His Statement as Made to His Grandchildren Joseph,*

18

Gervas and Reuben During the Hard Winter of 1734, and takes the form of a narrative related by an old man about his adventures as a youth. The novel is more history than fiction in some respects, and includes a short appendix of notes explaining and clarifying historical details in the story.

Essentially the book recounts the ill-fated 1685 campaign of James Scott, the Duke of Monmouth. Monmouth, the illegitimate son of Charles II, groomed himself for accession to the throne and was encouraged to some degree by Charles. Charles's brother, the Duke of York, who was the heir presumptive, was unpopular because of his Catholicism, so a struggle for the right to succeed Charles evolved between the Duke of York and the handsome and popular Monmouth. Charles finally threw his support to his brother, but Monmouth, who had fallen under the influence of the Duke of York's enemies, continued his campaign, encouraging public demonstrations of support. With the death of Charles early in 1685 the stage was set for a showdown. Monmouth, who had been living in exile on the continent, returned to England with a small group of men and assembled an army from the citizens who joined his cause.

It is at this point that Doyle picks up Monmouth's struggle. Micah Clarke is turning twenty-one in the spring of 1685 when Monmouth returns to claim the throne. The question of whether Monmouth's claims have merit is a vexing one for Clarke, but he becomes convinced that the real issue is not Monmouth's right to accession, but the struggle against James II's Catholicism. If James II is not removed, he is told, Protestantism cannot be preserved in England. Clarke joins Monmouth's army then, and embarks on what amounts to a religious crusade. There are frequent references to the Civil War that had taken place less than fifty years before when

Charles I had lost his throne (and his head) to the Puritans.

The high points of the novel are also the high points of Monmouth's campaign–his triumphant entry and "coronation" at Taunton, and his rebel army's final defeat at Sedgemoor. Through this Doyle weaves the adventures of Clarke, who comes of age by narrowly escaping death several times in his perilous fight on behalf of the losing side. What is most interesting about the novel is Doyle's attitude about the uprising. It is not clear there was a "right side" in this conflict. Monmouth was to some extent the people's choice, but he was technically a rebel and his self-coronation illegal. James II won the battle and retained the crown in 1685, but fled the country in 1688 during the "Glorious Revolution," and lost the throne to William and Mary in 1689.

Doyle captures the ambivalence many Britons must have felt in this conflict. Monmouth is seen by Clarke as a fundamentally weak leader, yet he is nevertheless attracted to the pretender's dashing, aristocratic manner. Micah cannot summarily dismiss the man or his campaign. In the final pages, for example, Clarke says that Monmouth "showed in his last moments some faint traces of that spirit which spurted up now and again from his feeble nature, like the momentary flash of an expiring fire." Of course, at the time he writes these words Clarke is an old man and aware of the way the historical drama ended, an insight he did not have when he was twenty-one. Finally, it is this ambivalent attitude about Monmouth and the revolution that makes the book interesting, for these ambiguities elevate it above the status of an historical adventure novel. It is a bildungsroman that ends neither in triumph or tragedy–a rarity to say the least.

Doyle's next historical novel, *The White Company* (1891), is his most famous and also one of his favorite works, but may not appeal to most twentieth-century readers. Set midway in the Hundred Years War, during the reign of Edward II, the novel opens in 1366 with the expulsion of John of Hordle from the Abbey of Beaulieu. On the same day Alleyne Edricson, a clerk and ward of the Abbey, turns twenty and sets forth to explore the world outside its walls. Together they join the forces of Sir Nigel Loring, leader of the White Company, in his campaign against France and Spain. This is an age of heroism with which Doyle was always in love, the source of endless stories he had heard as a boy. His description of the troops of the White Company preparing for their march reflects his awe:

In front stood the bowmen, ten deep, with a fringe of under-officers, who paced hither and thither marshalling the ranks with curt precept or short rebuke. Behind were the little clump of steel-clad horsemen, their lances raised, with long pensils drooping down the oaken shafts. So silent and still were they, that they might have been metal-sheathed statues, were it not for the occasional quick, impatient stamp of their chargers, or the rattle of chamfron against neckplates as they tossed and strained. A spear's length in front of them sat the spare and long-limbed figure of Black Simon, the Norwich fighting man, his fierce, deep-lined face framed in steel, and the silk guidon marked with the five scarlet roses slanting over his right shoulder.[1]

It should not come as a surprise to learn that Doyle, obviously impressed by this image of "metal-sheathed fighting machines," should later advocate a return to body armor and metal shields for Britain's twentieth-century army.

In the battles that ensue we see heroic ideals and manly courage displayed on every side. Sir Nigel, for example, places a black patch over one eye, and pledges not to remove it until he has demonstrated his valor in battle.

(Sir Nigel, it should be added, is well into gray-headed middle age, and is not a young knight.) Such a self-imposed handicap he accepts willingly as "the path of honour" (WC, p. 169). Later, when Sir Nigel defeats a Spanish soldier, "the picked lance of the monkish Knights of Santiago, who had won fame in a hundred bloody combats with the Moors of Andalusia" (WC, p. 333), he removes the patch, saying the knight "was a person from whom much honor might be won" (WC, pp. 335–36). There are jousts, shooting matches, brawls in taverns, encounters with maidens in distress, and castles under siege. The novel culminates in a massive battle against sixty-five thousand Spanish and French troops. Undaunted by the challenge, the White Company follows Sir Nigel's commands—"Now order the ranks, and fling wide the banners, for our souls are God's and our bodies the king's, and our swords for Saint George and for England!" (WC, p.330)—and its troops are decimated in the struggle. Except for a handful of men the White Company is no more.

Alleyne Edricson, who was sent from the battle to seek assistance, survives, as does his friend John of Hordle. Alleyne is knighted and marries Sir Nigel's daughter Maude, snatching her from the door of the church just before she, grieving because she has heard all in the White Company are dead, enters a nunnery. Even Sir Nigel, who was taken prisoner and believed to be dead, turns up again in England and the family can live happily ever after. "So they lived," Doyle concludes, "these men, in their own lusty cheery fashion—rude and rough, but honest, kindly and true. Let us thank God if we have outgrown their vices. Let us pray to God that we may ever hold their virtues" (wc, p. 352). Although the novel was a moderate success, it never gained the reputation Doyle had hoped it would. Still, he was so impressed by the spirit of this chivalric age he returned to it several years later in a second novel, one he described in his memoirs as his most solid contribution to literature.

Sir Nigel (1906), first serialized in *The Strand*, returns to several of the characters of *The White Company* and tells the story of their exploits as youths. (It is what has recently been dubbed a "prequel" rather than a sequel, because its action precedes that found in the original work.) In *Sir Nigel* we follow the exploits of Squire Nigel Loring from 1348 to 1356 and the eve of his wedding. Although Doyle was quite proud of this novel, the book contains little that cannot be found in *The White Company*. Nevertheless there are more fierce battles, brave knights, strong bowmen, dastardly villains, and innocent maidens. Furthermore, given the list of books Doyle claims in his preface to have consulted, we must assume it is all historically accurate.

Although the novel is a bildungsroman of sorts, there is no real psychological development on the part of Nigel. The book is essentially an adventure story, and its climax coincides with the peak of the physical action—the Battle of Poitiers in 1356. Historically, in this struggle King John II of France was captured by English soldiers and then imprisoned. In Doyle's fictional account it is Squire Nigel Loring to whom King John surrenders, and Squire Nigel is knighted Sir Nigel because of this heroic deed and his selfless actions. In knighting Sir Nigel the young Prince of Wales says to his men, "I swear by my father's soul that I had rather have the honor this Squire has gathered than all the richest ransoms of France."[2] After such praise there is no higher plane Sir Nigel can aspire to (in this novel at least), so the book quickly ends with Doyle reflecting on the past and the "men who loved honor more than life" (*SN*, p.346).

Not all of Doyle's historical fiction involves the distant past, however. Like Hardy, who was roughly his contemporary, Doyle was interested in the early years of the nineteenth century, the age of Napoleon. *Rodney Stone* (1896) is set in that era and, like many of Doyle's historical novels, is a tale told by an aging narrator about his youth. As a child, young Conan Doyle had of course sat at the knees of aging relatives and listened to just such histories; in an age when the oral tradition was so much stronger than it is today, this convention must then have seemed to Doyle to be the perfect format for his storytelling.

In this case the setting is England, shortly after the turn of the century and just before the Regency, a time of fops, dandies, and "sporting gentlemen." The novel is more complicated than some of his, weaving the story of the coming of age of the narrator, Rodney Stone, with a Dickensian murder mystery and a detailed portrait of the sport of boxing as it existed in the early nineteenth century. Doyle writes his better books when he combines multiple themes, and he is obviously fascinated by this culture that provides such a study in contrasts.

On the one hand there is the brutality of bareknuckle boxing matches. Held under the open sky and ready to be transported to the next county at the approach of an unfriendly magistrate, such matches could last forty rounds or more, continuing until both opponents were bloodied and exhausted and one finally could not stand. On the other hand there are the promoters of this violence, whom Doyle calls a "circle of dandies, . . . [with] their dainty little hats, their wonderful waistcoats, and their boots in which one could arrange one's cravat."[3]

In the middle of this world Doyle drops his narrator, who (like the athletic Doyle, one might assume) admires the "manliness" of the boxing, and attempts to find some redeeming values in the foppery. Although he cannot find much sympathy with those who debated endlessly about velvet and lace, Doyle (in the persona of Stone) maintains a somewhat neutral stance, noting finally only that "they

lived strange lives, these men, and died strange deaths"
(*RS*, p.168). The novel's climax comes with the conclusion of a monumental boxing match and the nearly simul-
taneous solution of the murder mystery. Stone's story of
his brush with the world of Beau Brummel closes with his
looking forward to telling of his sea adventures in the
Napoleonic wars, but that book, if it was foreseen by
Doyle, was never written.

Other Napoleonic tales were written, however. The
first of these was the very short novel *The Great Shadow*
(1892). The "shadow" in the title is that of Napoleon
Bonaparte, the man "who had cast that great shadow over
Europe, which darkened the nations for five-and-twenty
years."[4] The novel is the story of Jack Calder, a young
man living on the coast of Scotland who falls in love with
his cousin Edie. Edie, however, is attracted to a mysterious stranger, "Bonaventure de Lapp," who arrives in
their village one day. In his disappointment Calder and
his best friend Jim Horscroft join the army to fight Napoleon, who was an exile on Elba at the opening of the
novel. The action moves quickly to the battle of Waterloo, which occupies a good portion of the book, and
which even those who do not like action must admit is
excellently treated and extremely exciting. "Bonaventure
de Lapp," who has married cousin Edie, turns out to be
B. de Lissac, aide-de-camp to Napoleon. At the battle of
Waterloo, the climax of the novel, both Jim and de Lissac
are killed. (Jim kills him and is promptly bayoneted on
the spot.) But de Lissac lives long enough to give Jack a
final message for Edie. Jack delivers it to Edie, whom he
now sees for the shallow person she is, and then leaves her
forever. She remarries and dies in childbirth; he goes to
Scotland, marries, rears seven children and lives happily
ever after. According to Jack, "the great shadow had been
cleared away from Europe, and should no longer be
thrown across the breadth of the lands, . . . darkening

lives which should have been so happy" (*GS*, p. 183). As for himself, he is content to live a quiet life in relative isolation, because, in his words, "we have had our romance, when Jim and I went a-wooing, and the man with cat's whiskers came up from the sea" (*GS*, p. 184).

But Doyle's best Napoleonic fiction was yet to come. It was not his two other Napoleonic novels, *Uncle Bernac* and *The Refugees*, which according to one biographer "represent the reef on which his historical fiction foundered,"[5] but a series of short stories about a French cavalryman, Brigadier Gerard. After Holmes and Professor Challenger, Doyle's next most popular fictional creation was Gerard. Doyle wrote a total of sixteen stories about this gallant soldier of Napoleon. The first eight were published in *The Strand* in 1894–95 and collected as *The Exploits of Brigadier Gerard* (1896); the second eight stories were published in *The Strand* in 1900–03 and collected as *Adventures of Gerard* (1903). During most of this time, it should be noted, Sherlock Holmes was "dead" and not a character Doyle was planning to resurrect.

Although at first Gerard seems to resemble no other major character in Doyle, if one looks closely one can see resemblances to an assortment of military figures sprinkled throughout his historical fiction. Gerard is a braggart who is never more happy than when singing his own praises. He is also an excellent swordsman, the best rider in Napoleon's entire army, and a lover who bewitches (and is in turn bewitched by) every attractive woman he meets. Although Gerard's bravado might put off readers at times, this flaw in his character is more than offset by his overwhelming sense of loyalty to his emperor Napoleon, and his intense belief in honor and chivalry.

It is somewhat ironic that Doyle the patriot chose as a hero a French soldier, particularly a soldier who fought directly against the British in one of their most bitter struggles. Yet it is perhaps because the French cause was defeated by the British that it seemed more romantic to him. Gerard represents an attitude about war that Conan Doyle always found glamorous, and whether the French soldiers were in fact more dashing, more reckless, and more devoted to achieving glory for its own sake than were the more pedestrian and businesslike British soldiers (whom Gerard regularly refers to as "English beef"), Doyle seems to have believed that they were and thus was able to incorporate Arthurian ideals into a work of fairly recent history. The British, after all, were led into battle by a bureaucracy of generals; the French were led by a single man, an emperor who, like Caesar or Alexander or Arthur, could be found on the battlefield as well as in court; it was the scope and daring of Napoleon's struggle against most of Europe that caught Doyle's imagination. Gerard, by frequently being a special envoi for the emperor, is freed from the mundane necessity of being tied to a specific unit or military action. He is free to wander through most of Europe (and his exploits take him everywhere–Russia, Italy, England, Germany, Spain, Poland) in a series of swashbuckling episodes, accompanied only by one of his fast and faithful horses.

The stories are told in the first person by an elderly Etienne Gerard, whom we usually find sitting in a café drinking wine and reminiscing over his past. The stories he tells span the period from 1807 to 1815, taking him from the rank of lieutenant to colonel. The first story in the series, "How the Brigadier Came to the Castle of Gloom," establishes that he is both a fearless fighter (he has recently dueled with six fencing masters) and a reckless soul when the safety of a woman is involved. Gerard, imprisoned in a cheese cellar, sets off an explosive charge to blast his way free, even though a nearby powder magazine might also explode and bring the whole castle down. When the fire does spread to the magazine Gerard is outside, but the ensuing blast renders him unconscious for weeks. Such a mishap is a fairly minor occurrence for Gerard, however, whose life is threatened regularly in the rather bloody series.

In "How the Brigadier Slew the Brothers of Ajaccio," for example, Gerard is asked by Napoleon to serve as the emperor's bodyguard on a secret mission. Gerard is not alert enough, however, to prevent an assassin from sinking a dagger to the hilt in the emperor's chest. A furious and humiliated Gerard kills the assassin and his companion, then learns that the murdered man was not Napoleon but a servant Napoleon had asked to masquerade as himself. The assassination attempt, like other nonfactual elements of the series, was "kept secret" by Napoleon and Gerard during Napoleon's lifetime, and can only be told now that many years have passed.

In the next story in the series, "How the Brigadier Held the King," Gerard is taken prisoner. He then plays cards and wins his freedom, but meets Wellington who refuses to honor the arrangement and grant that freedom. "See, my lord," cries Gerard, "I played for my freedom and I won, for as you perceive, I hold the king."[6] To this plea Wellington only responds, "On the contrary. . . . It is I who won, for, as you perceive, my King holds you." Thrown into Dartmoor prison in "How the King Held the Brigadier," Gerard languishes only briefly, then effects a breathtaking escape (involving both an attractive lady and an English prizefighter), is recaptured, and finally exchanged for an English colonel and returned to France where he can begin his adventures anew.

In "How the Brigadier Played for a Kingdom," we find Gerard betrayed by a German princess and nearly hanged while trying to deliver a message for Napoleon. In "How the Brigadier Won His Medal" he resolutely and against all odds delivers what turns out to be a false message that Napoleon assumed would be intercepted and would deceive the enemy. Gerard, in tears, tells Bonaparte, "Had I known that you wished the despatch to fall into the hands of the enemy, I would have seen that it came there. As I believed that I was to guard it, I was prepared to sacrifice my life for it. I do not believe, sire, that any man in the world ever met with more toils and perils than I have done in trying to carry out what I thought was your will" (*EBG*, p.316). Napoleon's response to this is to give Gerard a special medal of honor, because, in Napoleon's words, "if he had the thickest head he has also the stoutest heart in my army" (*EBG*, p.316).

Such a stout heart is remembered by Bonaparte in "How the Brigadier was Tempted by the Devil," the last story in *The Exploits*. In it Gerard is summoned and asked to join in a coup against Napoleon because the fight looks lost. Gerard refuses, absolutely indignant, and it is this loyalty to his emperor that causes him to be sent on yet another secret mission (involving yet another beautiful countess) to retrieve important papers. After a perilous adventure Napoleon and Gerard bury the papers in a secret hiding place and Gerard explains that he understands Napoleon thrice attempted to write Gerard from St. Helena about them. Because these letters were intercepted, Napoleon's secret documents remain buried, their exact location known only to Etienne Gerard who has remained loyal to his leader and silent about their whereabouts. Gerard promises to tell how he dug these papers up in a later story (in fact, Doyle never relates that episode), and the first series of adventures ends.

In the second volume, *Adventures of Gerard* (1903), Doyle quickly reestablishes the gallant nature of his hero in "How the Brigadier Lost His Ear" by having Gerard, who is imprisoned by Venetian terrorists, exchange cells with a young female prisoner, who is to be punished for fraternizing with him by having her ear cut off. The ear is removed in the dark (inexplicably), so no one notices that

Gerard is in her place until too late. French soldiers arrive to release him and the young woman retires to a convent. "Youth is past and passion is gone," the elderly Gerard muses at the tale's conclusion, "but the soul of the gentleman can never change, and still Etienne Gerard would bow his grey head before her and would very gladly lose this other ear if he might do her a service."[7]

In two stories in this volume Gerard experiences the British sensibility firsthand. In "How the Brigadier Slew the Fox," Gerard, while in Spain, infiltrates an English fox hunt and finds himself both emotionally and physically caught up in the pursuit. As the best horseman in Napoleon's army, Gerard is able to outdistance the British riders and kills the quarry before breaking off from the hunt and rejoining his companions. Tongue in cheek, Doyle creates his conversion of Gerard to a "British sportsman" in a high-spirited fashion. "Then it was that the strangest thing of all happened," proclaims Gerard. "I, too, went mad–I, Etienne Gerard! In a moment it came upon me, this spirit of sport, this desire to excel, this hatred of the fox. Accursed animal, should he defy us?" (AG, p. 96). Gerard, not as familiar with the details of the hunt as he might be, uses his saber to cut the "accursed animal" in two; in the next story he receives the dismembered fox as a present from the English along with a note urging him to eat it now that he has slaughtered it.

In "How the Brigadier Triumphed in England," Gerard returns to the sojourn he spent in England as a prisoner, an adventure described in The Exploits. While waiting to be exchanged for an English colonel he becomes embroiled in a duel fought over a beautiful woman. When the woman intervenes before the duel is completed, Gerard attempts to show off by discharging his pistol in a playful fashion and nearly kills a bystander. His gracious and charming apology gets him out of this scrape and wins him the praise of his rival, Lord Dacre, who says "I never thought to feel towards a Frenchman as I do to you. You're a man and a gentleman, and I can't say more" (*AG*, p.169).

"How the Brigadier Bore Himself at Waterloo" is a two-part story that covers Gerard's heroic action in Napoleon's last battle. In the first part, Gerard infiltrates enemy lines where among the soldiers he meets he encounters an English officer who remembers him from the fox hunt. Surrounded by the enemy on all sides, Gerard takes refuge in the loft of an inn and is able to escape when the wife of the innkeeper creates a diversion. In the second part of the story he passes back through the Prussian army to the front by posing as a Prussian messenger carrying a special dispatch. Reaching the front lines, he discards his Prussian disguise and crosses to the French side to rejoin Napoleon, who first disbelieves, then grudgingly accepts, the bad news Gerard brings. While on the other side Gerard has learned that a select crew of nine horsemen has been picked from the Prussian army and assigned to capture Bonaparte. Seeing this team approaching, Gerard suddenly shoves Napoleon into his carriage, takes Bonaparte's overcoat and white horse, and rides off hoping to decoy the raiders away from their true quarry. The trick works and in a hair-raising chase Gerard systematically eliminates and eludes eight of the nine horsemen while Bonaparte effects his escape. Finally having Napoleon's horse shot from beneath him, Gerard arrives safely in a French encampment just as the last pursuer closes in. The action, of course, only temporarily staves off the inevitable, for Napoleon surrenders a few weeks later. "Had others been as loyal as I," Gerard remarks, "the history of the world might have been changed" (*AG*, pp.271–72).

Although Gerard called his Waterloo ride his "last and most famous exploit," his adventures, like those of Watson and Holmes, were hard to conclude. In "The Last

Adventure of the Brigadier" Conan Doyle brought him back for an attempt to rescue Napoleon from St. Helena. Put ashore with the assignment of escorting Napoleon back to the rescue ship, Gerard discovers that the attempt is ill-fated. He arrives to find his emperor has just died. Sadly, Gerard views Napoleon lying on his bier surrounded by rows of burning candles. Gerard pulls himself to attention, gives his fallen leader a final salute, and solemnly takes his leave.

"You have seen through my dim eyes something of the sparkle and splendour of those great days" Gerard says in his closing remarks, "and I have brought back to you some shadow of those men whose tread shook the earth" (AG, pp.271–72). In this series of stories Doyle creates some of his best historical fiction, perhaps proving once and for all that he was far better at writing short stories than writing novels. There is an excitement and dash to these adventures that appears only episodically in the longer fiction, largely because Doyle keeps the plot uppermost and does not bury himself under a mass of historical description, detailing the technicalities of chamfrons, arbalests, or greaves.

Instead he is left to sketch the portrait of a man who is the abstraction of an age, or at least an age as Doyle idealized it. "Long after Etienne Gerard is forgotten," the old soldier muses, "a heart may be warmed or a spirit braced by some faint echo of the words that he has spoken" (AG, p.297). This is essentially how Conan Doyle viewed the tales, as moral and psychological props to brace the spirit of an age that seemed to be in need of heroes. The aftermath of the Boer War brought a good deal of criticism to the British military, an organization that Doyle knew from his firsthand experience had performed heroically on the battlefield. Histories, such as Doyle's own books on the Boer War and World War I, could record the factual data, but in fiction Doyle could record the emotional truths of heroism, the "sparkle and splendour" of great days and actions where gallantry was recognized no matter what uniform it was wearing.

Gerard is not so much a French soldier as he is an ideal soldier, devoted to principles he will never abandon. It is because Gerard represents these ideal truths that Doyle chose to make him French–the enemy in the eyes of most of Doyle's countrymen. Making him British could have turned the series into another nationalistic gesture on Doyle's part, and perhaps have tempted him to repeat the patriotic stereotypes one might expect in such fiction. In these stories Doyle is trying to do something much larger than reinforce the average Englishman's stereotyped responses to queen, flag, and country. In Gerard he creates a figure–not completely noble and perhaps therefore more believable–who represents the true embodiment of a chivalric code. To what end? "As the tree is nurtured by its own cast leaves," notes Gerard, "so it is these dead men and vanished days which may bring out another blossoming of heroes, of rulers, and of sages" (*AG*, p.297). By Gerard's example, and by the examples throughout his historical fiction–fiction in which courage, loyalty, and truth are the supreme values–Doyle hopes to invoke such an age.

3

Sherlock Holmes: 1887–1894

It has been said that Sherlock Holmes, the legendary detective, owes at least part of his fame to an equally legendary criminal–Jack the Ripper. While such an assertion cannot be proved, it is certainly true that Holmes and the Ripper burst onto the scene only a few months apart, Holmes in December, 1887, and the Ripper in the late summer of 1888. Initially, however, it was the Whitechapel murderer who received the greater amount of attention. The lurid murders that were being described in the daily papers had a fictional counterpart in Doyle's short novel–which had an appropriately lurid name–*A Study in Scarlet*. The chief difference, of course, was that in the fiction the murderous criminals were undone by the masterful Holmes, while in real life the Ripper was not caught.

The bloody crimes of Jack the Ripper galvanized London, making the public aware of brutality in the streets and the need for efficient police work. The relatively ineffective actions of Scotland Yard one usually finds in the Holmes stories, in fact, may simply reflect what the public felt was all too true (as the inability to catch the Ripper proved). Conversely, the ability of Holmes to foil every criminal made him the very figure that a crime-conscious England was seeking. Without the Ripper to terrify London, the interest in the work of a super detective such as Sherlock Holmes might never have arisen.

Sherlock Holmes did not begin as Sherlock Holmes,

however. Conan Doyle's original manuscript for *A Study in Scarlet* clearly shows (and Doyle's manuscripts are surely the most legible and orderly of all time) that the famous detective was first to be named Ormond Sacker. Doyle also considered the name Sherrinford Holmes before settling on Sherlock. John H. Watson, as we might expect, was the only name considered for Watson (although Doyle, much to the distress of his avid readers, mistakenly alludes to the trusty doctor as James in some of the tales).

There have been many theories proposed about the source of these fictional characters. Doyle himself, of course, has been most frequently named as the pattern for Watson; the many parallels between the two men are obvious. Doyle's friend and secretary Major Alfred Wood has also been nominated as the "real" Watson, for Wood's character and appearance resembled the fictional character's in many ways. If two possible originals for Watson are not enough, there was also a real Dr. James Watson whom Doyle knew; this Watson was actually practicing medicine in Southsea when Doyle created his famous characters. The originals for Sherlock Holmes are most often thought to have been Doyle again, for as the creator of Holmes he himself must have possessed some of Holmes's remarkable insights, and Dr. Joseph Bell, one of Doyle's professors at medical school. Bell's reputation for being a keen and skilled observer was well established among the medical students, so well established, in fact, that when Holmes became famous some former students believed they recognized Dr. Bell, and Doyle acknowledged the fact. In his later years Doyle related in his memoirs an often repeated anecdote about Bell, describing a scene in which Bell, after examining a patient before his class, correctly deduced that the man had served in the army in a Highland Regiment, was a recently discharged noncommissioned officer, and had been stationed at Barbados. Bell then explained his conclusions to an astonished class: "You see, gentlemen, the man was a respectful man but did not remove his hat. They do not in the army, but he would have learned civilian ways had he been long discharged. He has an air of authority and he is obviously Scottish. As to Barbados, his complaint is Elephantiasis, which is West Indian, and not British." Here we certainly have the essence of Holmes. Bell publicly denied that he had any direct connection with Holmes, but the evidence seems to indicate clearly that he at least had a strong indirect connection.

Of course we do not have to assume that Conan Doyle's famous pair is based on anyone. In forty years of writing fiction Doyle created literally hundreds of original characters, and Holmes and Watson may chiefly have been the product of his wonderful imagination. It is only Doyle's skill in depicting these two that has made readers insist on the existence of real-life sources for the detective and his best friend.

In *A Study in Scarlet* Conan Doyle established the pattern that he elaborated on for the next forty years, but did not substantially change. The novel opens with John H. Watson, recently discharged from the army (because of an injury) and "as free as air" in London, though running short of funds and looking for an inexpensive place to live. He is tapped on the shoulder by an old friend, Stamford, who tells Watson he has just spoken to another individual who would like to save money by sharing his rooms. Watson is then taken to the chemical laboratory of St. Bartholomew's hospital where Stamford introduces him with a simple statement, "Dr. Watson, Mr. Sherlock Holmes." Holmes surprises Watson by immediately deducing Watson has been in Afghanistan, and the two men hit it off quickly. They make an agreement to share rooms at 221B Baker Street and their famous partnership is formed.

Holmes shocks Watson with his erratic habits and his unusual philosophic bent. "A man's brain originally is like a little empty attic," Holmes explains, modifying Locke's metaphor of the blank tablet; there is, he believes, just so much room available in it. Holmes therefore does not believe in remembering unnecessary information, what he calls "useless facts elbowing out the useful ones."[1] Watson draws up a list of what Holmes's interests (and, accordingly, his limits of knowledge) are, and finds that Holmes has a peculiarly skewed mind. When Watson discovers a magazine article that argues "From a drop of water . . . a logician could infer the possibility of an Atlantic or a Niagara, without having seen or heard of one or the other," he dismisses it as "ineffable twaddle" (*CSH*, p.23). Sherlock Holmes, it turns out, is actually the author of the article and he justifies his "twaddle" to Watson by explaining how he had deduced at their first meeting that Watson had served in Afghanistan. When Watson is still doubtful, Holmes correctly identifies a messenger as a retired sergeant of marines. Watson is then convinced, and Doyle, having fully apprised his readers of the powers of Sherlock Holmes, then opens up the mystery itself.

Summoned by Scotland Yard's Inspector Gregson to the scene of a murder, Holmes carefully examines the grounds before entering the house where the crime was committed. There he and Watson find Gregson and his associate Lestrade, and the corpse of Enoch J. Drebber, an American. On the wall in letters of blood is found the word RACHE. Interpreted by Lestrade to be part of the name *Rachel*, the letters are instead identified by Holmes as the German word for revenge. With a great deal of evidence he has gathered Holmes leaves the scene, after giving the inspectors a thumbnail sketch of the killer: "He was more than six feet high, was in the prime of his life, had small feet for his height, wore coarse, square-toed boots and smoked a Trichinopoly cigar. He came here with his victim in a four-wheeled cab, which was drawn by a horse with three old shoes and one new one on his off fore-leg. In all probability the murderer had a florid face, and the finger-nails of his right hand were remarkably long" (*CSH*, p.32).

Holmes has deduced all this, as he explains to Watson, from the evidence at the scene, evidence Scotland Yard has not been observant enough to notice. He then sets a trap by placing in the newspaper an advertisement stating that a wedding ring (similar to a ring found on the body) has been found. Surprisingly, a bedraggled old woman shows up in response to the advertisement and claims the ring. Suspicious, Holmes then follows the old woman, but loses her; she seems to be a young man in disguise.

The next day inspector Gregson shows up to announce proudly that he has solved the case and arrested the killer. The man Gregson has in jail, Arthur Charpentier, is the son of the proprietor of the boarding house where the dead man Drebber was staying. Gregson (who of course has arrested the wrong man) is particularly pleased with himself because he knows that Lestrade has gone off to arrest Drebber's secretary Joseph Stangerson.

Stangerson, however, has also been murdered, and the discovery of his body, accompanied by the word RACHE in letters of blood, throws everyone (but Holmes) into total confusion. Holmes, who has sent his Baker Street irregulars, a group of ragged street urchins, out to locate a certain cab, is pleased when one of the boys appears to announce that the cab is outside. Summoning the cabman upstairs to help with a suitcase, Holmes suddenly snaps handcuffs on the man and introduces him as Mr. Jefferson Hope, the murderer they have been seeking. The first part of the novel closes at this point.

The second part presents a flashback recounting events that took place in the United States thirty-five years before. There, wandering in an alkali desert, a man and his young daughter are dying of exposure and thirst. The man is John Ferrier, and he and his daughter Lucy are the only survivors of a doomed wagon train. Just as Ferrier abandons hope and settles down to die, help arrives in the form of Brigham Young and his band of Mormons, among them the Elders Stangerson and Drebber. Ferrier and his daughter are pronounced members of the sect "now and for ever" by Young, and they travel with the Mormons to Utah where they establish a home and Lucy grows into womanhood.

Trouble arrives in this paradise when Jefferson Hope, the son of an old friend of Ferrier's, arrives and romances Lucy, urging her to run off with him. The Mormon Elders hear of Lucy's romance, however, and Brigham Young himself arrives to remind Ferrier that she may not marry outside her religion. He advises her to consider the sons of Stangerson and Drebber, gives Ferrier a month to resolve this problem, and suggests Lucy will not be allowed to carry out any marriage with a non-Mormon. Jefferson Hope arrives and helps the Ferriers attempt an escape to Nevada, but the Mormons follow, kill Ferrier, and carry Lucy back to force her to marry young Drebber. Lucy dies and Jefferson Hope vows revenge. When Drebber and Stangerson themselves split with the Elders of the church, they leave Utah and go to Ohio, then to the continent, then London, all the while doggedly pursued by Hope.

When Jefferson Hope is in the custody of Scotland Yard he recounts his motives for the murders and relates his crimes, explaining that his bad heart will soon give out. As a cabman he was able to locate and trail his victims. Trying to be fair even as he cornered his prey, he gave Drebber the choice of two capsules, promising to swallow the other himself. Drebber took the poisoned one and Hope wrote the word RACHE on the wall to confuse the police. When he caught Stangerson he gave him the same opportunity to choose life or death, but Stangerson attacked him and was killed, according to Hope, in self-defense. Hope was then summoned to 221B by one of the irregulars and arrested.

With this confession the case closes. Hope is led off to jail where he dies of a burst aneurism, just as he predicted. Holmes reveals to Watson that he had telegraphed the police in Cleveland and had learned that Drebber had asked for protection there from a Jefferson Hope. Piecing all the evidence together, Holmes then sent the irregulars off through London to find a cabman by that name. "The whole thing," he explains to Watson, "is a chain of logical sequences without a break or flaw" (*CSH*, p.85). Watson is amazed and delighted with the crime's solution, but is somewhat disappointed to find that the papers have credited Lestrade and Gregson with solving the crime. He promises to set that wrong right by publishing the notes in his journal; the result of that promise is of course the story that the reader has just read.

A Study in Scarlet has several major flaws. The American flashback is awkward and unnecessarily long. It takes the reader away from the truly fascinating story taking place in London. One wonders why Doyle, who had never been to Utah, and in fact had probably never even met a Mormon, decided to write his novel about this element of American history. It was certainly not because he was an expert on the subject, for his depiction of the religion is both inaccurate and extremely unfair. He had no doubt read some distorted contemporary accounts, and his novel may owe something to Robert Louis Stevenson's 1885 novel *The Dynamiter*, in which one character claimed Mormon connections. There are some elements of the story that are factual. The Mormons were polygamous, and this polygamy must have upset the moral principles of the chivalric Doyle. Lucy is carried back, Doyle says, to become part of a Mormon "harem." Mormon leaders like Young were hailed as prophets and their word was obeyed as law. Such authority could and sometimes did lead to the kind of murder and kidnapping we see the Mormons carry out.

Paradoxically, however, it was probably the fact that Doyle knew so little about the Mormons that made him choose them for his story. They were mysterious, and, like many aspects of the American frontier, rather "exotic" to someone living in staid Victorian England. (When the spiritualist movement became popular, for example, a high proportion of the "spirit guides" turned out to be American Indians. No one seemed to find this bizarre, presumably because the Indians were already recognized as mysterious and romantic figures.) In addition, although Watson mentions only Poe and Gaboriau in *A Study in Scarlet*, Wilkie Collins' novel *The Moonstone* (1848), an extremely popular book acknowledged to have been the first detective novel, was also probably an influence on Doyle. *The Moonstone* has a religious cult at its center, and Doyle, imitating Collins, very likely tried to give his story a similar touch by including what seemed to him to be a cult–Mormonism.

Afficionados of detective fiction may feel slightly cheated when Holmes explains the case. The story violates the unwritten principle of giving the readers all the facts and allowing them to solve the mystery. Holmes's sudden arrest of the cabman startles us because even though he has "solved" the crime in principle by deducing what took place, the murderer could have been anyone in London. The all-important name of the assailant–for that, after all, is what allows him to be located–has been forwarded to Holmes unknown to the readers or Scotland Yard. If the Cleveland police did not happen to have Hope's name in their files, Holmes would not have had any way of catching the criminal. There is indeed a "chain of logical sequences without break or flaw," but there is also some very good luck involved. One might question, for instance, why Hope came so willingly to 221B at the close of the action. Suspecting a trap, he had sent his accomplice there to pick up the wedding ring. It seems very unlikely that a cautious man would then endanger himself by returning to the apartment, unless the specific address has simply slipped his mind.

Despite these flaws there is much that is excellent about *A Study in Scarlet*. There is the essence of all that will make the later adventures popular—the skepticism of Watson, the unjustified self-assuredness of Scotland Yard, the wit of Holmes ("To a great mind, nothing is little," he says to Lestrade, acknowledging the detective's ineptitude with acidly ironic praise). The fundamental formula for the series is also established: Holmes and Watson are snug in their rooms when a mysterious visitor arrives with a problem; they travel to the scene and Holmes asks curious questions and makes enigmatic remarks while Watson either appears to be puzzled or convinced that there is a very obvious solution; the obvious solution is swept aside with the sudden revelation of the true facts; the pair then returns to Baker Street where Holmes wraps up the story by explaining how he reached his conclusions. Doyle's repetition of this basic plot line for the remaining fifty-six stories and three novels does not damage the series. On the contrary, it adds a certain familiarity to the adventures that readers have come to expect. Although many have returned to Holmes and Watson time and again because of the puzzles the mysteries have provided, it is the characterization of the principal figures themselves that has made them known worldwide. Doyle, like Dickens before him, realized that it was repetition of certain traits and patterns that made characters memorable. It is a sign of his talent that he chose not to alter his formula, rather than a limitation of it.

The second Holmes novel, *The Sign of Four* (published first as *The Sign of THE Four*), was commissioned by *Lippincott's* magazine and first appeared in February, 1890. It begins with the infamous scene in which Holmes is injecting himself with his "seven-per-cent solution" of cocaine. He has resorted to the drug to stimulate his mind during a slow time in which no puzzling crimes have come his way. Holmes, having finished his injection, then summarizes the principles of observation and deduction for Watson, demonstrates them by correctly deducing where Watson has been that morning, and then reaches some startling conclusions based on his observations of Watson's pocket watch. This recapitulative touch is necessary because it has been three years since the public has seen the pair. (Doyle, too, needed to refresh his memory for he unconsciously moved Watson's old war wound from his shoulder to his leg.) Fortunately these doldrums soon are to end; immediately after Holmes laments, "What is the use of having powers, Doctor, when one has no field upon which to exert them?" (*CSH*, p.93), a young lady is ushered into the room and the adventure begins.

Miss Mary Morstan's father mysteriously disappeared from a London hotel ten years previously, shortly after returning from India. Four years later an anonymous advertisement appeared in the *Times* asking for the address of Mary Morstan. She replied and quickly received a single pearl in the mail with no note of explanation. The gift was repeated every year on the same date and she has received a collection of six pearls. Now she has received an unsigned note calling her a "wronged woman" and asking her to appear that night outside the Lyceum Theater. Holmes and Watson agree to accompany her.

Holmes spends the afternoon researching the case and returns with the information that a Major Sholto, a close friend of the missing Captain Morstan, died only a few days before Mary Morstan received the first of the pearls. Holmes feels the fact is relevant; Watson is doubtful. Miss Morstan arrives for their trip to the theater, bringing with her a curious document she has found in her father's desk. It seems to be a map or plan of a building, and it is inscribed with a hieroglyph annotated "The sign of the four." There are four names signed to this document, three of them apparently the names of Indians.

At the theater the three are approached by a man who asks them to enter a carriage and then quickly drives them away. When they arrive at a dark house after a long drive, they are introduced to Mr. Thaddeus Sholto, who is the son of Major Sholto. Sholto mysteriously invites Dr. Watson to listen to his heart, a strange request because nothing seems wrong with it. He then goes on to explain that Captain Morstan is in fact dead, and he makes several allusions to his twin brother Bartholomew whom they will soon visit. Sholto describes how his father received a devastating letter four years after the disappearance of Morstan. Major Sholto was sent to his deathbed by the news contained in this letter—news of Morstan's orphan, Mary, and of Morstan's death. Sholto had brought a treasure back from India with him, and Morstan, upon his return, met him to divide the booty. They quarreled, and Morstan died from a heart attack. Sholto, out of fear he would be accused of murder, disposed of the body and hid the treasure. At the moment he was about to tell his sons where the treasure was, however, he saw a hideous face staring in the window—and died of fright. That night the house was ransacked by intruders and a note with the inscription "The sign of the four" was left on his body. The brothers searched the house and garden for the treasure, but found nothing beyond a string of pearls their father had removed from the treasure hoard. They decided to send a pearl to Mary Morstan at yearly inter-

vals as a symbol of her share in the only part of the treasure they could locate. This story told, Sholto accompanies them as they drive to Pondicherry Lodge to meet
his brother Bartholomew. The treasure, he explains, has
now been found, and it is worth half a million pounds.

At Pondicherry Lodge they find the body of Bartholomew. He is seated at a table with a strange smile on his
face. On the table is a peculiar stone hammer and a paper
with the words "The sign of the four." The only sign of
the cause of death is a thorn, which Holmes assumes to be
poisoned, that is removed from just above Sholto's ear.
The treasure has been stolen. Holmes goes to work at the
scene and discovers a trapdoor leading to the roof, along
with the print of a bare foot. Returning to the body for a
further examination, he concludes that the poisoned
thorn has been shot into the scalp. Any more investigation at the scene of the crime is brought to an end by the
arrival of police detectives and ensuing confusion; the
police arrest all servants in the house as suspects.

Watson obtains a bloodhound with which Holmes
hopes to track the barefooted individual, who has stepped
in some creosote while climbing about the attic and roof.
This trail of creosote takes them through London to the
docks, where it appears the culprits have rented a launch;
the launch owner's wife has grown anxious at the length
of their absence. The trail seems cold at this point so
Holmes returns to Baker Street and employs the irregulars to search for the launch. Nothing turns up and a
newspaper advertisement also produces no response, so
finally, in desperation, Holmes disguises himself as an old
sailor and finds the launch by inquiries at the yards of
boat repairmen. He, Watson, and Athelney Jones of
Scotland Yard plan to intercept the launch that night as
the suspects move to Gravesend where they will transfer
to a passenger ship bound for Brazil. After a high-speed
chase down the Thames the launch and its passengers are

apprehended. A pygmy with a blowgun is shot and killed
in the struggle; his poisonous darts have just missed
Holmes and Watson.

The remaining captive, Jonathan Small, recounts his
story in a long flashback. He had been a soldier in India
where he lost his leg to a crocodile. Discharged from the
army, he worked for a planter until the Sepoy uprising in
1857. He then took refuge in an old fort in the city of
Agra. There, on nightwatch with two Indians, an unusual
thing happened. They seized him and threatened to kill
him, offering mercy only if he joined them in their plot to
murder a rich merchant seeking safety in Agra. Small
agreed, and these two, along with a confederate traveling
with the merchant, entered into a pact, promising to share
the merchant's treasure four ways. The merchant arrived
and was killed, and the treasure hidden in the fort, its
location noted on a map similar to the one recently discovered by Mary Morstan. Their plans were upset, however, when all four were arrested for the murder (the
jewels were never mentioned) and sentenced to hard
labor.

The years passed and Small was eventually transferred
to the Andaman Islands where he met Sholto and
Morstan. Small hoped to use the treasure to bribe Sholto
and Morstan into helping him escape, so he told them the
story, offering them a fifth share for their assistance. A
bargain was soon reached. Sholto would go to India and
find the treasure box. He would then arrange for a boat so
that the prisoners could escape to Agra where they would
meet Morstan and divide the treasure. Sholto left and
doublecrossed them all, taking the treasure and returning
to England. Small then made an ally of a native, Tonga,
and stole a boat, escaping but leaving his comrades
behind. With revenge as his sole motivation he returned
to England to kill Sholto. When Major Sholto died in bed
it was Small's face he saw peering through the window,

and it was Small who ransacked the house. Small stayed near the house until the treasure was finally located, then made his move, stealing the treasure. Tonga killed Bartholomew Sholto with his deadly blowgun dart. Together they had planned to escape to Brazil, but when the pursuit got hot Small dumped all the jewels into the river rather than have any descendant of Morstan or Sholto own them. The treasure, therefore, has been lost again.

Jonathan Small is taken off to jail by Athelney Jones, and Watson gives the novel a final twist by announcing that he is to marry Mary Morstan. Holmes responds by saying that because he does not value emotion he cannot congratulate Watson. "I should never marry myself," Holmes adds, "lest I bias my judgment" (CSH, p.157). The novel ends as it began with Holmes reaching for his cocaine bottle.

Although *The Sign of Four* is very different from *A Study in Scarlet*, we can see that its plot, involving Indian treasure unfairly appropriated by Englishmen, also owes much to *The Moonstone*. Like *A Study in Scarlet*, this novel utilizes revenge as the chief motive for the murder that takes place. Although there is not a religious cult present in this second Holmes novel, the "threefold oath" that is sworn by "the four" has all the fervent intensity we would expect any cult to possess, and the mysterious "sign of the four" notes that are found lying about repeatedly suggest that some secret organization is at work.

Structurally this novel is a great improvement over the first Holmes novel. The flashback explanation is much shorter than the American scenes in *A Study in Scarlet*, and Doyle is able to keep the mystery moving. There is the initial problem of the pearls, then there are the clandestine visits to not one but two mysterious houses, culminating in the discovery of Bartholomew Sholto's body. This is quickly followed by the bloodhound episode,

Holmes appearing in a disguise so authentic he fools Watson, and the exciting chase down the Thames. The aborigine Tonga and his blowgun add just the touch of the fantastic that Doyle loved to include. Even though the story demonstrates that Conan Doyle had his formula fully under control, we can see that he had no plans to continue the saga. Watson's marriage will separate Holmes from his chronicler and the "series" will end with this second and final story.

The success of the new magazine *The Strand* in 1891 convinced Doyle that he might write for this popular illustrated monthly. Rather than serialize a Holmes novel, either Doyle or *The Strand* (it is not clear which) hit upon the idea of a series of short stories based upon a single set of characters, in this case Holmes and Watson. Doyle wrote a series of six stories, then another six, collecting these first twelve into a book, *The Adventures of Sherlock Holmes* (1892). Written very quickly and apparently very easily by Doyle (he wrote the first two in two weeks), these first twelve stories, published over the course of a year, became immediately popular and once and for all established the detective and his friend as permanent figures in literature.

In *The Adventures of Sherlock Holmes* we see Conan Doyle refining the formula he created for the first novels and distilling it into the shortened form this new kind of literary venture required. As it turned out, the short story was a better vehicle for Holmes and Watson than the short novels in which they had already appeared. Plots had to be simpler and more quickly sketched. There was no room for the extended flashbacks of the earlier books. Although Doyle was to return to the novel form twice more with Holmes, only one of these books—*The Hound of the Baskervilles*—is first-rate. As most mystery writers have discovered, successfully sustaining suspense for several hundred pages is not an easy task; the short story is a much more efficient medium for maintaining a mood, as Poe pointed out. Doyle's series of related stories in *The Strand* was a fortunate accident for him and the detective; as a group they are virtually unique in literature.

In "A Scandal in Bohemia," the first of the *Adventures*, it is necessary for Doyle to reunite Holmes and Watson after Watson's marriage to Mary Morstan. To do this he simply has Watson pass the familiar Baker Street doorway, notice a light, and drop in for an unannounced visit. After an obligatory demonstration of Holmes's powers of observation and deduction to acquaint new readers with the detective's method, the case is introduced. Holmes is visited by no less a personage than the King of Bohemia, who is being blackmailed by an American opera singer, Irene Adler. Adler, who once had an affair with the king, says that she, apparently out of jealousy, will reveal this affair on the day of his impending marriage. Holmes attempts to retrieve an incriminating photograph for the king, appearing in two different disguises and employing Watson to throw an incendiary device into Irene Adler's house, hoping that in her panic she will reveal the photograph's hiding place. She does tip her hand, but, to his frustration, she recognizes Holmes. She marries and leaves the country with her new husband saying she will never use the incriminating photograph except in some form of self-defense. Presumably such an action will never be necessary for the king would prefer not to hear of her again; he trusts her word and therefore feels the problem is solved.

The case is an interesting one for Doyle to begin his new series with, because Holmes fails in his attempt to secure the photograph. Irene Adler not only sees through Holmes's disguise, she actually tricks him by following him home in a disguise of her own. Curiously, Holmes turns down the king's offer of an emerald ring as payment in favor of a photograph of Irene. Even Watson notes that

Holmes seems affected by the episode and always refers to Irene after this as "the woman." Although Holmes once told Watson "the fair sex is your department" (*CSH*, p.657), many critics wonder whether "the woman" might potentially have been the one great love in the detective's life.

"The Red-Headed League," the second story in the volume, is a classic episode, with a plot Doyle was to reuse in other forms. A pawn broker, Mr. Jabez Wilson, answers, at his new assistant's urging, an advertisement in the paper announcing a vacancy in the "Red-headed League." Wilson gets the position and learns that through the gift of an eccentric millionaire he, solely because he has red hair, will be paid four pounds a week to copy the *Encyclopedia Britannica*. He reports to work, copies away diligently for eight weeks, almost finishes all the "A's," then discovers one morning the job and the "league" have been dissolved. His investigation turns up no evidence of his former employers and the whole situation seems to have been a prank. Holmes declares the case "a three-pipe problem" and after some meditation visits Wilson's pawnshop. A short visit with Wilson's assistant convinces Holmes his assumptions are correct. A tunnel is being dug into the cellar of a nearby bank–from Wilson's pawnshop. The copying job Wilson has taken is only a ruse intended to keep him out of the shop while the assistant and his confederates dig the tunnel. Holmes, Watson, and Athelney Jones wait in the cellar and apprehend the criminals as they dig into the cellar for the special gold shipment stored there. Holmes calls the case "remarkable" and certainly it is. Wilson's red hair and the job of copying the encyclopedia are perfect red herrings. Wilson and Watson are completely baffled by these bizarre details and with them Doyle is able to throw his readers completely off the track also.

In "A Case of Identity" the mystery and its resolution

are far less satisfying. Miss Mary Sutherland, a part-time typist, has had a disappointing affair of the heart. She has met a Mr. Hosmer Angel at the "gasfitters ball" and he has proposed marriage, but he seems terrified of her stepfather whom he avoids at all costs. On the way to the altar Hosmer inexplicably disappears from a cab and vanishes. Holmes solves the case by deducing that Hosmer is really her stepfather in disguise. The stepfather, benefiting from Mary Sutherland's income while she lived at home, hoped to perpetuate this arrangement. First he tried to discourage her from seeing young men her age, then he hoped to sour her on romance by masquerading as her lover and jilting her at the church. Holmes partly solves the case by matching a typewriter's worn keys to notes that "Hosmer" has written. In this episode, as in "The Red-Headed League," Doyle seems intentionally to select a working-class client for Holmes in order to establish a varied clientele. Doyle documents his detective's history for new readers by mentioning the King of Bohemia twice in the story, as well as by references to *A Study in Scarlet* and *The Sign of Four*, far more "serious" cases than this one. Although no real crime has been committed in this story, we see Holmes rising to the occasion and gallantly defending the wronged Mary Sutherland by threatening to assault her stepfather with his riding crop. Doyle thus demonstrates early in the series that Holmes is interested most of all in justice, not in the magnitude of the crime that has been committed or the social class of his clients.

"The Boscombe Valley Mystery" begins with Watson's reception of a telegram at breakfast and his departure from his wife to travel with Holmes to Boscombe Valley, where one James McCarthy has been arrested for bludgeoning his father to death. Lestrade is on the scene, but is puzzled as always, so Holmes goes to work, performing an exhaustive observation of the area of the crime with his magnifying glass. He concludes the murderer "is a tall man, left-handed, limps with the right leg, wears thick-soled shooting-boots and a gray cloak, smokes Indian cigars, uses a cigar-holder, and carries a blunt pen-knife in his pocket" (*CHS*, p.213). This amazing description points directly towards a neighbor of the late McCarthy's, Mr. John Turner. Turner, who lived as an outlaw in Australia, was being blackmailed by McCarthy who recognized him and threatened to expose his past. Turner then killed McCarthy in a rage. Dying himself from diabetes, Turner plaintively urges Holmes to show him mercy and not reveal his actions. Strangely, Holmes takes the law into his own hands and says he will not divulge who the true murderer is unless the son of the murdered McCarthy is actually condemned to die. Young McCarthy is acquitted because of evidence Holmes brings forward, Turner dies, and the identity of the killer is known only to Holmes and Watson. This case represents the first time (but certainly not the last) that Holmes acts as judge and jury and refuses to report what he knows to authorities. It is a rather bold step on Doyle's part.

The next story, "The Five Orange Pips," is most remarkable not for its mystery, but for its atmosphere. It begins with a classic Baker Street scene. Holmes and Watson (whose wife is visiting her mother and who is rapidly becoming something of a nuisance for Doyle to explain away) are snugly sequestered at 221B on a day on which "equinoctial gales had set in with exceptional force." As the evening closes in they settle deeper into their easy chairs while the wind "cried and sobbed like a child in the chimney" (*CSH*, p.218). Into this bastion of Victorian security, however, comes the inevitable visitor with the inevitable problem.

John Openshaw's Uncle Elias had emigrated to the United States during the Civil War and had lived there for several years fighting for the Confederacy. After returning to England, Elias Openshaw received a letter containing five orange pips; the envelope is marked K.K.K. Openshaw seems terrified, immediately burns some personal papers and asks to have his will witnessed. He takes to drinking, seems afraid to leave his locked room, and is finally discovered, seven weeks after receiving the orange pips, face down in a pool of water, apparently a suicide.

Two years later John Openshaw's father receives a similar letter also containing orange pips and marked K.K.K. He does not understand the message, but is also discovered dead shortly afterwards. Now John Openshaw himself has received a letter with orange pips and the instructions "Put the papers on the sundial" (*CSH*, p. 222). The papers are apparently the ones his uncle burned years before, and he feels there is no escaping the fate of his uncle and father. One page of his uncle's papers has survived the fire. He shows this to Holmes, who advises him to place it on the sundial with an explanation of what has happened. Ruminating on the case, Holmes deduces that the marking K.K.K. stands for the Ku Klux Klan (a connection modern readers perhaps find more obvious than Doyle's London contemporaries did). Curiously, Holmes's encyclopedia solves the mystery by explaining that the orange pips were used by the Klan to signal their imminent revenge upon a victim. Elias Openshaw evidently possessed, and then burned, a diary or register naming many Klan members; the Klan was willing to stop at nothing to retrieve this secret list.

Unfortunately Holmes's solution comes too late to save John Openshaw. The morning papers reveal that his body has been found in the river. Holmes is devastated because he has not been able to prevent his client's death. After a good deal of legwork he discovers that a particular American ship has put into port in the appropriate city at the same time each victim has received the orange pips. He checks the logs and discovers there are three Americans on this ship. Concluding, perhaps far too quickly, that these men are the "gang" responsible for the murders, he then sends them five orange pips and plans to have them arrested when they dock in Savannah. The ship sinks in the Atlantic, however, and the Klansmen are evidently lost at sea.

Although Doyle comes up with a believable cult or conspiracy in this story, Holmes's conclusions seem a bit strained. If the Klan wanted the diary enough to murder for it, one would assume that those seeking it would do so in a more intense and less sporadic manner, because the names could be made public at any time. Although the legend of the great detective would have him be infallible, we should note that here, as in "A Scandal in Bohemia," Holmes fails to capture his culprits even though he technically solves the case.

"The Man with the Twisted Lip" provides a much more bizarre mystery. It begins not in Baker Street, but at Watson's house, when a friend comes to ask the advice of Watson and his wife (who inexplicably addresses Watson as *James* rather than John, a sure sign Watson has been spending too much of his free time in Baker Street). Their friend's husband, Isa Whitney, has been missing for two days, so Watson agrees to escort Kate Whitney to an opium den Whitney has been known to frequent. Watson finds Whitney, but much to his surprise also discovers Holmes, who is visiting the opium den in disguise. Holmes persuades Watson to stay with him in a nearby room rather than return home, and on the way Holmes explains the very complicated case he is working on. A Mr. Neville St. Clair was last seen by his wife beckoning strangely from a second-floor window above an opium den (the same den Holmes and Watson have just visited). When Mrs. St. Clair summons the police and enters the room where she saw her husband, she finds only a hideously crippled derelict and her husband's clothes, along with some bloodstains. The cripple, a professional beggar named Hugh Boone, claims he has no knowledge of how the clothes came to be in his otherwise bare room.

It looks as though St. Clair has been murdered, although there is no real evidence of this. A note from him suggests that he is alive and well, but is attempting to rectify "a huge error." Holmes ponders this problem all night long, smoking pipe after pipe while Watson sleeps. The next morning Holmes goes to the jail where Boone is being held and astonishes Watson by revealing Boone to be Neville St. Clair rather than his murderer.

St. Clair has become a professional beggar in order to pay debts. He takes in a great deal of money, and performs no work other than the ordeal of putting on his disguise daily. No crime has been committed; he is set free with his secret and urged not to continue his dual life. The story owes a good deal to the earlier "A Case of Identity." Again a person who has "vanished" turns out to be someone else masquerading in disguise. In both stories Doyle strains our imagination by having us believe that average citizens can disguise their appearances and voices so well that even their own family members cannot recognize them. Holmes, of course, frequently fools Watson with his disguises, but Holmes is supposed to be an expert at such matters. This story completed Doyle's original *Strand Magazine* contract for a series of six stories.

"The Adventure of the Blue Carbuncle" was first published in the January, 1892, issue of *The Strand Magazine*, appearing in late December. Appropriately, then, it is the first seasonal Holmes adventure—a Christmas story. Watson calls on Holmes shortly after Christmas and finds that his latest problem involves a goose and a hat dropped by a man attacked by a street gang. Holmes is trying to find the owner of the hat, an inconsequential task, until it is discovered that a large blue carbuncle, recently stolen from a countess, is lodged in the crop of the goose. The man who dropped the hat and goose in the street responds to an advertisement placed by Holmes, retrieves his hat and gladly settles for a replacement of the original goose, indicating that he knew nothing of the valuable stone it contained. Holmes and Watson then proceed to locate the poultry supplier so they can determine how and when the goose swallowed the carbuncle. When they find another man, James Ryder, making similar inquiries, they invite him back to Baker Street and reveal that they know about the jewel. He confesses he had conspired with the countess's maid, stolen the jewel, and, fearing apprehension, had forced the stone down the throat of a goose belonging to his sister. He planned to kill the goose later when he was certain he was safely beyond suspicion. Holmes listens to the story, then dispatches Ryder, planning to return the stolen jewel but keep the name of the thief a secret. He and Watson then sit down to a holiday meal of roast goose.

In "The Adventure of the Speckled Band" Conan Doyle created what may be Sherlock Holmes's most famous adventure. The popularity of the story caused him to create a stage version of it in 1910 that was also very popular. The story has been a favorite partly because it presents the classic problem of a crime committed in a "locked room"–a plot formula that writers since Poe have enjoyed attempting. Doyle's locked-room mystery involves the mysterious death of Julia Stoner, the stepdaughter of Dr. Grimesby Roylott of Stoke Moran. An old and once wealthy family has been destroyed by intemperance and wastefulness, and is now in danger of disappearing. The last survivors are Helen Stoner, twin sister of the deceased Julia, and Dr. Roylott. The precise cause of Julia Stoner's death was never determined. In the middle of a stormy night she suddenly screamed and then staggered from her locked bedroom shrieking "It was the speckled band"; she died in her twin sister's arms. The only clue to the mystery Helen Stoner can provide is that her sister mentioned hearing a low whistle about three in the morning for several consecutive nights before her death. Now Helen has heard the same low whistle and, terrified that her death is imminent, has come to Holmes for help. Holmes agrees to assist her, but shortly after Helen Stoner leaves an angry Dr. Roylott shows up, demanding to know what she has told Holmes and Watson. Holmes will tell him nothing and Roylott warns them to stay out of his affairs.

At Stoke Moran, which is crumbling into ruin, Holmes inspects the bedrooms of Roylott, Helen, and the late Julia. Because of some repair work to the decaying building Helen has moved into her sister's old room, next door to her stepfather's bedroom. Holmes finds the shutters to be impenetrable, and is satisfied that when locked the room is secure. He is interested in what appears to be a dummy bell rope hanging onto the bed. In Roylott's room he finds a safe, a saucer of milk, and a small lash with a loop tied in the end. Holmes and Watson plan to sneak into the bedroom and spend the night after Roylott has retired. They wait there in the dark until three in the morning, when they hear the low whistle the sisters reported hearing. Holmes then suddenly springs into action and beats at the bell rope with his cane. A terrified scream from the next bedroom then takes them to Roylott's chamber where they find him dead, a yellow band with brown speckles around his head. It is a snake, a swamp adder, "the deadliest snake in India" according to Holmes.

Holmes reports to Helen Stoner that her grandfather was accidentally bitten while handling his pet snake (Roylott also kept a pet baboon and cheetah). To Watson he explains that if either of the stepdaughters had married, the little estate left would have been severely reduced. Roylott planned to murder the two sisters by sending the swamp adder into their room through the ventilator and down the fake bell rope. It could take several nights for the snake to attack whoever was sleeping in the room, so Roylott would call the snake back into his bedroom each night with the whistle. He would feed it milk from the saucer and then lock it in his iron safe. When Holmes attacked the snake on the bell rope it was driven back at Roylott and killed him. Holmes realizes that he is thus indirectly responsible for Roylott's death, but feels absolutely no guilt.

There has been much discussion of this famous story. A good deal of it questions the details. What kind of snake is a "swamp adder" anyway, and could it or any snake be trained "to come at the sound of a whistle," or climb up and down a bell rope? What snake's bite kills in ten seconds, and why did it take much longer than that for Julia Stoner to die? These problems, however, do not detract from the story's real strengths. The puzzle itself is excellent. The mysterious sounds and clues all lead directly to the conclusion when one knows the solution (there are certainly some Holmes stories in which the facts do not add up nearly so neatly), but the mystery is so baffling the reader cannot reach the conclusion before Holmes explains it. The atmosphere is magnificent. Holmes and Watson crouch in the chill dark outside Stoke Moran and they along with readers are startled by the sudden grotesque appearance of the baboon roaming the grounds; there is also the constant danger of the cheetah that lurks somewhere in the shadows to keep the detectives on their toes. The dangerous vigil in the darkened bedroom that gives even Holmes second thoughts adds to the tension that peaks (but does not conclude) with Holmes frantically beating at the bell rope in the dark.

The tale may owe something to Poe's "The Fall of the House of Usher." In each story we see the final survivors of aristocratic families living in decadence and fear. The Stoner girls are twins, as are Roderick and Madeline

Usher, and in both stories the mysteries are accompanied by the sounds of wild stormy nights and clanging heavy metal doors. The description of Julia Stoner standing in her bedroom doorway in her nightgown, "her face blanched with terror, her hands groping for help, her whole figure swaying to and fro" (*CSH*, p.242), suggests Poe's description of Madeline in her shroud "trembling and reeling to and fro upon the threshold."[2] Both women immediately die in the arms of their twins. Madeline falls "heavily inward upon the person of her brother . . . in her violent and now final death agonies"; Helen Stoner throws her arms about her sister Julia, whose "knees seemed to give way and she fell to the ground." Julia "writhed as one in terrible pain, and her limbs were dreadfully convulsed" (*CSH*, p.262). The parallels between the scenes seem too strong to be purely coincidental.

We should also note in this story that Doyle has apparently run out of excuses for getting Watson out of the house and has dropped the chronological pattern created for the series so far. From now on Doyle will have Watson telling stories about cases that took place at various times in his association with Holmes, including some cases that took place before the ones published so far in the series. This change in Conan Doyle's method has allowed Holmes fans to spend countless hours dating the adventures and working out their "true chronology." Because Doyle was somewhat careless in his references to dates and facts (the confusion over Watson's first name and the precise location of his old war wound has already been noted), critics are able to use these chronologies to "prove" that Watson must have been married several times, or that the dates cited by Watson for a number of cases are absolutely "wrong." Naturally this obsession for dating the cases is not something Doyle expected, or perhaps he would have been more precise. He could not, however, have anticipated the degree to which the Holmes cult would expand.

The next story in the series, "The Adventure of the Engineer's Thumb," is a far less satisfying tale than "The Adventure of the Speckled Band." It presents the story of Victor Hatherly, a hydraulic engineer who comes to Watson for treatment, having had his thumb amputated in what he calls a "murderous attack." Curious, Watson introduces Hatherly to Holmes, and the engineer tells how he was approached by Colonel Lysander Stark, who offered him a large sum of money to examine a hydraulic stamping machine that was malfunctioning. The work would take only an hour but must be performed in absolute secrecy. Hatherly agreed and was placed in a closed carriage to travel to his appointment so that he could not see exactly where he was taken. He was led into a dark house and shown into a small room, actually the compression chamber of a huge press. Hatherly inspected the machine, discovered why it was not working properly, but demanded to know what the press was used for, sensing he had been lied to and led into some clandestine operation. Stark replied by throwing him into the press chamber and starting the machine. As the ceiling descended, Hatherly noticed a small opening in the wall through which he forced himself to freedom. He ran through the strange house, assisted by an unknown woman who suddenly appeared, and dropped from an upper-story window. While he was hanging from the window, Hatherly's thumb was severed by Stark, wielding a cleaver.

Holmes and Watson accompany Hatherly to the station where he entered the closed cab, attempting to determine where he might have been taken from there. Their questions are answered when they see a large fire in a nearby house. In his escape Hatherly dropped an oil-lamp which started the conflagration and exposed the location of a counterfeiting ring that had been using the press to produce coins. The counterfeiters themselves have disappeared and are never caught, although their work at this location is finished. Hatherly has lost his thumb and his fee, but has gained "experience" in the words of Holmes.

In "The Adventure of the Noble Bachelor" the case opens with Holmes receiving a letter from a Lord St. Simon, whose marriage to Hatty Doran, the daughter of a California millionaire, was somewhat dampened when the bride vanished shortly after the wedding and never appeared at the wedding breakfast. Holmes claims to have solved the case before St. Simon comes to explain the details of the mystery, and when Lestrade, who has been dragging the river, arrives, Holmes tells him that "there is not, and there never has been, any such person" as Lady St. Simon. Holmes then goes out for the afternoon and returns to stage a dinner at which many surprises will be revealed. Lord St. Simon arrives, and then a Mr. and Mrs. Francis Hay Moulton; Mrs. Moulton is St. Simon's recent "bride." The Moultons were married in the American west; Francis Moulton went prospecting in Arizona and Mrs. Moulton heard he had been killed by Indians. After a year passed and there was no word from him she assumed the story was indeed true, and so she felt free to seek a new husband. Francis had in fact only been captured, rather than killed, by the Indians, and when he escaped he attempted to find her, showing up in the church on her wedding day. She saw him and "vanished" soon afterwards. Holmes has solved the problem by simply thinking over the facts of the case and then checking London hotels until he found the couple, a solution that is much more easily accomplished in fiction than in real life.

"The Adventure of the Beryl Coronet" brings a frantic man to 221B Baker Street who seems more distraught by his problem than any client yet seen. The man is Alexander Holder, senior partner of the second largest bank in London. He has been approached by an extremely important client (whom he will not name) who has borrowed fifty thousand pounds and left as collateral a beryl coronet, an invaluable artifact apparently belonging to the royal family. Holder is so stunned by having this national treasure left in his care that he decides to take it home and guard it around the clock. Needless to say, the worst happens and Holder awakens in the night to find his son holding the damaged coronet and three of its jewels missing. He explodes in anger and his son responds in kind by refusing to answer any questions about the crime. The police are brought in and the son is arrested. The missing piece of the coronet has not been found.

Holmes points out that there are many problems in assuming young Arthur Holder is responsible, not the least of which is the fact that the jewels he allegedly took cannot be found. He goes to Holder's home to examine the scene and questions the other members of the household. Holder tells Holmes that he will pay any sum for the return of the jewels, and Holmes works late into the night roaming the streets. The next morning when Holder arrives at Baker Street even more distraught, Holmes asks him to write a check for four-thousand pounds and then Holmes dramatically presents him with the missing jewels.

The true thieves turn out to be Holder's trusted niece Mary and her lover George Burnwell, a gambler. Arthur saw Mary pass the coronet out the window to Burnwell, and so he quickly jumped into the street and fought to get it back. When Arthur returned the coronet to his father's room he discovered it had been damaged; his father awoke and apprehended him at just that moment. Holmes has deduced much of this from the story he had been told, and from footprints he has found around the house. Holmes confronted Burnwell and discovered he had already fenced the jewels, but Holmes was able to locate them and buy them back. Holder will have to make peace with his unjustly accused son, repair the coronet, and adjust to the loss of his favorite niece. Conan Doyle would have liked to kill off Holmes at this point. His mother, among others, urged him not to, and she sent him the idea he used for the final story in the series.

"The Adventure of the Copper Beeches" rounds out the first twelve short stories. It begins with Holmes praising Watson for choosing for publication a representative sample of his cases, although Holmes feels Watson does "embellish" somewhat and tends to focus on the crime rather than the logic that solves the crime. According to Holmes, Watson has "degraded what should have been a course of lectures into a series of tales." Holmes feels his own practice has reached its nadir, for he has just received a letter from a young woman, Violet Hunter, seeking his advice on whether she should accept a position as a governess. She has been offered a job at a salary over twice what she expected, and will receive half of her annual salary in advance. One of the conditions of the position, however, is that she must cut her hair and agree to dress as her employers request. She is reluctant to cut her hair and so declines the position, but comes to Holmes when the offer is renewed and the salary increased even more. She takes the job when Holmes agrees to come to her if she needs help.

The call for help comes very quickly. Holmes and Watson arrive at the scene and Miss Hunter explains that on several occasions she has been asked to sit in front of a window in a blue dress, while her employer marches up and down and tells her humorous stories. She is not allowed to look out the window, but one day uses a small mirror to see a man watching the window from the road. Mr. Rucastle, her employer, keeps a huge mastiff for a guard dog, and he and his wife have apparently sealed off one wing of the house, although Miss Hunter sees them occasionally visiting these deserted rooms. She sneaks into this wing one evening and thinks she hears footsteps; she is certain all this evidence indicates something untoward is happening.

Holmes deduces that Violet Hunter has been hired to impersonate the Rucastle's daughter, who for some reason is being hidden in the closed wing. He and Watson enter the house, but the Rucastle girl has gone. An angry Rucastle discovers them and releases the mastiff, which in its confusion attacks and nearly kills him. Alice Rucastle, they learn, has been kept out of sight by her father to discourage an eager suitor, for marriage would deprive Rucastle of his daughter's income. Violet Hunter's impersonation was intended to convince the young man that Alice was happy and content, with no interest in leaving her father and stepmother.

Although the idea for this story came from Doyle's mother, the tale owes a good deal to gothic romance, particularly the novel *Jane Eyre*, in which a young governess is hired by an employer who keeps a woman–his mad wife–locked away in his house in a secret chamber. Many details have been changed, of course, but Rucastle, like Rochester, has the ability to be both charming and witty, and then suddenly explode in angry fury. The huge hound Rucastle keeps resembles Rochester's gigantic dog Pilot, and, like Rochester, Rucastle survives his tragedy, but lives out a diminished life, chastened somewhat by his experiences. Doyle's turning to other literary works for ideas suggests that the pressure of constantly coming up with new and inventive situations was already wearing on him. Even so, he paused only briefly before beginning a new series of twelve tales, the series he assumed would finally be the last of the saga of Holmes and Watson. Interest in the first dozen stories was so great that they were collected in one volume (a practice that was to become the standard procedure for all the Holmes short stories) as *The Adventures of Sherlock Holmes* (1892).[3]

The Memoirs of Sherlock Holmes (1894) contains eleven of the twelve adventures that were published in *The Strand* in 1892–93. The first of these stories, "The Adventure of Silver Blaze," is one of the best of the whole cycle. As Holmes and Watson speed off via train for Dartmoor to look into the disappearance of a race horse, Silver Blaze, and the murder of its trainer, Holmes reestablishes his credentials for his readers after a six-month absence from print by estimating the speed of their train to be exactly fifty-three and one-half miles per hour. The calculation, he says, "is a simple one" (*CSH*, p.335). At Dartmoor he and Watson meet with Inspector Gregory, who is investigating the case, and examine the possessions of Straker, the murdered trainer, finding among them a curious surgical knife. Holmes pursues his investigation and discovers Silver Blaze, found wandering on the moors and concealed by a horse dealer who has bet on Silver Blaze's rival. Holmes does not reveal to Colonel Ross, the owner, that he has found the horse. He returns to London with Watson, but the murder has still not been solved.

At the race for the Wessex Cup a few days later a strange horse wearing Ross's colors wins. The horse is Silver Blaze, his markings camouflaged just as they were when Holmes found him. The murderer, Holmes dramatically reveals, is the horse itself. Straker had taken the horse onto the moors where he hoped to nick its tendon with the surgical knife just enough to damage its chances in the race. Silver Blaze, however, was startled and kicked the trainer in the head before Straker could do his damage. The horse then wandered onto the moors where it was found and correspondingly hidden.

Doyle is able to baffle his reader by the linking together of several different puzzles. Straker intended to injure the horse, but not hide it. The man who held the horse did so because he found it loose; he would not have had the courage to try to injure it or even steal it. The death of Straker was completely accidental and might have oc- curred whet   her he approached the horse with criminal intent or not. By weaving these situations together Conan Doyle creates a mystery that stems from the juxtaposition of several coincidences, thereby writing a story that reflects the complexities of life itself. Holmes is of course attuned to the complexities of "everyday life," and this is what allows him to observe what others do not.

The most famous piece of dialogue in this story cap- tures perfectly Holmes's ability to notice the unnotice- able ripples on the surface of life. Inspector Gregory is speaking to Holmes about the clues he has found:

> "Is there any point to which you would wish to draw my attention?"
> "To the curious incident of the dog in the night-time."
> "The dog did nothing in the night-time."
> "That was the curious incident," remarked Sherlock Holmes.
> (CSH, p.347)

The essence of Holmes's power, we should note, is his ability to notice when things do not happen, as well as when they do.

In "The Adventure of the Yellow Face" Watson begins with a short preface explaining that the case is unusual because Holmes could not successfully solve it. Grant Munro, a well-established hop merchant, comes to Holmes concerned about the renters of a small cottage near his home. He has seen a strange face peering from the window of this house; furthermore, his wife has begun acting suspiciously, has requested a large sum of money, and has now begun to visit this cottage. When confronted she tells him he must not examine the case any further for their lives are at stake. Nevertheless, Munro visits the house, finds no one there, but discovers a recent photograph of his wife prominently displayed.

Holmes surmises that the wife's first husband is living in the cottage and blackmailing her. Munro decides to force his way into the cottage, despite his wife's protest, so he calls Holmes and Watson to the scene to assist. When the three of them enter the house they do not discover a husband, but rather find a little black girl wearing a mask—the "yellow face." The child is the result of Mrs. Munro's first marriage to an American black, and the girl has been hidden away because of her racial heritage. The Munros are reconciled and Holmes and Watson return to London.

Interracial marriage was of course much less socially acceptable in Doyle's time than it is today, and the marriage Mrs. Munro describes would have in fact been illegal in the state of Georgia where it supposedly took place. It is to Doyle's credit that, as a product of an imperialistic culture, he does not take a racist stand on this issue, although he does use the sudden unmasking of the black child to shock his readers. The case is nevertheless one of the least satisfying that Doyle has published to this point, because the case is "solved" largely through strong-arm tactics. Holmes has a theory (which he quite uncharacteristically reveals to Watson *before* he knows it is valid), but he is wrong. In the end, Holmes, Watson, and Munro simply force their way into the cottage; even Lestrade could have done that.

"The Adventure of the Stockbroker's Clerk" is not a much better effort, and essentially repeats the fundamental structure of "The Red-Headed League": a man is hired and paid a great sum of money to do a largely inconsequential task in an isolated office while a crime is committed in his absence. In this instance, Mr. Hall Pycroft, a stockbroker's clerk, is hired away from a new job before he can report for his first day of work. While he is directed to a shabby office to do minor secretarial jobs, an imposter reports to his original job at a financial house and uses his name. The imposter attempts a robbery, but is captured. His brother, an accomplice, tries suicide when Holmes and Watson arrive at Pycroft's "office" to investigate; Holmes and Watson thwart the suicide but are forced to discover the details of the crime by reading them in the newspaper. The entire episode is similar to "The Adventure of the Yellow Face" in that Holmes does little to solve the crime other than visit Pycroft's "employer." It is at this point that the "employer" panics and the deception is revealed. Again, Lestrade could have handled the case as well.

The next story in the volume, "The Adventure of the 'Gloria Scott,'" is also somewhat weak, but has the distinction of being the first case Holmes ever handled, a case that occurred, of course, before Watson came into his life. It involves the father of a friend Holmes had met at college, Victor Trevor. One evening while Holmes is present, Trevor senior is visited by an old acquaintance named Hudson, a sailor whom Mr. Trevor has not seen for thirty years. Mr. Trevor's health declines from the point of this visit and Holmes is later summoned by Victor when his father's death seems imminent. Mr. Trevor has kept the mysterious Hudson on at the house, making him gardener and then butler; Hudson has risen to become a dominant figure in the household, even seeming to acquire some power over the senior Trevor. After Hudson leaves to visit Beddoes, another acquaintance known to both him and Trevor, Mr. Trevor receives a mysterious letter that sends him to his deathbed.

Holmes decodes this curious letter, and then Victor produces a statement his father had written shortly before his death. The statement explains that Mr. Trevor was actually James Armitage, convicted of embezzlement and placed in the prison ship *Gloria Scott* for transportation to

Australia. The *Gloria Scott* never completed its journey, however, but was taken over by its prisoners. Jack Prendergast, another prisoner, was a leader in the rebellion and responsible for the deaths of many of the crew. Armitage and others objected to the brutality of Prendergast, so they were put adrift in a small boat. Picked up by a passing craft, they pretended to be survivors of a foundered passenger ship. Armitage and a friend (Beddoes) changed their names, prospered in Australia, and then returned to England with their secrets. All was fine until Prendergast/Hudson showed up to blackmail the pair. Holmes, who admittedly is a novice detective, does really nothing in the case besides cracking the code in the letter received by Trevor; all the facts are revealed in Trevor's written statement.

If Conan Doyle's inventiveness seemed to be sagging in "The Adventure of the Yellow Face," "The Adventure of the Stockbroker's Clerk," and "The Adventure of the 'Gloria Scott,'" he made up for their weaknesses and demonstrated he still had the ability to write a first-class story by creating one of his best adventures in "The Musgrave Ritual." It, like "The Adventure of the 'Gloria Scott,'" was one of Holmes's very early cases, taking place when he lived alone in Montague Street, before he and Watson moved into 221B. Like the "Gloria Scott" case, it involves a college friend, Reginald Musgrave, and that friend's father. Musgrave lives at Hurlstone, a large rambling house that employs a sizable staff. As Reginald Musgrave wanders through the house one evening, he finds the butler, Brunton, in the library examining a map and what appear to be family papers. Musgrave is outraged by this snooping into private documents; he gives Brunton a week to leave the household, greatly distressing the butler who has served for over twenty years. After two days Brunton disappears; his clothes are still in his room so he apparently has not packed and left. Another employee and former lover of Brunton's, Rachel Howells, becomes hysterical over his absence, and two days later she too mysteriously disappears. The lake is dragged; no bodies are discovered, but a bag containing what seems to be a lump of shapeless metal and glass is found. Its relevance to the problem is not clear to Musgrave.

Holmes examines the paper Brunton was found studying. It is a copy of a family ceremony, the "Musgrave Ritual," which consists of a set of questions and answers read by each Musgrave on coming of age. The ritual has been in the family for centuries. Reginald has no understanding of its meaning or importance, but simply dismisses the ritual as a curious family tradition. Here is the ritual:

"Whose was it?"
"His who is gone."
"Who shall have it?"
"He who will come."[4]
"Where was the sun?"
"Over the oak."
"Where was the shadow?"
"Under the elm."
"How was it stepped?"
"North by ten and by ten, east by five and by five, south by two and by two, west by one and by one, and so under."
"What shall we give for it?"
"All that is ours."
"Why should we give it?"
"For the sake of the trust." (CSH, p.392)

Holmes travels to Hurlstone and examines the grounds. The house itself dates back to 1607 and parts of it may be older still. Holmes concludes that certain measurements are alluded to in the ritual, so he takes a fishing line and compass and paces off his calculations. There are signs that someone else has done this recently, and Holmes assumes it was Brunton. Holmes's measurements take him to the cellar, where a large stone in the floor is lifted to reveal the body of Brunton. With the assistance of Rachel Howells, Brunton apparently had lifted the stone so that he could lower himself into a small room beneath the floor where a chest was hidden. Then the heavy stone either slipped or was caused to fall by Rachel, who was jealous of Brunton's interest in another woman, and Brunton was trapped and left to die beneath the floor. Rachel threw into the lake the bag Brunton had passed up to her in order to conceal her part in the tragedy; then, after several days of hysterical panic, she left the neighborhood and apparently the country as well.

The chest Brunton was seeking is discovered to contain a few metal coins dating from the reign of Charles the First, but not enough to make the cache valuable. The real treasure turns out to be the twisted metal retrieved from the lake. It is the crown of the Stuarts, hidden after the execution of Charles I so that it could be returned to Charles II following the Puritan revolution. The questions of the ritual clearly refer to this, as Holmes points out. Over the centuries, however, somehow the explanation of what the ritual signified was forgotten by the Musgraves, although the ritual itself was carefully passed on.

There are several reasons for this story's success. Doyle uses the ritual as a centerpiece for what is essentially a treasure hunt, always a subject that intrigues readers. Robert Louis Stevenson's *Treasure Island* and Poe's "The Gold-Bug" have quite similar searches for buried treasure, but Doyle was able to include the mystique of these exotic adventure stories without having Holmes leave England. More important, in this story Conan Doyle was able to bring to the Holmes cycle his love of historical fiction, giving the Musgrave family a role in one of his country's most significant events and allowing Holmes actually to hold a fabled historical treasure. Hurlstone, centuries old, with its elegant park and trophy-covered walls represents the Romantic traditions Doyle had read about in Scotland and had been told about since he was a child. The fact that a family could survive and pass a ritual or custom down for centuries in itself fascinated Doyle, who was always charmed by the family legends his mother told him. Even Reginald Musgrave himself has a Romantic aura about him. Holmes tells Watson that he "never looked at his [Reginald's] pale, keen face or the poise of his head without associating him with gray archways and mullioned windows and all the venerable wreckage of a feudal keep" (*CSH*, p.388). By combining his enthusiasm for Romantic historical fiction and adventure tales with his detective story, Doyle was able to create the very distinctive atmosphere of "The Adventure of the Musgrave Ritual" that makes it one of the best and most popular stories in the series, even though Watson is not an active participant in the episode. As a general rule, the few stories in which Watson does not play an important part are considered to be among the weaker ones in the series; in this story, however, the atmosphere is so powerful that Watson's absence is not noticed.

"The Adventure of the Reigate Squire" begins with Holmes suffering from the stresses of overwork. Watson proposes that they spend a few days in the country at the home of Colonel Hayter where Holmes can recuperate. A burglary at one neighbor's house and a murder at another quickly ends Holmes's vacation, however, when the police seek his assistance. The murdered man, William Kirwan, was a servant who had apparently surprised a burglar; in his hand is found a piece of a note that suggests he may have been keeping an appointment.

To solve the case Holmes goes to great length to throw his suspects off the track. He fakes a fainting spell, feigns forgetfulness, and even clumsily knocks over a table and blames it on Watson, hoping to create the image of an inept detective and cause the murderers to reveal their hand. They do, and nearly strangle him, but help comes in time. The killers, a father and son, murdered William Kirwan, who was threatening to reveal that they had broken in the home of a neighbor hoping to find a document that would aid them in a lawsuit. Holmes solves the case primarily by using handwriting analysis; he also finds a good many inconsistencies in the killers' alibis. The story's chief interest, however, lies in Holmes's own clever use of deceptiveness; he demonstrates convincingly that when he appears to be baffled he may in fact be bluffing in order to gain a greater advantage.

In "The Adventure of the Crooked Man" Holmes invites Watson to join him in an investigation of the murder of Colonel James Barclay, a military officer who dies under suspicious circumstances. He was heard arguing with his wife behind a locked parlor door; her sudden screams brought the servants who entered through open French windows off the garden. Barclay is dead from an apparent blow to the head; his wife is unconscious in a fainting spell. The most curious point is that the key to the locked room has never been found; a locksmith is required to open the door. On the scene Holmes finds some mysterious footprints that indicate another man had entered the room through the open window, along with a strange animal. It is this intruder, Holmes feels, who took the key. There are, however, no suspects.

Holmes interviews Mrs. Barclay's friend Miss Morrison, who had been out with her the evening the murder took place. Miss Morrison tells Holmes of a chance encounter Mrs. Barclay had with a deformed man, a man Mrs. Barclay said was an old acquaintance she had not seen for thirty years. Holmes locates the deformed man, Henry Wood, and asks Watson to accompany him when he questions Wood about the murder. Wood denies the murder, but has a story to tell all the same. He had served in India with Colonel Barclay and both were rivals for the same woman's hand. Barclay betrayed Wood and caused him to be captured by rebel outlaws. Wood was tortured and eventually crippled by the rebels; Barclay married the woman. Their paths had never crossed until recently.

Wood had determined he would see the couple before he died, so he returned to England and took a room near Barclay's regiment. He met Mrs. Barclay, told her how Barclay had betrayed him, then, unknown to her, followed her home and witnessed the argument that took place when she confronted her husband with this knowledge. Wood, in distress, came to the window where he was seen by Barclay, who instantly died "from fright," hitting his head as he fell. Wood, afraid he would be charged with murder, entered the room, took the key from the door and fled. The strange footprints Holmes had seen belonged to Wood's pet mongoose, an animal he used like an organ-grinder's monkey to make his living. Holmes does not tell the police about Wood's role in the incident because the official inquest determines that Barclay died of apoplexy; no crime took place.

In "The Adventure of the Resident Patient," Holmes and Watson are visited by Dr. Percy Trevelyan, who was set up in his practice by a man named Blessington, a benefactor who suddenly appeared one day. Blessington, who has a weak heart, agreed to finance Trevelyan's new practice and pay Trevelyan a percentage of its total income, on the condition that Blessington become a kind of resident patient; Blessington will live in the house and always have access to the doctor so his condition can constantly be monitored. Trevelyan agrees and the business is a success; he prospers, quite pleased with the arrangement.

As Trevelyan explains to Holmes, however, Blessington's condition has deteriorated rapidly and he seems to live in fear of something he will not identify. When it appears that a patient has left the consulting room and visited Blessington's quarters, Blessington becomes hysterical and asks that Trevelyan bring Holmes to the scene. Holmes visits Blessington but feels the man is not revealing the true reasons for his anxiety. The next morning Holmes and Watson find that Blessington has committed suicide.

When Holmes visits Blessington's residence he concludes that the apparent suicide is actually a case of murder. Holmes takes a photo of Blessington to the police headquarters and returns with the news that he was actually a bank robber named Sutton. When arrested, Sutton turned informer and the rest of his gang was captured and convicted. Sutton/Blessington then used some of the stolen money to finance Trevelyan and lived an isolated life in comparative freedom until his gang was released from prison. Two of them pretended to be patients in order to get at Sutton/Blessington; his death proves they finally succeeded. The murderers are not caught but apparently die on a ship that is lost at sea.

In "The Adventure of the Greek Interpreter" we meet for the first time one of the more interesting characters in the cycle–Holmes's brother Mycroft. Holmes feels that Mycroft's powers of observation are much superior to his own, but explains that Mycroft spends most of his time idling away the hours in the Diogenes club, a gathering place for the "most unsociable and unclubable men in town." When Watson visits the Diogenes Club with Holmes he finds Mycroft to be a rather large and fat man, and certainly every bit as observant and clever as Sherlock has made him out to be.

Mycroft introduces them to a friend, Mr. Melas, who has a problem. Melas is a Greek interpreter for the courts, and frequently finds himself visited by foreign travelers with problems. One night his services are requested and he is driven about for several hours, in a cab with the windows covered, before stopping at a large house. In this house Melas is told to question in Greek a man whose mouth is bound; the man responds by writing his replies on a slate. Melas, quickly sensing that his employers understand no Greek at all, begins to add his own queries to the questions he is forced to ask; Paul Kratides, the prisoner, responds to these questions, unbeknownst to his captors. A woman suddenly bursts into the room and the prisoner jumps up to embrace her. He is restrained and the interview is over.

Melas is paid for his services, told never to mention the incident to anyone, and driven about in the sealed carriage for a time. Melas has told only Mycroft and the police about the episode, and Mycroft has placed an advertisement in the paper seeking information. When a response does come to the advertisement, it mentions a house that is very likely the place where the episode took place. Holmes, Watson, and Mycroft drive to the house after discovering that Melas has apparently been kidnapped by the same people who employed him. They enter the house and discover Melas and Kratides nearly dead from suffocation. Upon being revived the two men tell a story that matches almost exactly Holmes's deductions up to this point, although some of the story is never completely explained. Sophy Kratides, the sister of Paul, had met a young Englishman on a visit to England, and was either persuaded by him to stay or simply prevented from returning to Greece. When her brother Paul arrived to bring her home, he was held prisoner and concealed from his sister while his captors attempted to force him to sign away his and her estates. Betrayed by Melas, the pair of kidnappers are forced to flee the country with the girl. Both are later found stabbed and Holmes suspects that Sophy Kratides has had her revenge. Despite Holmes's praise, Mycroft is really not instrumental in solving the case.

"The Adventure of the Naval Treaty," although only

slightly longer than some of the adventures, was first published in two parts in October and November, 1893. Doyle presumably did this to allow the December issue of *The Strand* to carry the last Holmes story, "The Adventure of the Final Problem." The holiday issues of magazines were "special," as they still are today; it would not do to let Holmes die in November, leaving the December issue without him and Watson, so "The Adventure of the Naval Treaty" was stretched a bit to allow it to run in October and November, leaving December for the finale.

In this story it is Watson who is actually approached by the client, an old friend, Percy Phelps, who would like Watson to bring Holmes into an investigation. Holmes agrees and the pair are soon on the train bound for Woking. There they find Watson's friend recuperating from nervous strain and exhaustion, cared for principally by his fiancée Annie Harrison and her brother Joseph. Phelps, who works at the Foreign Office, was entrusted with the original of a treaty between England and Italy. Phelps was to copy the document in his office, but was warned to take extreme care to ensure that the contents of this document remain absolutely secret. Working late at copying the treaty, Phelps sent for a cup of coffee, and when it did not come he wandered down the hall to get it himself. While doing so he heard the signal bell in his office ring, indicating someone was in there; he ran back to the office but the treaty was gone. Phelps searched the streets for a culprit, but found nothing. Scotland Yard was instantly called in and the commissionaire and his wife (the only other people in the building at the time of the theft) were questioned and searched; nothing was found. Phelps is confined to bed from the strain of the situation and has been there for over nine weeks when he recovers enough energy to summon Watson and Holmes.

Holmes and Watson talk with Phelps, then return to

London and place an advertisement in the paper seeking a cabman who might have dropped off a fare at the Foreign Office on the night the treaty was taken. Holmes feels that the fact no news of the secret treaty has appeared in the press after nearly two months is very significant. The case takes a different turn when Phelps is awakened in the night by the sounds of a man attempting to break into his room. Holmes and Watson again visit the ailing man, then Holmes announces they will all return to London together. At the last minute, however, Holmes sends only Phelps and Watson back while he remains in Woking to spend the night. The next morning Holmes returns to Baker Street with his head bandaged, looking a bit haggard. He says little, but insists that Phelps sit down to breakfast; when the cover on the dish is raised there lies the missing treaty.

Holmes then explains how he waited outside Phelps's home with the expectation that the intruder of the previous night would return. A man did appear, opened the window, and climbed into Phelps's bedroom, where he removed the missing treaty from an opening beneath the carpet. Holmes apprehended the burglar, who turned out to be Joseph Harrison, the brother of Phelps's fiancée.

Holmes explains that Joseph Harrison had stopped at the Foreign Office to pick up Phelps so they could take the train home together. Entering by a side door, Harrison went to Phelps's office just after Phelps had stepped out. Harrison rang the bell, then noticed the treaty lying on the desk. Sensing it was an important document, he instantly grabbed it, took it to Woking and hid it under the floor in his bedroom, but was immediately moved from that room when it became a sickroom for the distressed Phelps. In short, Phelps has been "guarding" the treaty with his presence for ten weeks, because Harrison has no way of removing the treaty while the room is occupied.

The story is one of the better ones in the series, and actually benefits from Doyle's story-stretching. The extra length allows Holmes to wax philosophically while he rides the train with Watson, and also allows the pair to engage in some interviews for which there would not normally have been space. The nature of the crime–the treaty was taken on impulse by someone who only accidentally happened across it–makes the mystery particularly puzzling, because the nature of the theft suggests a carefully premeditated plan. The charm of the story is that the episode was far more simple than it appeared to be, and only Holmes was not fooled by its simplicity.

In "The Adventure of the Final Problem," Doyle makes it clear from Watson's very first words–"It is with a heavy heart that I take up my pen to write these last words in which I shall ever record the singular gifts by which my friend Mr. Sherlock Holmes was distinguished"–that this will be the conclusion of the series (*CSH*, p.469). Strangely, perhaps, the story contains no real mystery, but only records a pursuit. Holmes arrives in Watson's consulting room looking quite nervous and harried. He explains to Watson that his nemesis, Professor Moriarty, the "Napoleon of crime [and] . . . organizer of half that is evil and of nearly all that is undetected" in London has been haunting him (*CSH*, p.471). Moriarty has been threatening Holmes's life and is now acting to carry out those threats; Holmes has already had three very close calls. He sees himself as being in such danger that he refuses even to spend the night with Watson, for fear he might endanger his old friend. Watson does agree to go with Holmes to the continent, however, where they plan to stay for a few days until the police, acting upon the information Holmes has given them, arrest Moriarty.

Watson arrives at the train station to depart and finds Holmes there disguised as a priest. Moriarty has set fire to their rooms in Baker Street, Holmes tells an astonished Watson. Despite their elaborate precautions, Moriarty is in hot pursuit, so Holmes and Watson change trains before boarding the ship to France, where they telegraph London and discover that the London police have arrested all of Moriarty's gang, but Moriarty himself has escaped. Holmes and Watson pass into Switzerland and stay in a small hotel at Meiringen, near the Reichenbach Falls. While visiting the falls Watson receives a message that a traveler is in need of a physician. He hurries back to the inn, leaving Holmes on the narrow path overlooking the chasm. When Watson reaches the inn he discovers the note was faked. Watson rushes back to the falls but finds only Holmes's alpine-stock, his silver cigarette case, and a short note. In the note Holmes says that he suspected the message for Watson was a ruse, but allowed Watson to leave to permit a confrontation with Moriarty. Watson concludes that a struggle occurred on the narrow pathway, and that both combatants tumbled to their deaths in the falls far below. Such was the end, Watson tells us, of "the best and wisest man whom I have ever known" (*CSH*, p.480).

Several things about the story are noteworthy. First, Doyle does very little with the narrative plot; the reader is never told, for example, what Moriarty and his gang have specifically done, nor does the reader learn exactly what Holmes has done to "inconvenience" and "incommode" him. (Although after this episode Moriarty's villainy would make his name famous as Holmes's nemesis–he is the only criminal Holmes combats in more than one adventure–Doyle's readers in 1893 might, like Watson, have wondered why they had never heard of him in the series before, particularly given the magnitude of his evil influence.) The reader is given only a chase and the end of Holmes; Doyle is able to make the pursuit high-pitched and exciting and thus maintain interest. Second, although

Doyle said he wanted to do away with Holmes for good, he did not firmly close the door. No body is discovered, and thus the revival of Holmes at a later date is fairly simple. Why did not Doyle do a better job of killing off Holmes? Perhaps he wanted to spare his readers the sight of their hero's corpse and the awkwardness of a funeral and burial. Perhaps though he consciously wanted to eliminate Holmes, he knew that someday he might need him again. No writer who lives by his creativity is absolutely certain that he will always be able to please his public. With Holmes, Doyle was certain of pleasing, but the stories, which had appeared monthly for a total of two years, were preventing him from doing other things. If he could, he would do without Holmes; if he needed Holmes again at a later date, he still had not really provided an absolute end for the cycle.

Many readers feel that the best of Holmes and Watson is found in the first half of the stories, before the "death" at Reichenbach Falls. It is clear that Doyle returned time and again to a certain formula. Only a handful of the stories, for example, deal with the planning and commission of a contemporary crime. In most of the adventures the important action has occurred in the previous generation. A great many children in the Holmes cycle are trying to untangle the sins and indiscretions of their fathers. Two-thirds of the cases in the series involve either revenge being taken for a past action, or an attempt to cover up or conceal a past action, usually through blackmail. In a large number of these situations the disposition of an estate is also an issue. Doyle's extraordinary concern with truth and fair play may explain the direction these stories have taken. In the first half of the Holmes cycle justice may be delayed, but it is not defeated. Crimes that are committed may go unpunished for twenty or thirty years, but sooner or later a crooked man appears on the sidewalk, or a mysterious note arrives in the mail, and all the years of guilt and concealment are overturned. In the few cases where the culprits manage to elude Holmes or Scotland Yard, the villains invariably drown in a shipwreck, or die of a heart attack, or meet some other horrible fate neatly recorded in a postscript by Watson. There is, then, a highly intense moral tone in the fiction. Wrong is wrong and right is right, although it should be pointed out that right is not always what the law dictates. Holmes is emblematic of an even higher law than Britain's, a moral code of conduct true to eternal values and as idealistically pure as King Arthur's. When Holmes sees fit, for example, he does not report some questionable actions and chooses to ignore some crimes. In this respect he closely resembles Conan Doyle himself, who willingly tangled with the legal system (as he did in the Slater and Edalji cases) when he felt that true justice had not been achieved.

4

Holmes Redux: 1901–1904

Holmes lay "dead" for eight years while Conan Doyle turned to other subjects. When we look at the fiction he produced between 1894 and 1901 we find very little that is significant. It is, in fact, the period of his life in which his imaginative writing is weakest, although his very important and well-received nonfiction history *The Great Boer War* was published in 1900. Doyle's reputation, particularly after his book on the Boer war, was still strong, but he had written a great many books since the death of Holmes and had not achieved more than a moderate commercial success with any of them. It was still primarily as the creator of Holmes and Watson that he was known to the public. He did not need more money, and he could scarcely acquire more fame, but there was always the simple matter of pride. William Gillette's play *Sherlock Holmes*, which Gillette had written and produced with Doyle's assistance and blessing, was an amazing success and opened in London after a triumphant tour of the United States. The time was right for a return of Holmes, but a return under circumstances fully agreeable to Doyle. A Holmes novel, for example, unlike a series of Holmes stories, could be written at Doyle's own pace. It would not repeatedly demand, as a series of adventures would, a new plot, a new idea each month; it was never the character of Holmes that had bothered Conan Doyle so much as the pressure of the contracts he had signed. Freed from that pressure, and given the renewed popularity Gillette's dramatization had created, it is really not surprising that Doyle should turn back to his touchstone, Sherlock Holmes.

Doyle himself, however, explained the return of Holmes in a slightly different way. While on a vacation at Dartmoor with his friend Fletcher Robinson, Doyle heard from Robinson a folk legend about a ghostly hound that roamed the moors. Doyle (who dedicated the finished book to Robinson) wanted to work this legend into a novel, and decided that rather than create an entirely new set of characters for this book, it would be simpler to return to the well-drawn figures he already had in his repertoire–Holmes and Watson. Of course now that we have the novel in hand it is difficult to imagine it could have been written with a different set of characters, for it seems to be the perfect vehicle for the great detective and his friend; many readers, in fact, feel it is the best Holmes story of all. Nevertheless, it is not improper to see the book as a kind of experiment on Conan Doyle's part. He carefully set this adventure prior to Holmes's "death" at Reichenbach Falls, in the period before Watson's marriage when he and Holmes were happily residing in Baker Street.[1] If the return of Holmes were not particularly successful, Conan Doyle could leave him safely "dead"; if the book were popular, Doyle could rethink the whole matter of Holmes's resurrection, but he still had no commitment beyond this novel.

As it turned out Doyle had nothing to worry about. The Hound of the Baskervilles appeared in The Strand Magazine in nine parts, beginning in August, 1901, and was an immediate popular and critical success. The story begins with Watson contemplating a walking stick, from which Holmes makes several deductions. When the owner of the walking stick returns to present his problem, Holmes's conclusions turn out (naturally) to be absolutely correct. Dr. James Mortimer, owner of the stick and physician to the late Sir Charles Baskerville, brings with him a manuscript, dated 1742, that contains the legend of Baskerville Hall. According to the legend, Hugo Baskerville, a man of intemperate habits, once kidnapped and held captive a local peasant girl to whom he was attracted. When she escaped from him across the moors he promised to "render his body and soul to the Powers of Evil" if he could recapture her. In a drunken frenzy he unleashed a pack of dogs to pursue the young girl. Her body was found later by his cohorts; the hounds ran her to death. Near her body, though, was also found the body of Hugo Baskerville; a huge black hound standing over him had ripped out his throat, apparently fulfilling the agreement Baskerville made with the forces of evil. The manuscript urges all future Baskervilles to use caution on the moors because the hound has returned to haunt the family ever since.

Holmes dismisses the story as a fairy tale, but Mortimer produces a newspaper account describing the recent death of Sir Charles Baskerville, who died under mysterious circumstances. Apparently the victim of a heart attack, Baskerville died on a midnight walk, a look of terror frozen on his face. Near his body were found the footprints of a giant hound. Holmes interrogates Mortimer about the details of the death scene; the most mysterious fact is that several people reported seeing a creature on the moor that was "luminous, ghastly and spectral." Holmes then sits down with a large-scale map of the area and a pound of tobacco, and contemplates the case. He concludes that Sir Charles Baskerville died running for his life; what Baskerville was running from is not clear.

The next morning Holmes is again visited by Dr. Mortimer, accompanied by the last of the Baskervilles, Sir Henry, a nephew of the deceased. He has just received a mysterious letter formed of words cut from a newspaper, warning him to keep away from the moor. One of his new boots is also missing and has apparently been stolen. Holmes is intrigued and agrees to meet with Baskerville again to discuss the problem further. When Baskerville and Dr. Mortimer leave 221B, however, Holmes and Watson immediately follow them. In the streets they observe what Holmes has suspected; Baskerville is being shadowed by someone else.

Arriving at Baskerville's hotel later they find Sir Henry furious because a second boot has now been stolen. Upon questioning Dr. Mortimer and Sir Henry about the man he had seen following them, Holmes learns that the man strongly resembles Barrymore, butler of the late Sir Charles. Barrymore, however, is supposed to be at Baskerville Hall, so Holmes wires Barrymore at the Hall in an attempt to confirm this. They agree that Watson will travel with Sir Henry to Baskerville Hall while Holmes remains in London on another case. Before they part, Sir Henry finds that his missing new boot has been mysteriously returned, although the second stolen boot remains missing.

While Watson rides to Baskerville Hall with Sir Henry and Dr. Mortimer, he is given a description of all the people living on the moors at or near the Hall. They are somewhat surprised, however, arriving at the edge of the desolate moor, to find soldiers looking for an escaped murderer in the area. Baskerville Hall itself is an old, elegant, and somewhat gloomy place that Sir Henry promises to renovate. As Watson lies in bed that night, staring out at the bleak landscape, he hears the muffled sobs of a woman crying in the house. The sounds stop as abruptly as they begin.

The next morning Watson meets Mrs. Barrymore, the butler's wife, and it is apparent she is the woman who was crying in the night. He also learns that the telegram Holmes sent from London was not actually delivered to Barrymore, but given to his wife instead. There is no proof, then, that Barrymore was not in London. Watson meets Stapleton, a naturalist who often hunts butterflies on the moor; he points out to Watson the great Grimpen Mire, a treacherous place full of bogs and quicksand, although Stapleton is able to pick his way through it on the narrow paths. While Stapleton is off pursuing a butterfly, his sister Beryl approaches Watson and tells him to get off the moor and to go back to London. She drops this discussion when her brother approaches, but it is soon apparent that she has mistaken Watson for Sir Henry. Watson later questions her in private about her remarks, but she refuses to elaborate beyond saying the moor is a dangerous place.

The narrative then changes slightly, taking the form of Watson's written "reports" to Holmes in London. In these letters Watson tells how Sir Henry seems to be developing a romantic attraction for Miss Stapleton. The most curious aspect of Watson's report is his description of the behavior of Barrymore, who has been seen at night staring out onto the black moor and apparently signaling from the window. When caught in the act and questioned about this activity Barrymore refuses to explain. Mrs. Barrymore, however, says that her husband was signaling to Selden the escaped convict, who is her brother. Watson and Sir Henry go out onto the moor to capture Selden. In the darkness they hear a noise that Watson identifies as the cry of the hound. They close in on Selden, but are unable to catch him. When they give up the chase they then see in the distance the figure of a man silhouetted against the sky; the man does not, however, seem to be Selden.

The narrative then undergoes another change and we are given extracts from Watson's daily diary. In these he records Barrymore's observation that Sir Charles had gone to meet a woman on the night that he died. Watson's detective work determines that the rendevous was to be with Laura Lyons, the daughter of a neighbor. The diary then ends and the narrative resumes. When Watson visits Mrs. Lyons she admits having contacted Sir Charles, but claims her reasons for doing so had nothing to do with his death. Watson accepts her story and, having been warned of some suspicious activity on the moor, he follows a boy who seems to be carrying food. The boy leads Watson to a crude camp located in some ancient stone huts. Watson waits, pistol in hand, for what he assumes will be the convict's return; instead he is greeted by Holmes.

Holmes was the silhouetted man Watson had seen on his midnight chase. He has been living in the stone hut for some time, receiving Watson's reports that were being forwarded from London. He reveals to Watson that "Miss" Stapleton, who has attracted Sir Henry's attentions, is really Stapleton's wife and not his sister. Mrs. Lyons, who is planning a divorce from her husband, is contemplating a marriage to Stapleton, whom she believes to be unmarried. Holmes is telling Watson that he believes Stapleton is involved in murder when their discussion is interrupted by a scream of terror and the cry of the hound. They charge into the darkness and soon discover the body of a man who has fallen off a cliff in panic. His clothes identify him first as Sir Henry, but closer investigation reveals him to be Selden the convict. While they examine the body Stapleton appears, claiming that he too heard the cries and came to assist. On their way back to Baskerville Hall, Holmes tells Watson that Stapleton is one of their most worthy opponents.

At the Hall Holmes inspects some of the family portraits lining the walls, and points out to Watson that Stapleton resembles the figure in one of the pictures. Holmes concludes "the fellow is a Baskerville." He sets his trap for Stapleton by summoning Lestrade from London, and then telling Sir Henry that he and Watson will be forced to return to London; in fact, they actually plan to stay. Holmes then calls on Mrs. Lyons and reveals to her that Stapleton is married. She is very angry and discloses that Stapleton, promising her marriage, was the one who urged her to arrange a rendezvous with Sir Charles and ask for financial assistance with her divorce expenses. It was also Stapleton who, after she made the appointment, asked her not to keep it. Holmes then feels he has all the information he needs, and he, Watson, and the recently arrived Lestrade, prepare to spend the evening on the moor.

They wait in the dark outside Stapleton's home, where Sir Henry has been invited for dinner, and from which, on Holmes's advice, Sir Henry intends to walk home. As the party breaks up a fog moves in, somewhat hampering their plans to follow Sir Henry. Suddenly they hear the sound of a running dog and then it is upon them, a huge black hound, with "fire burst[ing] from its open mouth" (*CSH*, p.757). Sir Henry sees the dog bearing down upon him and bolts in terror, while Holmes empties his revolver at the creature. The dog, which falls lifeless, is not a supernatural beast, but is simply a very large dog, its jaws painted with phosphorus to give it a ghastly appearance. Rushing back to Stapleton's, Holmes finds Mrs. Stapleton tied up and beaten. Stapleton has left her there and escaped into the dangerous Grimpen Mire.

The next morning Holmes and Watson inspect the Mire. There they find a hideout where Stapleton had kept the dangerous hound; they also find Sir Henry's missing boot, stolen by Stapleton to set the hound upon Baskerville's track (the other boot that had been taken and then returned was brand new and therefore of no use in such a situation). There is no sign of Stapleton himself and Watson assumes that "somewhere in the heart of the great Grimpen Mire, down in the foul slime of the huge morass which had sucked him in, this cold and cruel-hearted man is for ever buried" (*CSH*, p.760).

In the final chapter of the novel, Holmes, as usual, explains the case. Holmes has discovered that Stapleton was in fact Rodger Baskerville, nephew to Sir Charles and son of a brother who was thought to have died childless. Stapleton/Baskerville moved to Dartmoor with the intention of gaining the Baskerville estate, but with no firm plan. It was from Sir Charles himself that he learned the legend of the hound and set his plan in action. He had shadowed Sir Henry and stolen his boots, while his wife, suspicious of his actions, had sent Sir Henry the warning message. Stapleton/Baskerville wished her to draw Sir Henry into his trap, so he encouraged the affair Sir Henry was cultivating; ultimately he hoped only that Sir Henry's frequent visits would often place him on the moor alone.

The Hound of the Baskervilles is extremely successful for many reasons. Of the four novels it is easily the best plotted, and the only one that does not require a lengthy flashback; unlike the other novels (and many of the stories), it does not involve a crime motivated by revenge, so the obligatory explanation of the motive for the revenge is not needed. Doyle is also able to incorporate a subplot (something we seldom see in his fiction) very effectively with the episode of the escaped convict Selden; by weaving this subplot skillfully into the narrative he is able to maintain the suspense at a level we usually find only in the short stories. Like many of the adventures, *The Hound of the Baskervilles* does focus upon an attempt to usurp an estate. It is generally superior to the other tales with a similar theme, however, because of the very powerful atmosphere that distinguishes it.

Doyle had visited Dartmoor just before writing the novel, of course, and had experienced this bleak expanse firsthand. There are other fictional works, however, which may have influenced the novel. Poe's "The Fall of the House of Usher," for instance, a story that Doyle had previously drawn upon for "The Adventure of the Speck-led Band," contains an ancient estate, surrounded by a swampy tarn, and isolated in a bleak countryside. Poe's description of the approach to Usher's house–"During the whole of a dull, dark, and soundless day in the autumn of the year, when the clouds hung oppressively low in the heavens, I had been passing alone, on horse-back, through a singularly dreary tract of country; and at length found myself, as the shades of the evening drew on, within view of the melancholy House of Usher"[2]–is remarkably like Doyle's version of the journey to Basker-ville Hall:

> To his eyes all seemed beautiful, but to me a tinge of melan-choly lay upon the countryside, which bore so clearly the mark of the waning year. Yellow leaves carpeted the lanes and flut-tered down upon us as we passed. The rattle of our wheels died away as we drove through drifts of rotting vegetation–sad gifts, as it seemed to me, for Nature to throw before the carriage of the returning heir of the Baskervilles. (*CSH*, p.700–01)

The buildings themselves resemble each other also. The House of Usher, with its "sense of insufferable gloom," "bleak walls," "vacant eye-like windows," surrounded by "a few white trunks of decayed trees" is no more foreboding than Baskerville Hall "glimmer[ing] like a ghost," "draped in ivy," encircled by "stunted oaks and firs which had been twisted and bent by the fury of years of storm" (*CSH*, p.701–02).

The atmosphere of *The Hound of the Baskervilles* transcends these simple gothic touches, however, largely because Doyle so effectively incorporates the force of Nature into his story. Two other very powerful nineteenth-century novels, Emily Brontë's *Wuthering Heights* and Thomas Hardy's *The Return of the Native*, also employ natural settings that are quite similar to that of *The Hound of the Baskervilles*. On this moor, as on

Hardy's Egdon Heath, primal forces dominate. There are, for example, the prehistoric stone huts where Holmes resides. Dr. Mortimer, in fact, spends his time excavating the ancient barrows and discovering the bones of neolithic man. These prehistoric traces, like the decaying Baskerville Hall or even the Baskerville legend itself, surround Holmes and Watson with the evidence of a universe much older and more powerful than themselves. Darwin's evolutionary theories frightened the Victorians because they suggested an indifferent universe, operating by chance ("natural selection"), in which man, like other species, was also a changing (and therefore not permanent) creature.

By plucking his characters from their snug Baker Street flat and placing them in the middle of such a desolate and primitive atmosphere, miles from civilization, Doyle increases their vulnerability. On the moors they are alone in a way they can never be alone in London, alone in space and time and far from the achievements of a civilized world, facing the fundamental forces of the universe. It is this confrontation with cosmic powers that increases the terror of the novel. In such a place as Dartmoor forces may exist that civilized man has forgotten and long ago ceased to believe in, creatures that battled and perhaps destroyed the neolithic man whose bones now lie scattered and whose huts remain barren under the indifferent sky. In such a place, Watson's trusty revolver, which is always so reassuring in most adventures, may be absolutely worthless and of no more real advantage than the neolithic man's stone axes. The supernatural hound turns out to be something largely created by man rather than nature, but Doyle convincingly demonstrates that nature's power is not something with which to trifle when Grimpen Mire claims the body of Stapleton, much as it claimed the hapless heath pony earlier in the novel. For eons Grimpen Mire has become the final resting place for the bones of thousands of victims, both human and animal. In the "foul slime of the huge morass" one could find an evolutionary record of the creatures who have inhabited these moors, for the moor is the ultimate conqueror of the temporal life upon it.

Doyle, however, unlike the more pessimistic Hardy, is not going to leave us speculating upon our powerlessness in an indifferent universe; ultimately such contemplation can lead to a nihilistic hopelessness that would be completely alien to his fundamentally positive view of the human spirit. Masterful artist that he is, he can take us to the moors and freeze us with horror as the "enormous coal-black hound, but not such a hound as mortal eyes have ever seen" (*CSH*, p.757) bursts out of the fog; but once we have totally suspended our disbelief and accepted this supernatural phenomenon, he can return us to the logical and orderly world of Holmes the rational thinker. Doyle therefore ends the novel by moving us directly from Holmes looking out across "the huge mottled expanse of green-splotched bog which stretched away until it merged into the russet slopes of the moor" to Holmes and Watson relaxing "upon a raw and foggy night, on either side of a blazing fire in our sitting-room in Baker Street" (*CSH*, pp.760–61). The immediate juxtaposition of scenes restores us to the safe world of London, where Watson's revolver is the ultimate security and where dinner and the opera are only a few steps away. We are once again safe, and Holmes has once again been the agent of our salvation.

The reaction to *The Hound of the Baskervilles* was even more positive than Doyle might have hoped. The circulation of *The Strand* increased by thirty thousand copies an issue and people literally were lining up to buy the magazine. Doyle was once again the best-selling author in England and he was given the opportunity to become the best paid author if he would write more Holmes stories.

Few men could have resisted the flattering pressure, and so, after a year of hesitation, he began a new series of thirteen stories in the fall of 1903. Appearing monthly in *The Strand Magazine* in England and in *Collier's* magazine in the United States, these stories were later published in book form as *The Return of Sherlock Holmes* (1905).

One of the conditions set down by the publisher of *Collier's*, however, was that Holmes would need to be resurrected; naturally, allowing Holmes to survive the episode at the Reichenbach Falls would allow Doyle more creative possibilities in his series, so the only question was how it was to be accomplished. In the first story of the new series, then, "The Adventure of the Empty House," Watson acts both as doctor and amateur detective, puzzling over the details of the unsolved murder of Robert Adair, a prominent London socialite. It is a situation that at first appears to be suicide; Adair is found shot to death in a locked room. There is, however, no trace of a weapon in the room. Futhermore, there is no evidence that anyone entered or left the house, and although the house is located on a well-frequented street, no one has heard any gunshot. Adair has been shot in the head with a single soft-nosed bullet, but no one is exactly sure how the crime was committed.

When Watson strolls by the house where Adair was killed, he stumbles into an elderly gentleman carrying an armful of books, knocking some of them to the ground. The old man is very surly about the accident, so Watson is surprised to find the gentleman awaiting him when he returns home. The book collector explains to Watson he could use some more books, pointing to a gap on his shelves. Watson turns to look, and when he turns back, Sherlock Holmes, who has been disguised, is standing before him. Watson promptly faints, "for the first and last time" in his life, he claims (*CSH*, p.485).

Holmes then reveals to Watson what really happened

at Reichenbach Falls. After he had written the note that Watson found, Holmes grappled with Moriarty, finally throwing him into the abyss. Holmes then climbed the very steep rock face to a ledge above the path. There he was nearly crushed when a confederate of Moriarty's rolled a rock down towards him from the top of the cliff. Holmes then scrambled back onto the path and off into the darkness, but because some of Moriarty's men were still at large, decided to let the world believe he was dead. Only Mycroft was aware of the truth, Holmes reveals, and tells Watson that he spent his three missing years traveling, visiting Tibet, Persia, Khartoum, and finally living in France. When he heard that only one of Moriarty's men was still alive, Holmes felt it was safe enough to return to England to look into the same murder that Watson is investigating. According to Holmes, Mycroft has kept the rooms in Baker Street preserved as they were (there is no mention of the fire Moriarty set in "The Final Problem"), so Holmes invites Watson to join him that evening as he attempts to solve the murder (Watson's wife is also not mentioned in this story). The old friends are together again and the game is afoot. Even Watson is excited, noting that "it was indeed like old time when . . . I found myself seated beside him in a hansom, my revolver in my pocket and the thrill of adventure in my heart" (*CSH*, p.488).

Their journey that night takes them not to their rooms in Baker Street, but to the empty house across the street from their apartment. There they look up to their rooms and see the silhouette of Holmes on the drawn shade. The shadow is cast by a bust of Holmes he has placed there by the window and is moved by Mrs. Hudson every few minutes to give the impression of reality. Suddenly the pair hear footsteps in the house and a figure, unaware of their presence, silently enters the room, opens the window, aims a weapon at the figure of Holmes across the

street and fires. Holmes and Watson then jump onto the
assailant and whistle for the police who have been waiting
in the street. The gunman is Colonel Sebastian Moran,
"once of Her Majesty's Indian Army, and the best heavy
game shot that [the] Eastern Empire has ever produced"
(*CSH*, p.492). Moran, a former tiger hunter, is the last
member of Moriarty's gang on the loose and the same
man who had attempted to kill Holmes at Reichenbach
Falls. Although maintaining a public front of respectabil-
ity, Moran is, according to Holmes, "the second most
dangerous man in London"; he has used the same high-
powered air rifle in his attempt upon Holmes that he used
in the murder of Ronald Adair.

Back in the familiar Baker Street apartment Holmes
theorizes that Adair had gambled with Moran, caught
him cheating and threatened to expose him. Moran, who
made his living gambling at private clubs, could not toler-
ate exposure, so he followed Adair home and shot him
through an open window with his silent air rifle. Moran,
knowing that Holmes was still alive, had his apartment
watched, and was aware that Holmes was back in London, so he made his move. Fortunately, of course,
Holmes was one step ahead of Moran and now, in the
words of Holmes himself, he "is free to devote his life to
examining those interesting little problems which the
complex life of London so plentifully presents."

The first of these "interesting little problems" that
Holmes examines, "The Adventure of the Norwood
Builder," begins with Holmes lamenting the lack of
interesting crime since the demise of Moriarty. This temporary lull is soon broken, however, by the sudden
appearance of a frantic and disheveled young man—John
Hector McFarlane—who bursts into their rooms. McFarlane announces that he soon may be arrested for the murder of Mr. Jonas Oldacre, of Lower Norwood. Oldacre
has disappeared after a mysterious fire in a timber yard at

this residence. There are some mysterious bloodstains and the trace of some unidentifiable remains, but no body.

McFarlane, whose parents were briefly acquainted with Oldacre, was stunned when Oldacre appeared in his law office the previous day with a will naming McFarlane as his beneficiary. Oldacre's only explanation was that he was a bachelor and had heard that McFarlane was deserving. He invited McFarlane to come to his house with the will to examine some other documents. McFarlane did, but claims that Oldacre was alive when he left later that evening. As predicted, Lestrade arrives to arrest McFarlane for the crime, but Holmes notes several inconsistencies in Lestrade's case.

When Holmes visits McFarlane's parents he learns that Oldacre was once a suitor of McFarlane's mother; she characterizes the missing man as "more like a malignant and cunning ape than a human being" (*CSH*, p.503). She was once engaged to Oldacre, but rejected him because of his brutality. At Norwood Holmes examines the evidence Lestrade has collected, but is unable to come up with much of anything new beyond the fact that some important documents seem to be missing. He goes to bed feeling that Lestrade may be correct in his conclusions for once, but a morning telegram from Lestrade announcing that new evidence has been discovered gives Holmes renewed interest.

Lestrade shows Holmes a newly discovered bloody thumbprint on the wall. The print matches McFarlane's and Lestrade feels it is the final piece of evidence needed to link McFarlane to the crime. Holmes seems curiously amused by this new evidence and confides to Watson that he is certain this thumbprint was not there when he examined the premises the day before. He tells Lestrade he will produce a very important witness; he then gathers some straw and proceeds to build a fire in an upstairs corridor. The smoke and accompanying cries of "fire" indeed do produce an important witness. A concealed door at the end of the hall swings open and out darts Mr. Jonas Oldacre, the missing Norwood builder, who has been flushed from hiding by the flames.

Holmes explains that Oldacre, being a builder, was able to create a small hiding place for himself in his house, where, known only to his housekeeper, he could conceal himself. Oldacre has gone to such lengths so that he can fake his own murder, "disappear," and throw off his numerous creditors; he has transferred large sums of money to himself under an alias, and had his plan been successful he would have assumed this second identity permanently. McFarlane was implicated in this scheme only because Oldacre had been rejected by McFarlane's mother; Oldacre wanted revenge upon his old sweetheart and decided to use her child to achieve it. Holmes acknowledges that the crime was nearly perfect, but Oldacre could not resist adding the thumbprint to insure McFarlane would be accused. It was one piece of evidence too much. If one can accept the premise that Oldacre can burn with the desire for revenge for nearly thirty years the story is plausible. If one cannot accept this premise the story is still memorable for its use of fingerprints as evidence, a technique that had been adopted by Scotland Yard in 1901, only two years previous to the story's publication.

The next story in the series, "The Adventure of the Dancing Men," is far superior and is one of the most famous and popular of Holmes's exploits. It begins with a classic opening, Holmes putting together an incredible string of inferences from a bit of chalk dust on Watson's finger. Their discussion is suddenly interrupted by the arrival of Mr. Hilton Cubitt, whose American wife has received a series of curious messages. These messages, for that is what they seem to be although Cubitt can make nothing out of them, are terrifying his wife. They take the form of hieroglyphics–Watson says they resemble "a child's drawing" (*CSH*, p.511)–and seem to be stick figures of little dancing men in various postures. The first message arrived in a letter from America; the second one was drawn in chalk on the windowsill; the third was found on the sundial in the garden. Cubitt refuses to ask his wife to explain the meaning of this disturbing correspondence, because he promised her when they married that he would never ask her to talk about any aspect of her past; he is determined to keep his word and so has come to Holmes for assistance.

Holmes studies the hieroglyph for several days and does not seem to be making any headway, when Cubitt returns with several new pictures that have appeared around his house. He also reports that he has chased a figure from his lawn one night. The new data delights Holmes tremendously and he excitedly sets to work with the new hieroglyphs. After a few hours of work Holmes seems satisfied and dispatches a telegram to Cubitt. When the answer comes enclosed with another dancing-man message Holmes and Watson immediately leave for Riding Thorpe Manor, Cubitt's home. They arrive too late to avert a tragedy; they discover that Cubitt has been shot dead and his wife seriously wounded. Holmes questions the servants and inspects the room where Mr. and Mrs. Cubitt were found. Because the Cubitts were discovered with a revolver from which two shots had been fired, it was assumed by the servants that one of the Cubitts (and it could have been either) had attempted a murder-suicide. Holmes, however, discovers evidence that a third shot has been fired in the room, and deduces that another person (and gun) was present. He searches the flowerbed outside the window and finds footprints and another cartridge shell. Holmes questions the servants about a nearby farm, then creates his own dancing-man hieroglyph and dispatches it, addressed to a Mr. Abe Slaney at that farm. Soon a tall bearded man appears at the door, and when he enters the police take him into custody.

Slaney, an American, confesses to having shot Cubitt, and explains that he himself, a former member of a gang organized by Mrs. Cubitt's father in the United States, had once been engaged to marry her. She wished to live an honest life and rejected Slaney, now known as "the most dangerous crook in Chicago," and fled to England and married Cubitt, after securing his pledge never to question her about her past. Slaney tracked her down and had been sending her messages in a code her father had invented for the gang. Mrs. Cubitt agreed to meet him in the middle of the night, and attempted to bribe him into going away forever. Cubitt discovered them, fired a shot at Slaney and then was killed by Slaney's returned shot. Slaney fled and Mrs. Cubitt attempted suicide with her husband's pistol. Holmes was able to draw Slaney back to the house with a message purporting to be from Mrs. Cubitt saying, "Come here at once." Slaney, who ran after firing at Cubitt, was unaware of the actions Mrs. Cubitt had taken and did not know she was injured. Slaney is imprisoned; Mrs. Cubitt survives the gunshot and lives as a lonely widow.

It is the code of the dancing men that has drawn so much attention to this story. Holmes explains that using the order of frequency in which letters appear in English—which is roughly E,T,A,O,I,N,S,H,R,D, etc.—he is able to substitute letters for the appropriate dancing men, and break the code. To those uninitiated in cryptography, or those who are unaware that someone has ever bothered to calculate the frequency with which the letters of the alphabet are used, the solution seems remarkable. To those who are knowledgeable about crytography, or who amuse themselves with anagrams, the code is ridiculously simple and Holmes seems remarkably obtuse for not solving it more quickly; it is while he toys with it, after all, that Cubitt is killed. Some Holmes fans have constructed an entire alphabet for the code (we are given only a few letters in the story), and Doyle was once welcomed on a tour of the United States by a group of men posed in formation like the dancing men in the hieroglyph. Some of the charm of the story comes from the pictograph itself. Watson, as we have noted, calls it "a child's drawing"; Slaney says that "it would pass as a child's scrawl unless you just happened to have the key to it" (*CSH*, p.525). There is an innocence in these simple stick figures who dance across the page, waving flags and standing on their heads, that belies the seriousness of their nature. As readers, we experience shock when we learn of the shootings of Cubitt and his wife, because Doyle, with his quaint dancing imps, has convincingly led us to believe that there is little truly sinister about the problem—and once again he has surprised us.

"The Adventure of the Solitary Cyclist" introduces Miss Violet Smith (critics have noted what a high percentage of female clients are named Violet), who, responding to an advertisement in the *Times*, has been told that a forgotten uncle has recently died in poverty in Africa, and asked two gentlemen, Mr. Carruthers and Mr. Woodley, to look up his niece and do what they could to look after her. Mr. Carruthers, finding that Violet, soon to be married, is very poor, has offered her a job teaching music to his daughter. Violet takes the job, but is soon visited by the odious Mr. Woodley, who proposes marriage and promises her great wealth. She declines his advances and Carruthers sends Woodley from the house.

Strange incidents begin to happen. Violet, cycling to the train, notices she is shadowed by a bearded man on a bicycle. Violet cannot identify the man. Her troubles take an even stranger turn, however, when her employer Carruthers proposes marriage to her. She decides to leave her employment and Holmes determines that he and Watson will see that she departs safely. They wait by the roadside for her to pass, but when a driverless carriage appears Holmes excitedly jumps into it and they turn back down the road to Carruthers's house. As they drive they are suddenly confronted by the bearded cyclist, who pulls a gun and orders then to stop. He is looking for Violet also.

The three of them run for the house and, in a wooded glade, discover the abducted Violet, Woodley, and a minister who has just completed a wedding service uniting the two. The bearded man removes his beard and reveals that he is in fact Carruthers. He pulls a revolver and shoots Woodley; the minister pulls a gun also but finds himself looking down the barrel of Holmes's revolver. After all this gunplay, unusual in a Holmes story, everyone returns to the house where the tangled events are explained.

Carruthers and Woodley were friends of Ralph Smith, Violet's uncle. They knew that when she died she would inherit a large estate, so they agreed that one of them would marry her, and then share the money with the other. Carruthers was to employ her and Woodley court her, but Carruthers fell in love with her. Her outright rejection of the villainous Woodley caused Carruthers to become her guardian angel; it was he who followed her on the bicycle, insuring that she did not fall into the hands of Woodley, who was determined to force a marriage. Woodley's marriage in the woods is not legal, so Violet is free to marry her fiancé as planned.

As Watson explains at the beginning of the story, Holmes does very little to solve this case other than be there when the abduction of Violet takes place. With its fast-paced chase and high-pitched shootout, the tale is one of the more dramatic of the stories, although virtually no true detective work is involved.

"The Adventure of the Priory School" has what may be

the most dramatic opening in the cycle when Dr. Thorn-
eycroft Huxtable (the names Doyle selects often seem to
be parodies of British culture) bursts through Holmes's
door and faints dead away on the bearskin rug. When
revived, he explains that he has traveled nonstop, without
eating, to summon Holmes's assistance in investigating
the abduction of the Duke of Holdernesse's son. Holdernesse is a former cabinet minister and, according to Huxtable, "one of the greatest subjects of the Crown" (*CSH*,
p.540). Huxtable is the founder and principal of the
Priory school, where Lord Saltire (the Duke's son) was
attending and from which he mysteriously vanished.
Also missing is Heidegger the German master and, curiously, a single bicycle. Holmes questions Huxtable
closely, particularly on the detail of the bicycle, and then
agrees to take on the case and visit the school.

When they arrive they find the duke awaiting them. He
is disturbed that Holmes has been called in without consulting him first and explains that he wishes to avoid scandal. The duke has no real explanation for the boy's disappearance, so after a few questions Holmes leaves and
plans his strategy. The next morning, exploring the area,
Holmes finds the track of a bicycle. He is able to identify
the tread and claims it is not from the missing bicycle of
Heidegger. Further search turns up the track of Heidegger's bicycle, then Heidegger himself–quite dead.
Holmes concludes that Heidegger, rather than being the
abductor, was pursuing the boy, attempting to bring him
back. It is not clear, however, whether Heidegger was
murdered, or whether he simply had a cycling accident on
a dark night on the moors.

Returning to the first bicycle track and following it as
far as they can brings them to a nearby inn where they
confront an angry innkeeper, Mr. Reuben Hayes. When
Hayes forces them to leave his stable where Holmes is
examining the hooves of two horses they follow a new

lead–James Wilder, the duke's secretary, flying along towards Holdernesse Hall on a bicycle. When they catch up, they examine his bicycle and see that its tire matches the track they have been following all day. Holmes stands on Watson's shoulders to peek through a lighted window, then, without saying what he has seen, remarks that they should conclude their investigations for the day.

The next morning Holmes and Watson make a formal visit to Holdernesse Hall. There Holmes requests that the duke make out the reward check he had promised to pay to the man who could find his son. The duke agrees to do so, but seems very apprehensive about the information Holmes is going to present. Suddenly the duke breaks down and asks Holmes for assistance. James Wilder, who has presented himself as the duke's secretary, is actually the duke's illegitimate son. Jealous of Lord Saltire, the legitimate heir, Wilder conspired with Reuben Hayes to kidnap the boy. By substituting a letter of his own for one the duke had written, Wilder was able to lure the boy onto the moor at midnight. There the boy met Hayes, who was on horseback with a led pony, and they left together (their horses shod with shoes that produced the tracks of cattle). They were pursued by Heidegger, who was then killed by Hayes. The boy has been hidden at the nearby inn for the last several days.

Wilder hoped to bargain with the duke and secure what he felt was his rightful share of the estate in return for the boy. The discovery of Heidegger's body, however, prompted the duke to suspect what Wilder was up to and force a confession from him. The duke agreed to keep silent a few days and allow Hayes to escape, thereby implicating himself in the conspiracy.

Holmes pockets the duke's reward check saying he is "a poor man" (a somewhat uncharacteristic action and remark) and promises not to disclose everything he knows about the case, agreeing to let justice takes its course. Hayes will presumably hang for murder; Wilder is emigrating to Australia. The chief problem of this story is this very curious dispensation of justice. Wilder of course invents the scheme; Hayes is only the accomplice who actually carries it out. The duke and his son, presumably because of their position, will go unpunished while, according to Holmes, "the gallows await [Hayes], and I would do nothing to save him from it" (*CSH*, p.558). By refusing to speak out and tell what he knows, and by pocketing the duke's generous reward check, Holmes comes very close to implicating himself in the crime.

Despite these moral dilemmas the story poses it has remained popular, because it shows Holmes clearly demonstrating how the careful observation of footprints and tire tracks will reveal more than one might suspect. In 1903 the pneumatic bicycle tire was an invention only about fifteen years old, so Holmes's ability to identify the tread patterns of various manufacturers was a bit less surprising than it might seem today. Holmes's assertion that one can tell the direction a bicycle is traveling by observing its track also seems ingenious, but his claim has been questioned by a number of critics, as has his illustration of the cantering "cow" tracks that make him suspicious in the first place. In both cases, however, as is so often true in the Holmes stories, we should admire Doyle for the principles his stories are based upon rather than the particulars. There are a great many things one can learn from the careful observation of evidence; until Holmes demonstrated that this was theoretically possible, few people, except for the detectives in Gaboriau and Poe, had bothered to look at physical evidence as closely as he did. Doyle helped establish the modern science of criminology, even though some of his own detective's "discoveries" are often dubious.

In "The Adventure of Black Peter," the next story in the series, Doyle perhaps felt a twinge of guilt for allow-

ing Holmes to accept a six-thousand-pound reward in
"The Adventure of the Priory School," for he begins with
Watson specifically mentioning that case and noting how
unusual it was for the "unworldly" Holmes ever to accept
a reward. In any case, Watson's narrative goes on to relate
how Holmes, who had been visited by several rough men
looking for "Captain Basil" (one of Holmes's disguised
identities Watson assumes), suddenly walked into their
apartment one day, carrying a large harpoon; Holmes has
been at a local butcher shop with the weapon, attempting
to transfix the carcass of a pig. When a police inspector
named Hopkins arrives to discuss Holmes's progress on
his case, Holmes has Hopkins explain to Watson that a
former sea captain named Peter Carey, also known as
Black Peter because of his foul personality, has been
found dead in a small blood-spattered house near his
home, literally pinned to the wall with a harpoon. There
are a number of potential clues lying about–a tobacco
pouch, a notebook, a sheath knife–but nothing Hopkins
can use to crack the case.

Holmes visits the scene of the crime and when they
arrive they find the door of the locked cabin has been tam-
pered with; after a brief inspection of the cabin Holmes
decides they should return that night and see whether or
not the tamperer returns. They wait in the cabin in the
dark and pounce upon the startled young man–John
Hopley Neligan–who breaks in. Neligan's story is complicated. He is the son of a banker who absconded years
before with stolen securities. His father had gone to sea
with some of these stolen securities, intending to return
and clear his name someday; unfortunately he disappeared at sea and was presumed lost. Now some of these
securities have appeared on the London market; Neligan
has traced them to Black Peter. He has visited the cabin
hoping to find a logbook for Carey's ship that might shed
some light on his father's fate. He has found the log, but
the relevant pages are missing. Hopkins produces a

notebook with Neligan's initials that was found in the
cabin when the body was discovered. He arrests Neligan
believing he has found his man.

Holmes, however, is not satisfied. Although Neligan
no doubt visited the cabin, he does not seem physically
capable of harpooning Carey in the manner in which he
was found. Holmes then sends a telegram to a shipping
agent asking him to send some more potential crew members to apply for a position on Holmes's "ship," signing
the request "Basil." The next morning there are three
sailors at Baker Street inquiring for "Captain Basil."
Holmes dismisses the first two, but agrees to "hire" the
third one, Patrick Cairns, handcuffing him when he
bends to sign his sailing agreement. Cairns struggles furiously at first, but soon calms enough to admit that he
killed Peter Carey.

Cairns tells how he was a harpooner on Carey's ship
when Carey picked Neligan's father up at sea. Carey
murdered Neligan and kept his securities; Cairns was the
only witness. Years passed and Cairns decided that he
could blackmail Carey about the incident, so he showed
up at Carey's cabin. Both were drinking and Carey
attempted to stab Cairns, so Cairns harpooned him.
When Cairns is led off to prison Holmes explains that
although Hopkins had assumed a sealskin tobacco pouch
with the initials P.C. belonged to Carey, Holmes had
found no pipe in Carey's cabin. He then concluded that
another seaman had been present the night of the murder,
one with the initials P.C. who had also once served on
Carey's ship. He had previously concluded that only a
very strong and skilled man–a professional harpooner
perhaps–could have committed the murder, so under the
name of "Captain Basil" he had spread word that he was
planning an Arctic expedition (Doyle had served on just
such a whaling ship himself as a youth), and invited harpooners to apply.

The story is a bad one, notable only for the extremely

vicious nature of the crime itself. The senior Neligan's motive in setting out to sea with his securities is never explained. It seems extremely improbable that Cairns, after years have passed, should decide he will blackmail Carey over the contents of a box Cairns has never seen inside. To have Cairns arrive and commit the crime on the very night that Neligan's son, whose motive in visiting Carey is to "clear" his father's name somehow, shows up, stretches our credulity to the limit. It is among the weakest stories of the cycle.

The next tale in the series, "The Adventure of Charles Augustus Milverton," has also been frequently criticized, because Holmes's actions cause him to break several laws. The case begins with Holmes receiving the card of Charles Augustus Milverton, a man he characterizes as "the worst man in London" (*CSH*, p.573). Milverton is a professional blackmailer who pays large sums of money for letters he can use to compromise the wealthy. He has successfully blackmailed hundreds and has avoided prosecution because those blackmailed do not want their situations revealed publicly. Milverton is coming to Holmes because Holmes has been approached by one of Milverton's victims, Lady Eva Brackwell, who is soon to be married. Milverton has secured some of Lady Brackwell's old love letters, which are apparently indiscreet enough to jeopardize her marriage; she has asked Holmes to serve as her agent and make the best deal he can with the blackmailer.

When Milverton arrives he is just as odious as Holmes said he would be, and Watson notices that Holmes is extremely upset with the negotiations. Milverton refuses to accept less than seven thousand pounds for the letters, despite Holmes's plea that Lady Brackell can not afford to pay anything near that sum. Holmes angrily attempts to detain Milverton by force, but Milverton's display of a revolver stops this move; the blackmailer disappears into the street and Holmes begins his campaign against him.

First he dons the disguise of a young workman and vanishes for several days, returning only at odd hours. When he does discuss his movements with Watson, he explains that under the identity of a plumber named Escott he has courted and become engaged to Milverton's housemaid. Furthermore, now that he has become acquainted with the establishment, he plans to burgle Milverton's house. Watson is aghast, but Holmes claims such an action is "morally justifiable." Holmes plans to commit this crime alone, but Watson persuades him that the two of them should attempt it.

Wearing masks and equipped with burglar's tools, the intrepid duo uses a glasscutter to remove a window pane and enter the house. There they find a large safe and Holmes proceeds to crack it with the skill of an accomplished bankrobber. Holmes discovers a number of documents inside the safe, but before he can find Lady Brackwell's letters a noise sends him and Watson to a hiding place behind the curtains. There they observe Milverton who is still roaming about the house, apparently smoking a final cigar before retiring. Suddenly there is a knock at the door and a veiled woman enters the room; Milverton has been up waiting for this late-night meeting with one of his "clients." The woman has seemingly come on the pretense of selling Milverton letters, but when she raises her veil she reveals to Milverton and the hidden detectives that she is instead a woman whom he has ruined when she would not pay his price. Angrily she pulls a revolver, empties it into Milverton and then flees. Holmes prevents Watson from interfering in this shooting, and when the woman has left Holmes empties the safe–all the blackmailer's incriminating documents–into the fire. The pair then escape into the garden, although Watson must kick free from the clutches of a pursuer as he scales the wall.

The next morning Lestrade comes to Holmes for assistance in solving the break-in and murder, but Holmes declines, saying his "sympathies are with the criminals rather than with the victim" (*CSH*, p.582). Later Holmes and Watson see in a window a picture of the woman they had watched shoot Milverton. Watson says he "caught [his] breath as [he] read the time-honoured title of the great nobleman and statesman whose wife she had been"; Holmes, however, "put his finger to his lips" and turned away (*CSH*, p.582).

This unusual conclusion adds another dimension to Holmes, and critics are split on whether it is a positive or negative one. On the positive side one can argue that Holmes in this case, as he has done in other cases, rises above the law and operates on a higher moral plane. One may remember his comment to Watson that breaking into Milverton's is "morally justifiable so long as our object is to take no articles save those which are used for an illegal purpose" (*CSH*, p.574). If we follow Holmes's reasoning, however, we might conclude that all crimes against criminals are justified. Those who feel the story does little to enhance the reputation of the great detective can point to a string of questionable actions. Holmes, besides breaking into the house, attempts to take the letters by force when Milverton is in Baker Street, thus coming close to committing robbery and assault. When he does get his hands on Milverton's papers, of course, he indiscriminately destroys everything in the safe, without knowing how much of this material is related to Milverton's criminal activities. He thereby violates his own code of taking nothing "save [those] articles which are used for an illegal purpose." Furthermore, Holmes lies to the housemaid Agatha and proposes marriage to her, thereby making himself eligible for a breach of promise suit and at the very least breaking the defrauded maiden's heart ("You can't help it," he tells Watson and shrugs his shoulders). Then there is the murder, a far more serious crime than the burglary Holmes set out to commit. In some

stories Holmes decides that he will not volunteer information to the police that they have not asked for, but he
has not gone so far as to suggest he will withhold evidence
if questioned.

In this adventure he is approached directly and yet still
keeps silent. Murder is murder, and whatever the extent
of Milverton's crimes, none would have brought him the
death penalty, so it is difficult to say that justice has been
served. Ironically, Holmes seems to act only out of
revenge, the motivation behind most of the crimes in the
cycle. As Holmes tells Watson, "[Milverton] had, as you
saw, the best of the first exchanges; but my self-respect
and my reputation are concerned to fight it to a finish"
(*CSH*, p.576). Holmes's pride has been hurt and he is
both frustrated and angry. If the story damages his credibility as a champion of justice, it does at least establish
that he is not simply a thinking machine; he is human.

In "The Adventure of the Six Napoleons" Doyle
returns to a more traditional case. Lestrade reports that a
singular series of vandalous acts has taken place, in which
a plaster bust of Napoleon was found smashed to pieces in
an art shop, and two other identical busts purchased from
this shop have also been smashed; to commit the latter
crime the criminal had to break into both the purchaser's
home and medical office where the busts were displayed.
Holmes is interested in the case and asks Lestrade to keep
him informed about the curious crime.

The next morning Holmes is summoned to the scene of
a murder. Horace Harker, a journalist, was working late
at night when he heard strange sounds in his house, followed by a scream. He hurried down to find an open window and his recently purchased plaster bust of Napoleon
missing. Outside on the front step was the body of a man
who had been stabbed to death. The plaster bust, shattered, was later found nearby; Holmes reasons that the
bust was carried to a street lamp before it was broken so

that the vandal could see clearly what he was doing.

Holmes and Watson proceed to track down the source of the busts. At the factory they learn that all the smashed busts were part of a batch of six; the manager of the factory also examines a photograph found on the body of the dead man and identifies it as a picture of a former employee named Beppo. At the store where the last broken statue was purchased Holmes learns the names of the two customers who bought the remaining two statues from the original batch of six. That night, with Lestrade, he and Watson wait outside the home of one of the purchasers. There they watch a man silently break into the house; when the man leaves he is carrying a bust, which he breaks into pieces just before Lestrade takes him into custody. The arrested man is Beppo, and he is carrying a bloodstained knife indicating that he is the murderer.

The next evening in Baker Street Holmes and Watson are visited by the owner of the last of the six Napoleons. Holmes pays the man ten pounds for the statue, and then carefully breaks the bust to pieces. In the center is a black pearl, "the famous black pearl of the Borgias" exclaims Holmes.

Holmes then explains the chain of events that brought this jewel to Baker Street. The pearl had been stolen by a maid who passed it to her brother Pietro Venucci, the murdered man. The pearl then fell into the hands of Venucci's friend Beppo, who hid it in one of the busts when he worked at the factory. Beppo was imprisoned, and upon his release tried to track down the six statues, which had since been sold. Venucci was stabbed in a dispute over the pearl, Holmes concludes, and another sequence of astonishing inductive assumptions is brought to a close.

In "The Adventure of the Three Students" Holmes and Watson visit a university town (it is not specified whether they visit Oxford or Cambridge and thus endless debates have been generated) so that Holmes can do some research in the library. While there he is summoned by Hilton Soames, a lecturer and tutor. Soames has been preparing an important examination for the Fortescue Scholarship. One thing the examination contains is a long Greek passage which the student must translate. When Soames left his rooms for tea that afternoon he left the Greek passage lying on his desk. Returning later, he found a key in the door and the examination papers disturbed. Someone has looked over the test.

Holmes visits the rooms and concludes that whoever entered the rooms carried the pages of the translation to the window where he could simultaneously copy the text and watch for Soames's return. There are other bits of evidence—shavings from a broken pencil, a scratch on a writing table's surface, some curious pellets of sawdust-impregnated dried mud. Holmes talks with the three students who are scheduled to take the examination and Soames's servant Bannister, who has the only duplicate key to the room. The next morning Holmes takes an early walk and returns with the announcement that he has solved the mystery.

Holmes calls in Bannister, whom he accuses of lying about his claim that he has played no part in the incident. Gilchrist, a scholar-athlete, is then summoned and accused of entering the room and looking at the examination. Gilchrist turns to Bannister, who denies he has said anything and thereby implicates himself in the act.

Holmes explains that Gilchrist, returning from track practice and carrying his spiked shoes, was tall enough to glance in Soames's window and see the translation. Finding the key in the door Gilchrist entered, put his shoes on the new table and thereby scratched it, and proceeded to copy the text. Hearing someone coming, Gilchrist hid himself upstairs. Soames returned, noted the disturbance and called Bannister. Bannister, upon entering the room, saw and recognized Gilchrist's gloves lying in a chair. Bannister then "fainted" in the chair and refused to move until Soames went for Holmes. When Soames departed, Gilchrist, to Bannister's surprise, came down the stairs. Bannister reveals to Holmes that he was once butler to Gilchrist's father and has never forgotten the kindnesses that man demonstrated. Although he has been Soames's trusted servant for ten years he has been entrapped by the circumstances. Gilchrist, guilt-ridden over his act, has prepared a letter of resignation for Soames and decided to leave the university.

The story provides an excellent demonstration of Holmes's ability to understand the importance of small details. The most important pieces of evidence at the scene were the unusually shaped pieces of dried mud that had come from Gilchrist's spiked shoes; Holmes visited the jumping pit to find similar samples. Gilchrist is the least suspected of the three students, but the evidence, as Holmes notes, clearly pointed only to him.

"The Adventure of the Golden Pince-Nez" begins with a scene that is emblematic of the mood we usually think of as dominating the series, a scene that once again demonstrates the Naturalistic philosophy Doyle sometimes displays.

It was a wild, tempestuous night towards the close of November. Holmes and I [i.e., Watson] sat together in silence all the evening, he engaged with a powerful lens deciphering the remains of the original inscription upon a palimpsest, I deep in a recent treatise upon surgery. Outside the wind howled down Baker Street, while the rain beat fiercely against the windows. It was strange there in the very depths of town, with ten miles of man's handiwork on every side of us, to feel the iron grip of Nature, and to be conscious that to the huge elemental forces all London was no more than the molehills that dot the fields. I walked to the window and looked out on the deserted street. The occasional lamps gleamed on the expanse of muddy road and shining pavement. A single cab was splashing its way from the Oxford street end. (*CSH*, p.607–08)

In the cab that Watson sees is Hopkins, a police detective who is bringing their next problem.

Professor Coram, an invalid residing at Yoxley Old Place, lives a very secluded life, surrounded by a few servants and a secretary, Mr. Willoughby Smith. Smith has been found one night at the point of death, his throat cut with a small desk knife. Smith's final words—"The professor . . . it was she"—seem confused and shed no light on who his assailant was. Hopkins has found no evidence that would indicate how someone might have entered or left the study where the crime took place. Furthermore, there is no sign that anything has been taken from the house. The only piece of solid evidence Hopkins has, besides the knife, is a golden pince-nez in the victim's hand, which has apparently been grabbed from the killer.

Holmes examines the glasses and concludes that they belong to a woman (because of their size), who is well-to-do (they are gold), with a wide nose, close-set eyes and a peering expression (the strength and configuration of the glasses reveal this), who has visited an optician in the last year (the glasses have recently been repaired). Hopkins sets off to make the rounds of London opticians and Holmes and Watson agree to visit Yoxley Old Place.

On the scene Holmes finds a new scratch that no one has noticed before on a locked bureau and hypothesizes that the murderer was attempting to open this bureau when surprised by Smith. Holmes decides to question Professor Coram and ask him what is kept in the bureau. Coram is bedridden, but offers Holmes an imported cigarette; Holmes quickly smokes four of these cigarettes in the course of the interview, and after leaving tells Watson that the case "depends upon those cigarettes."

Later that day they have a second interview with

Coram, which Holmes begins by knocking over a whole box of cigarettes. After everyone has bent to pick up after him, Holmes announces that he has solved the case right then. The murderer, after being surprised by Smith while attempting to open the bureau, killed him and fled to the professor's room. Professor Coram himself is an accomplice, Holmes asserts. A hinged bookcase in the corner swings open and a woman steps out and admits the crime. She is, surprisingly, Professor Coram's wife; Coram, in fact, is not really named Coram but is a Russian. The two of them were revolutionaries in Russia (this story was written in 1904, and set in 1894, several years before the Russian Revolution actually took place). Coram betrayed his wife and some friends to the police, then escaped to England. His wife's new lover has been working in a salt mine in Siberia (!) and could be saved by some letters and a diary in Coram's possession. It was these documents for which his wife was searching. On her way to the house the morning of the crime she had met Smith in the road and, not knowing who he was, asked him where Coram lived. Smith had mentioned this to Coram that day, so in his last words he was trying to tell the professor the murderer was the woman they had discussed earlier that day.

Holmes explains that when no trace of the assailant's footprints could be found on the grounds he began to consider the possibility the criminal was still in the house. Noticing that one of the bookcases in Coram's bedroom seemed suspicious, he purposely smoked a great many cigarettes there, dropping the ashes in front of the bookcase. When he saw these ashes disturbed on his second visit he concluded that the bookcase did move and that the suspect was indeed hiding in the room.

Although Holmes demonstrates convincingly with the pince-nez that he can draw startling conclusions from physical evidence, the speed with which he solves this crime is difficult to take seriously. His case is nearly complete when he enters the professor's bedroom the first time, although he has almost no proof to support his chain of reasoning. If the murderer were not hiding behind the hinged bookcase as Holmes suspects, the mystery would probably have gone unsolved for there is no evidence to lead Holmes anywhere else.

"The Adventure of the Missing Three-Quarter" begins with Holmes receiving a telegram containing the enigmatic message "Right wing three-quarter missing." The problem is soon cleared up when the sender of the telegram, a Mr. Cyril Overton of Trinity College, shows up and explains that Godfrey Staunton, a rugby player for the team Overton coaches, has disappeared. Overton explains that on the previous night, after the team had turned in, a man with a beard delivered a note for Staunton. The porter who gave the note to Staunton reported that Staunton seemed stunned when he read it; he left his room and was last seen running down the street with the man who brought the note. He has not returned.

Holmes agrees to enter the case and visits Staunton's room looking for clues. He finds on the blotting paper part of the response Staunton had written in reply to a telegram he received several hours before he disappeared. Holmes visits the telegraph office and through a subterfuge discovers the addresses of Staunton's telegram. He and Watson then travel to Cambridge to visit Dr. Leslie Armstrong, the recipient of the telegram, and ask him about the telegram and a bill from Armstrong found among Staunton's papers. Armstrong refuses to discuss these matters and angrily throws Holmes and Watson out; they take rooms at an inn directly across the street from Armstrong's house where they can watch his movements. Holmes tries to follow Armstrong on his trips into the country, and he spends a day exploring nearby villages, apparently convinced that a lead to Staunton's whereabouts will be found in the area.

When the papers report that Cambridge has lost its

rugby match to Oxford, principally because of Staunton's absence, Holmes acquires a dog and announces that he means to follow Armstrong "to his burrow." He and Watson follow the tracks of Armstrong's carriage to a cottage where they find Staunton and a young woman who has just died. The woman was Staunton's wife, whom he had secretly married fearing that her low birth would endanger his inheritance. She had lived happily in this cottage near the school, but contracted a serious illness which Armstrong had been treating. Her turn for the worse was the cause of the appearance of the bearded man (her father) at Staunton's room; Staunton has been in the cottage ever since, awaiting the end. No crime has been committed, so Holmes and Watson leave. It is not a memorable case and Holmes does little to solve the mystery beyond follow the dog to the cottage, a job one assumes even Watson could have handled.

"The Adventure of the Abbey Grange" is another story with a memorable beginning. Holmes suddenly awakes Watson on a dark and "bitterly cold and frosty morning during the winter of '97" with the often-quoted words "Come, Watson, come! . . . The game is afoot" (*CSH*, p.636). Summoned by Hopkins of Scotland Yard, the pair are soon in a dark cab on their way to the train station; Sir Eustace Brackenstall, "one of the richest men in Kent" has been murdered in an apparent burglary attempt.

At the Abbey Grange Holmes interviews Lady Brackenstall, who reveals that Sir Eustace was a "confirmed drunkard," a villainous man who physically abused her. She explains that late on the previous night she surprised three men who were entering the house through a window. They had tied her and gagged her when her husband entered the room and was felled by a blow with a poker. After taking the silver and then drinking some wine the trio left; Lady Brackenstall eventually worked free of her gag and her screams brought the servants. Holmes questions the maid and her story tends to confirm Lady Brackenstall's.

Holmes examines the room and seems intrigued by the bell rope that was used to tie up Lady Brackenstall, noting that it was unusual for the thieves to pull it down without knowing whether their action would summon a servant. He is also interested in the wineglasses the trio drank from, the wine bottle and the cork.

On the way back to Baker Street Holmes admits to Watson that he is bothered by many details of the case. Only one of the three glasses he examined contained beeswing, or residue, indicating that only two glasses were actually used, and their dregs then poured into a third glass to give the impression that three people had been drinking. He feels that Lady Brackenstall and her maid have been lying. He and Watson turn around and go back to the Abbey Grange, where Holmes examines the bell rope once more and discovers it has been cut, not pulled down. He also notices bloodstains in the chair in which Lady Brackenstall claimed to be seated at the time of the murder. Lady Brackenstall still maintains her story is true, however, so Holmes instructs Hopkins to drag a pond on the grounds and returns to London to check on passenger ships passing between South Australia and London (Lady Brackenstall has emigrated from Australia eighteen months previously). At Baker Street Hopkins reports that the missing silver was found in the pond on the estate's grounds. The case seems hopeless when Holmes is visited by a Captain Croker to whom he has sent a telegram earlier. Holmes demands the truth from the sailor about what happened at the Abbey Grange.

Croker explains that he fell in love with Mary Fraser (Lady Brackenstall) on board ship when she traveled from Australia. By accident he has met her maid in the road and learned how Lady Brackenstall was abused by her drunken husband. He decided to visit her and she confirmed that her husband mistreated her. When surprised by Sir Eustace, who promptly hit Lady Brackenstall with a stick he was carrying, Croker grabbed the poker and fought back. It was actually Theresa the maid who devised the plan and the story that was told to the police.

Holmes is sympathetic to Croker and advises him to disappear. Then, turning to Watson, Holmes says:

"Watson, you are a British jury, and I never met a man who was more eminently fitted to represent one. I am the judge. Now, gentlemen of the jury, you have heard the evidence. Do you find the prisoner guilty or not guilty?"

Watson replies "Not guilty, my lord," and Croker goes on his way, safe, Holmes assures, "so long as the law does not find some other victim" (*CSH*, p.650).

One must undoubtedly feel a bit uneasy to see Holmes more blatantly than ever set himself and Watson up as the judge and jury. Croker is the second murderer Holmes allows to go free in this new series of stories (the woman who shot Charles Augustus Milverton was also not reported). Doyle liked to repeat the remark of a Cornish boatman who once said to him, "I think, sir, when Holmes fell over the cliff, he may not have killed himself, but all the same he was never quite the same man afterwards."[3] There is more than a grain of truth in the observation.

Since the incident at Reichenbach Falls, Holmes has become more independent and assertive, breaking the law on several occasions and acting rather questionably on several others (by accepting a check and promising silence in "The Adventure of the Priory School," and by telling Watson to put the stolen black pearl he finds in "The Adventure of the Six Napoleons" in his own safe rather

than turning it over to Lestrade who stands right there).
Watson describes Holmes when he keeps the pearl as "the
cold and practical thinker once more" (*CSH*, p.595), but
we have to see Holmes, who has no right to this stolen
property, as something more than "practical" in these
matters. He is tougher than he used to be, perhaps a bit
more ruthless, perhaps even a bit selfish or greedy.

Conan Doyle was not necessarily conscious of this
change in his hero. If the years between Holmes's "death"
in 1893 and his resurrection in 1902 are examined, it can
be seen that the biggest single incident in Doyle's life was
the Boer War. Doyle's service in that war, and his
extended defense of Britain's role in that war–a defense
that was intended to convince his own doubting countrymen and a skeptical world–left him a more worldly individual than he was in 1893. It was Conan Doyle who
became a bit more assertive, a bit tougher and more suspicious, a bit more cynical, perhaps a bit more conservative
in his politics (we should also remember that although he
had been knighted, he had been soundly defeated in his
first bid for Parliament too). He was always to remain a
great Romantic and idealist, but there was undeniably a
change, if ever so slight, that had taken place. If nothing
else he had lost some of his youthful naiveté. After all,
when "The Adventure of the Abbey Grange" was published Doyle was forty-five years old; he and Holmes had
aged almost twenty years since *A Study in Scarlet* was
written. If Holmes became more independent and willful
("practical" in Watson's words), it is only because his
creator did also.

After completing a series of twelve stories for *The
Strand* in September, 1904, Doyle came back in the
December Christmas issue of the magazine with a thir-
teenth and apparently final Holmes story. Watson begins
"The Adventure of the Second Stain" acknowledging that
he had intended for "The Adventure of the Abbey

Grange" to be the last exploit he reported. Holmes has retired to bee farming and, according to Watson, "notoriety has become hateful to him." Holmes has, however, agreed that one more case can be revealed, so that "this long series of episodes should culminate in the most important international case which he has ever been called upon to handle" (*CSH*, p.650).

The story begins with Holmes being visited in Baker Street by Lord Bellinger, "twice Premier of Britain," and Trelawney Hope, Secretary for European Affairs. An important letter from a foreign ruler has disappeared from the home of Trelawney Hope. The letter is of such an extremely sensitive nature that its publication might lead to war. No one at his house but Hope knew of the whereabouts of the letter, which was taken from a locked dispatch box in his bedroom. Only Cabinet members and a handful of other high-ranking officials even knew of the letter's existence. The premier believes that the letter probably is already on its way to any one of a number of governments where it can do a great deal of political damage to Britain.

Holmes decides he will check on the chief spies in Britain who might serve as the agent for the transfer of such a document, but after his visitors leave he learns that one of the three spies, Eduardo Lucas, was murdered on the previous night. Before he can act on this information he is visited by Trelawney Hope's wife. She has been kept in the dark about the specifics of the crime (although she realizes from her husband's actions that something important is missing), and she requests that Holmes explain it all to her. He declines and she departs, asking him to keep her visit secret from her husband.

Holmes plunges into the case but makes little progress. The letter, as best British intelligence can tell, has apparently not been turned over to any government, but all leads that develop in the case come to nothing. Holmes

tells Watson that the case, "should I bring it to a successful conclusion . . . will certainly represent the crowning
glory of my career" (*CSH*, p.659).

The mystery begins to break when Lestrade summons
Holmes and Watson to the scene of the murder. He has
no new information, but wishes to report that while
cleaning the carpet where the murder took place they
have discovered that the bloodstain on the carpet and the
corresponding bloodstain on the woodwork beneath do
not match, indicating that the carpet has been moved at
some time since the killing. Holmes pulls up the carpet
and finds a secret compartment beneath the floor, then
learns that the constable on guard has allowed a young
woman to visit the room. The woman fainted when she
saw the bloodstain so the constable left to get her some
water; when he returned she was gone.

Holmes calls on Lady Trelawney Hope and asks for the
missing letter, accusing her of giving it to Eduardo Lucas,
and then returning to retrieve it from its hiding place
under the carpet. She first denies this and then, admitting
the crime, produces the letter. Holmes returns the letter
to the dispatch box from which it was taken and then listens to Lady Hope's explanation. Lucas had obtained an
old love letter with which he was blackmailing her; he
offered to trade this letter for a document in her husband's box. She agreed to the deal, but did not realize the
document she was trading was as important as it was.
When Trelawney Hope arrives, Holmes tells him to
check the dispatch box again. He of course finds the letter, and Holmes leaves with the Secretary and Premier
still guessing.

Charles Higham, in *The Adventures of Conan Doyle*,[4]
has argued that this new series of stories has a distinctly
international flavor, reflecting Doyle's own growing concern with the changing balance of power in the world.
This assertion, however, distorts the facts somewhat.

Although "The Adventure of the Second Stain" is concerned with international intrigue, only two other episodes ("The Adventure of the Six Napoleons" and "The Adventure of the Golden Pince-Nez") involve what might be called foreign criminals, and in both cases their crimes have little to do with politics or the balance of power. The content of this series of thirteen stories seems no more international or political than that of the stories written before Holmes's death. If anything, the stories have become more limited and focused in their subject matter. Revenge is still a central theme, as is blackmail. In most of these stories an old love affair—either a love affair that went wrong and is now being avenged by one of the injured parties, or a love affair that one of the parties involved would like to keep a secret—is at the center.

There are no premeditated murders in this series, although the body count has risen noticeably from the earlier collections; all killings are crimes of passion, the passion often arising when a former lover confronts a blackmailer, or when a former lover confronts a new rival. If one generalizes on what these stories show us about Doyle, one could conclude that rather than reflecting a growing concern with world politics, they instead demonstrate his very real concern with propriety, with proper appearances, with the threat of scandal. Time and time again Holmes is seen working either for or against people who want to keep their secret lives hidden, people who fear exposure. And if one looks at Conan Doyle's own life at this time one can see that he too had his secret life, his liason with Jean Leckie, whom he had met in 1897 and who was living nearby Doyle's home. Doyle visited her as often as he could while his wife Louise's health deteriorated steadily (Louise died in 1906, eighteen months after this series was completed).

Over two-thirds of the stories in the collection *The Return of Sherlock Holmes* contain characters who are hiding a secret love affair. "The Adventure of the Missing Three-Quarter" even contains a young rugby player (Doyle was of course a star athlete) who keeps a woman in a secret cottage in the woods and visits her when he can–a situation that veils Doyle's own circumstances about as thinly as one might dare. In Doyle's story, of course, he makes the athlete's hidden lover a secret wife who is dying of a lingering illness, and thereby remarkably merges the characters of his two loves Jean and Louise. In his autobiographical novel *David Copperfield*, Charles Dickens was able to kill off David's first wife Dora and replace her with a more suitable mate, something Dickens would have liked to do with his own wife Catherine, but was unable. Similarly, the death scene in the cottage in "The Adventure of the Missing Three-Quarter" may have reflected Conan Doyle's mixed feelings about his own marriage. This is not to say that Doyle wanted to see his wife die; the story contains a strong mixture of the love, loyalty, and grief Doyle no doubt felt. Still, in this story (and in the general theme of this collection of stories) there is a remarkable fictionalizing of the romantic unrest the author was experiencing for a ten-year period, an unrest that became even more intense during the years in which the stories that make up *The Return of Sherlock Holmes* were written. We also see in the story of the young athlete a realization of how uncomplicated his dual life would become when Louise finally passed on and he, like Holmes, would walk "from that house of grief into the pale sunlight of the winter day."

5

His Last Bows: 1908–1927

Although there were several Holmes stories published in *The Strand* in the period following *The Return of Sherlock Holmes*, the adventures appeared irregularly and there was no monthly series of tales again for fifteen years. The next Holmes volume actually to appear was the short novel *The Valley of Fear*, published in book form in 1915 and serialized in *The Strand* beginning in September, 1914.

The Valley of Fear, like *The Hound of the Baskervilles*, goes back to the time before the incident at Reichenbach Falls, "the early days at the end of the 'eighties'" according to Watson. It opens with Holmes musing over a curious cryptogram he has received from Porlock, a pseudonym used by one of his informers close to Moriarty. Holmes extracts from the cipher the message that apparently danger awaits someone named Douglas at Birlstone House. A visit from Police Inspector MacDonald confirms Holmes's decoding; MacDonald has come to invite Holmes to look into a case with him—the murder of John Douglas at Birlstone Manor House.

Holmes explains to MacDonald how he came by the message and fills him in on the career of Moriarty, who may be behind the murder somehow. On their way to Sussex, MacDonald explains that Douglas had been killed with a shotgun blast to the head. Beyond the fact that no arrest has been made and that he has been told the case presents "some very perplexing and extraordinary features," MacDonald knows nothing.

Arriving at Birlstone, a castlelike structure with a drawbridge and moat, Holmes and Watson learn that John Douglas (who apparently acquired his money in the California goldfields) and his wife have lived there about five years. She is about twenty years younger than her husband, and although she displays some nervousness in her manner she seems to have been generally content in her marriage. Staying with them at the time of the murder was Cecil Barker, an old friend of Douglas's who, although English, had known Douglas in America. Barker is an easygoing and quite wealthy individual, several years younger than Douglas. It was Barker who rushed to summon the police on the night Douglas was discovered murdered.

The police found Douglas in his night clothes. He received both barrels of a sawed-off-shotgun blast squarely in the face. Barker explains to the constable that he was sitting in his bedroom at about eleven-thirty when he heard the shot. He ran into the room within thirty seconds, he claims, but found only Douglas lying on the floor. Mrs. Douglas, the housekeeper Mrs. Allen, and the butler Ames also heard the shot and appeared instantly, but Mrs. Douglas was sent away while Barker and Ames searched the room. The drawbridge was up, causing them first to suspect suicide rather than murder, but an open window and a bloody footprint suggest that a murderer may have escaped by wading the moat. Because the bridge had been raised at six o'clock, the constable reasons the killer was hidden in the house until Douglas made his rounds checking the rooms before going to bed. Other clues that were found at the scene include a card found beside the body with V.V. 341 scrawled upon it, and a hammer found lying on the rug. The constable also notices what first seems to be a tattoo, but is actually a symbol--a triangle inside a circle--branded on the dead man's forearm. Finally, it is observed that Douglas's wedding ring is missing, although removing it required the killer to take it off and then replace another ring worn beside it. It is this bewildering array of confusing evidence that awaits Holmes and Watson when they arrive.

Holmes finds many problems with the theory of a killer lying in wait for six hours to commit a crime with a noisy weapon like a shotgun. He inspects the moat and grounds and then returns to the study for an even closer examination, noticing this time that one of Douglas's exercise dumbbells seems to be missing. He then questions those who were in the house on the previous evening and compares their stories.

Barker has a theory about the killing that comes out in the questioning. He feels that Douglas was once a member of a secret society and always lived in fear of danger, one of the reasons he moved to such an isolated spot and bought a house with a moat and drawbridge. He recalls that in California Douglas left his gold claim quite suddenly for Europe, and within a week several rough-looking men who were not miners arrived searching for him; Barker thinks Douglas had a warning and left before this crowd could do him harm. He notes that Douglas usually carried a gun with him, even in the house, but apparently felt safe on the fatal evening because the drawbridge was up. When Holmes questions Barker about Mrs. Douglas, Douglas becomes angry. He says that Douglas himself was jealous of Barker's friendship with Mrs. Douglas and would sometimes become angry because of it. Barker insists that he was a loyal friend to Douglas, however, and that Mrs. Douglas was a faithful wife.

Mrs. Douglas confirms most of the details that have already been presented to Holmes. Her husband had been going round the house as he did every night, she believes, because he was apprehensive about fire. She does not know, however, how long he had been gone when she heard the shot. When questioned about her husband's past, she agrees that he may have had some powerful enemies and seemed to be on his guard against them. He never spoke specifically about this to her, but sometimes alluded to a "Valley of Fear" in which he once lived. During a fever once he mentioned the name of Bodymaster McGinty, but never explained the reference. She has no explanation for the missing wedding ring.

Later that day, while strolling through the garden, Watson comes upon Mrs. Douglas and Barker laughing and talking together. They are obviously startled and attempt to convince him they are not as callous about Douglas's death as they seem. Watson reports this incident to Holmes and Holmes says that he thinks Barker's whole story about discovering the body is a lie; because Mrs. Douglas's story agrees with Barker's, Holmes concludes she is lying also. Although Barker and Mrs. Douglas seem to be joined in a conspiracy, Holmes is not quite ready to accuse them of the murder. Too many details of the crime—such as the American shotgun—seem incongruous. Holmes believes that a third party may have committed the murder and been discovered by Barker and Mrs. Douglas, who were then drawn into the crime and perhaps even assisted the killer to escape.

Inspector MacDonald then returns with information about a bicycle that has been found on the grounds. It belonged to an American named Hargrave who had registered at a nearby hotel two days before; Hargrave left the hotel on the bicycle but never returned. MacDonald has put out an alert for the missing American, but admittedly is confused by Holmes's new conspiracy theory. Holmes says that he wishes to spend some time alone in the study where he plans to meditate and conduct "a little investigation"; he borrows Watson's umbrella and is gone much of the night.

The next morning Holmes surprises the police by advising them to abandon the case. He promises to ex-

plain the mystery that evening and tells them to advise
Cecil Barker that it will be necessary to drain the moat the
following morning. That night, Holmes, Watson, and
the police detectives hide outside Birlstone Manor near
the study windows. There they see a man lean out of the
window and fish about in the waters of the moat, then
haul a bundle inside. Holmes springs to his feet and they
rush inside to find Cecil Barker and the bundle, which
had been weighted down with the missing dumbbell. In
the bundle is a set of clothes, including an overcoat with a
special pocket made to the conceal the sawed-off shotgun
used in the murder. Holmes stuns everyone by saying
that John Douglas himself should explain this mystery,
and suddenly the man who was believed dead emerges
from a secret passage in the wall.

Douglas has been hiding in a concealed room of the
building that dates back to the reign of King Charles. The
murdered man was actually Ted Baldwin, the missing
American cyclist; he had come to England to kill Douglas. Baldwin had hidden in the study and surprised Douglas; in the ensuing struggle the loaded gun went off accidentally, but Baldwin and not Douglas was killed. Both
men were about the same size and carried identical brands
on their arms. Douglas then decided to fake his own
death; with Barker's assistance he put his clothes on the
unrecognizably mutilated body and dropped Baldwin's
clothes into the moat. Douglas refused to part with his
wedding ring, however, so that detail of the switch was
ignored. Douglas hoped to hide out for a few days and
then leave the area, join his wife, and live out his life in a
new identity, free from the danger that has overshadowed
him. He has a large manuscript with him that he gives to
Watson; he has written this account while in hiding, and
this story constitutes the second part of the novel.

Douglas's story is told in a flashback set in the Vermissa
Valley, Pennsylvania, an iron and coal mining district.

There, in 1875, a secret society known as the Scowrers terrorized the community with extortion and murder. Douglas, whose real name is Birdy Edwards, was a Pinkerton detective who infiltrated the Scowrers and eventually caused their arrest. Most of the Scowrers went to prison or the scaffold. A small group, including Baldwin the murdered man, vowed to get Edwards when they were released from prison. He is chased to California, then to England, where, as John Douglas, he finally met Baldwin face to face again.

The novel returns to Baker Street for a brief epilogue. Edwards/Douglas stands trial for murder, is acquitted, and is warned by Holmes to leave the country. Months later Cecil Barker visits Holmes to announce that Edwards/Douglas has been lost overboard in an accident at sea. Holmes assumes that Douglas was murdered and that Moriarty is behind the crime. When first contacted by the American criminals, Moriarty located Douglas for them; then when their agent was unable to do the job Moriarty handled it himself. The story closes with Holmes sitting in silence contemplating his revenge against Moriarty.

The Valley of Fear has drawn a very mixed reaction. In some ways it is the best of the Holmes novels; in some ways it is the worst. We see Doyle returning to the structure of *A Study in Scarlet* here, combining an exciting Holmes story with an extended and somewhat diversionary flashback. And, like *A Study in Scarlet* and *The Sign of Four*, *The Valley of Fear* focuses on a crime generated by a secret society or a cult's quest for revenge. This flashback, based on Allan J. Pinkerton's book *The Molly Maguires and the Detectives* (the Scowrers are Doyle's fictional representation of the Molly Maguires), is very much a self-contained story and, although interesting in its own way, totally destroys the narrative line of the novel. The mystery has been solved, and, except for a few details, the story has essentially been told when the long flashback is begun, making for a very extended and anticlimactic filler.

Although the overall structure of the novel is badly flawed, the mystery and its solution are as well done as anything in the cycle, if not superior to most of it. Particularly interesting is Holmes, who seems to be friendlier and more human than he is in the earlier stories. There is a good deal of joking with Watson and Inspector Mac-Donald (whom Holmes playfully adresses as "Mr. Mac" throughout the story), and this sense of humor is somewhat uncharacteristic. There is, to be sure, the very awkward linking of Moriarty to the whole incident, which seems to be a way of including a familiar name and point of reference to interest the fans of the series more than anything else. Oddly enough, Conan Doyle first wrote this story in the third person, and then went back to cast it in the familiar form of Watson's narrative.

His Last Bow (1917) is the most diverse collection of Holmes stories, containing episodes that were published in *The Strand* in the period of 1893–1917. After the series that made up *The Return of Sherlock Holmes* (1904), Doyle turned out the tales of Holmes and Watson on an infrequent basis, with only a half-dozen stories being written between the appearance of *The Return* and *The Valley of Fear* (1915). During this period Conan Doyle tried to launch his new hero Professor Challenger, and was only moderately successful. His readers, of course, always wanted more Holmes, so he wrote a story or two occasionally to keep them appeased.

"The Adventure of Wisteria Lodge" was one such story. It originally appeared in two parts with two titles; the first half was titled "The Singular Experience of Mr. John Scott Eccles," the second "The Tiger of San Pedro." It begins with Holmes receiving a telegram from a John Scott Eccles, who claims to have had an "incredible and grotesque" experience. When he arrives, a ruffled and disheveled Eccles begins to plunge excitedly into a mixed-up narrative, only to be interrupted when Gregson of Scotland Yard, who has been following Eccles all morning, bursts in and demands a statement from him. Eccles then tells Holmes and the police his story. He is a bachelor who recently met Aloysius Garcia, a Spaniard connected with the embassy. Invited to spend a few days at Garcia's home, Wisteria Lodge, Eccles went to find a tumbled-down building in disrepair. He was hosted at dinner by a very nervous Garcia who talked incoherently at times and seemed rather distracted. Eccles went to bed at eleven, thankful for a release from the awkward situation. He was later awakened by Garcia at the door who said it was one o'clock, and asked if Eccles had rung for him.

Eccles awakened the next morning at nine and was stunned to find that Wisteria Lodge was uninhabited, and that Garcia's bed had never been slept in. Garcia and his servants seemingly vanished in the night. Angered at what appears to have been an elaborate practical joke, Eccles did some investigating before coming to Holmes. The agency that rents the house told him that the rent was paid in advance and all seemed to be in order; on the other hand, the friend who introduced Garcia to Eccles actually knows almost nothing about him, and the Spanish Embassy reports it has never heard of Garcia.

Gregson reports that Garcia has been found in a field near his home, his head crushed from a heavy blow; Gregson places the time of death before one o'clock. Garcia has not been robbed and in his pocket is Eccles's letter accepting Garcia's invitation; this document identified the body and put the police on Eccles's trail. The central clue to the crime that the police have found at Wisteria Lodge is a note Garcia received in Eccles's presence the night of his death. It appears to have been written by a

woman and gives a set of directions, but its precise meaning is not clear. Gregson takes Eccles away and Holmes
tells Watson he believes Eccles was summoned to Wisteria Lodge to serve as a creditable witness to Garcia's
presence in the house. Holmes obtains a list of other
homes within walking distance of Wisteria Lodge and
then he and Watson set off, on "a cold, dark March evening, with a sharp wind and a fine rain," a night that even
Watson acknowledges is "a fit setting" (*CSH*, p.877).

In the second half of the story Holmes and Watson
arrive at Wisteria Lodge to find a terrified constable. He
has just seen a horrible inhuman face peering in the window at him; he ran onto the lawn but could find no trace
of the creature. In his inspection of the house Holmes
uncovers a number of bizarre objects. There is a mum-
mified figure, although the object is so shrunken and
withered it is not clear whether it is the mummy of an
infant or of a monkey. In the kitchen are the remains of a
large bird, which has literally been torn to pieces. Under
the sink is a pail filled with blood; there are also a number
of pieces of charred bone in the fireplace. According to
Inspector Baynes, "Something has been killed and something has been burned."

Holmes meditates on the crime, but days pass with no
solution. Finally the morning paper announces that the
police have captured a huge mulatto with a hideous face—
the man seen outside the window of Wisteria Lodge. The
man is illiterate, however, and does not speak English
well enough to tell anything about the murder.

Holmes goes over the case again with Watson, explaining his theory that Garcia and his "servants" were conspirators on a mission. Garcia was to leave the house on a
dangerous assignment and then return. If whatever action
they were attempting went successfully, then Eccles
(sleeping soundly upstairs) would provide an alibi for
them. When Garcia did not return from his dangerous

mission, the rest of the conspirators fled, leaving Eccles to awaken in an empty house.

On walks through the countryside Holmes has attempted to determine where Garcia might have been heading when he was killed. He has discovered that at nearby High Gable a Mr. Henderson and Mr. Lucas, both foreigners, reside. Henderson and Lucas lead very secretive lives; Henderson never walks alone and has a violent temper. Holmes believes that the note Garcia received came from the only woman in this strange household, Miss Burnet, the governess of Henderson's two children. Holmes has had the house watched, but since nothing has turned up he has decided that he and Watson need to enter it that night. Movement on the part of the suspects, however, brings a rapid conclusion to the case. Miss Burnet, drugged with opium, escapes from Lucas and Henderson when they attempt to leave the countryside. Henderson, it turns out, is actually Don Murillo, also known as "The Tiger of San Pedro" (San Pedro being a mythical Central American country).

Murillo was a ferocious dictator who after ten years of despotism was overthrown, but who managed to disappear with his children and secretary, and a great deal of wealth, just before a coup took place. His enemies have been searching for him all over the world. Miss Burnet, who is actually the wife of a former diplomat Murillo killed, served as a governess to gain entrance to the household for the conspirators. She had signaled Garcia with the mysterious note, but her employers discovered her act and killed him as he was on his way to achieve his revenge. Miss Burnet has been held imprisoned until the mulatto was arrested for the murder and Murillo thought it safe to make his move out of the country. The mulatto, who is guilty only of practicing voodoo rituals in the kitchen of Wisteria Lodge and had returned there to retrieve his mummy fetish, was arrested to spur Murillo to do just what he did, and therefore is released. Murillo and his secretary are found murdered in Madrid six months later; their murderers are never caught but are undoubtedly from San Pedro.

According to *The World Bibliography of Sherlock Holmes and Dr. Watson*,[1] an exhaustive catalogue of articles written on the Holmes cycle, "The Adventure of Wisteria Lodge" is the least notable of the sixty adventures Doyle wrote. As late as 1974 the episode was the only story in the series about which absolutely nothing had ever been written. Although the story has an intriguing opening with the story of Scott Eccles's curious experience, Holmes and Watson remain well out of the action and this may account for the story's relative lack of popularity. The capture of the mulatto, the flight of Murillo and the escape of Miss Burnet, the final deaths of Murillo and his secretary, these events all occur offstage; Holmes and Watson only learn of these actions secondhand, serving primarily as listeners who unify the story by having the narratives repeated in their presence. Also, the voodoo relics introduce a large red herring into the case, for the mulatto and his mysterious rites have nothing to do with the crime. We have come to expect that such clues as orange pips or dancing men or enigmatic inscriptions play a significant role in, and eventually help explain, the mysteries Holmes investigates. In this case, however, we have an abundance of macabre evidence that leads to nothing. Although it first appears that the crime may involve at the very least a bizarre perverted killer, at the bottom there is nothing more exotic than political assassination. One must assume that Doyle included the voodoo relics just to heighten the suspense, a tactic that is usually not considered playing fair in mystery writing.

The next story in the volume, "The Adventure of the Cardboard Box," has a strange history in several respects.

First published in *The Strand* in January, 1893, it therefore should have followed "The Adventure of Silver
Blaze" in *The Memoirs of Sherlock Holmes*. The story
was removed from the American edition of the book after
the first printing, however, and was never included in the
British edition; it was not reprinted in either country until
His Last Bow–almost twenty-five years later. Even more
odd is the fact that "The Adventure of the Cardboard
Box" and "The Adventure of the Resident Patient" contain an identical passage, several pages long, in which
Holmes reads Watson's mind as Watson sits musing on
the American Civil War.[2]

There have been several theories proposed to explain
this omission, addition, and duplication. The mind-reading passage, which did not appear in the original *Strand*
version of "The Adventure of the Resident Patient" in
August, 1893, was added to the story when it was
reprinted in *The Memoirs*; the extra passage was rather
carelessly inserted into the story, for we now find Watson
complaining about the heat (90° on the thermometer) and
longing for the seashore on what is also called a "rainy day
in October" (*CSH*, p.422). In its original position in
"The Adventure of the Cardboard Box," the exchange
between Holmes and Watson took place on a "blazing
hot day in August" (*CSH*, p.888).

One writer has suggested that Doyle, who joined the
Society for Psychical Research the month after "The
Adventure of the Cardboard Box" was published, was
pressured by that organization to delete a story
demonstrating how easily mind reading could be faked.
The problem with this theory, of course, is that although
Doyle omitted the story from *The Memoirs*, he added the
critical mind-reading passage to another adventure,
thereby negating the need to drop "The Adventure of the
Cardboard Box" in the first place. A much more plausible
theory, however, exists. An article in *Collier's* magazine

in 1908 reported that Doyle decided not to reprint "The Adventure of the Cardboard Box" because it involved an illicit love affair.[3] Accepting that explanation for the moment, it should be noted that when *The Memoirs* were collected in 1894 Doyle believed that he had killed off Holmes and there would be no more stories or collections. Reluctant to lose the mind-reading sequence of the omitted story (which demonstrates Holmes's powers at their most brilliant) Doyle then inserted it in "The Adventure of the Resident Patient" (although it did not fit well). Then in 1917 when it again seemed the series would end with the volume *His Last Bow*, Doyle, needing material to finish out the collection, agreed to reprint "The Adventure of the Cardboard Box" as it was originally published, thereby duplicating the amended version of "The Adventure of the Resident Patient" (he had perhaps forgotten about the duplication after twenty-four years).[4]

"The Adventure of the Cardboard Box" opens with Watson, bored, lamenting the heat, and Holmes performing his mind-reading act. Holmes then calls Watson's attention to an item in the paper Watson has overlooked, a story about a woman receiving in the mail two freshly severed human ears, neatly packed in a cardboard box. Lestrade has asked for assistance, so Holmes and Watson are soon on their way to Croydon to look into the puzzle.

Holmes carefully examines the package and its grisly contents, and concludes the ears have not come from medical cadavers. He believes the ears belong to a man and a woman recently murdered, because no victims of mutilations have come forward to report the crime. Susan Cushing, the recipient of the ears, is interviewed by Holmes, who notices a photograph of her two sisters and asks her several questions about them. Susan Cushing has no idea why this package was sent to her, so Holmes then visits the home of her sister Sarah Cushing, but is told by her physician that Sarah is extremely ill and cannot see anyone for several days. Holmes then drops by the police station to give some instructions to Lestrade and tell him he has the case solved.

That evening in Baker Street Holmes explains to Watson his theory that the package, addressed only to S. Cushing, was meant for Sarah rather than Susan. He also calls to Watson's attention the fact that the shape of one's ears is both unique and genetically determined; one of the ears in the box, he fears, belongs to a very close relative of Susan Cushing. The sudden illness of Sarah Cushing confirms that she understands the message the package was intended to convey. Word comes from Lestrade that an arrest has been made based on Holmes's conclusions and he sends Holmes the suspect's statement, which becomes the explanation of the mystery and the conclusion of the story.

Jim Browner, a ship's steward, confessed that Sarah Cushing was in love with him, although he married her younger sister Mary. When he rejected Sarah's advances her love turned to hate and she attempted to gain her revenge through Mary. Sarah introduced Mary to Alec Fairbairn, another sailor, and then, to Browner's dismay, encouraged an affair between them. When he discovered Mary on an outing with Fairbairn, Browner went berserk; he killed them, cut off an ear from each, and sank the bodies in the ocean. In a mad, defiant gesture he then mailed the ears to Sarah at the address where she once lived with Susan.

Browner's statement reads like a Robert Browning monologue. He complains of a throbbing in his head and believes he is going insane. The murders and mutilations he commits, coupled with the sexual theme of the story, is of course reminiscent of the Jack the Ripper murders. What is tolerated in real life, however, may seem unnecessarily gruesome in art, and the story probably overstepped the limits of some Victorian tastes. Murder in Doyle's stories is invariably a crime of passion, as were these murders. But mailing the severed ears suggests a deliberate coldbloodedness that borders on perversion (the Ripper mailed a victim's kidney to the police). Browner's crime is indeed one of the most brutal in the cycle, but it was probably Sarah's scheme to entangle her sister in an extramarital affair that caused Doyle to have second thoughts about the story. Victorian ladies scarcely acknowledged their sexuality existed; it was racy indeed for a gentleman like Doyle to suggest that a woman might betray her sister by making advances to her sister's husband, then, when rejected, encourage her sister's infidelity as a form of revenge. Decorum dictated the story's suppression.

"The Adventure of the Red Circle" (1911) begins in the middle of a conversation, a different opening for the stories. A Mrs. Warren has come to Holmes because of a mysterious lodger who has taken a room with her. The man has locked himself in his room, asks for his meals to be left outside his door, and communicates his wants only with single-word messages printed on scraps of paper. Knowing that Holmes "can read great things out of small ones," she has brought two matches and a cigarette stub. From this evidence and a note the lodger has left, Holmes concludes that the lodger is in fact not the person who contracted the room. Checking the personal column of the paper for relevant messages, Holmes finds a series of enigmatic advertisements that began shortly after Mrs. Warren's lodger took his room. The messages, signed G, appear every few days and counsel impatience; the latest one describes a house and room window, but says nothing more.

Holmes and Watson plan to look through Mrs. Warren's neighborhood to see whether the house described in the advertisement might be found there. They locate an apartment building that indeed seems to be the one described in the personal advertisements. Holmes then enters Mrs. Warren's and he and Watson hide themselves in an empty room across from the lodger's. Using a mirror to watch the lodger's door, Holmes and Watson are surprised to learn that a woman is living in the room rather than a man.

That night they return and see a man using a candle to flash a signal toward their building from the apartment down the street. At first confused by the Morse-code message, they discover it is in Italian. Suddenly the candle disappears in the middle of a word, so Holmes and Watson decide to investigate more closely. They find Inspector Gregson at the apartment doorway with an American Pinkerton detective. The Pinkerton man is on the trail of a murderer named Giuseppe Gorgiano, whom he has tracked to this London apartment. Going upstairs, however, they find Gorgiano dead with a knife through his throat. Stepping to the window, Holmes signals with the candle and the woman from Mrs. Warren's apartment soon arrives. She is delighted to see Gorgiano dead and believes her husband Gennaro Lucca has done it.

She explains that she and her husband met Gorgiano in New York where her husband had gone to escape an Italian secret society—the Red Circle—of which he was once a member. Gorgiano was a brutish killer who made advances toward Mrs. Lucca; her rejections made her and her husband Gorgiano's bitter enemies, so Gorgiano selected Lucca to be the murderer of Lucca's best friend. Lucca and his wife escaped to London to hide, but Gorgiano was on their trail. Surprised by Gorgiano while signaling to his wife, Lucca stabbed him in self-defense. Since Lucca is not in custody the episode ends with the final verdict in doubt, although Mrs. Lucca believes that her husband has done the world a favor and the Pinkerton detective agrees.

Originally titled "The Adventure of the Bloomsbury

Lodger" in the manuscript, this story takes us back to one of Doyle's favorite plots, a mystery generated by a secret society attempting revenge. The change in the title suggests that Doyle was trying to find something exotic and exciting to attract readers. "Red Circle," like *Study in Scarlet*, implies blood, and readers would have to finish the second half of the story that was originally published in two parts to find that the title was somewhat misleading, referring only to a peripheral aspect of what in some ways is a very dull case.

"The Adventure of the Bruce-Partington Plans" (1908) reintroduces Mycroft, a figure alluded to but infrequently appearing in the cycle. Mycroft arrives at Baker Street, on one of those fog-enshrouded days we associate with Holmes's adventures, to discuss the case of Cadogan West, a government employee whose body was found near the tracks where he had apparently fallen from a train. Accompanied by Lestrade, Mycroft reports that West was carrying the plans for the Bruce-Partington submarine, top secret documents never allowed outside of the Woolwich Arsenal; although some of the documents were found on the body, others are missing. According to Mycroft, the case represents "a vital international problem" (*CSH*, p.916).

Holmes learns the details of the case from Mycroft, but no clear reconstruction of the crime can be made. Assuming that West took the plans to sell them to a foreigner, it is not clear why some of the drawings were found and some were missing, why no train ticket was found on the body, and why West was found at a location off the route between Woolwich Arsenal and London. Holmes feels it may be pointless to pursue the case because the plans are certainly already out of the country, but Mycroft is insistent that action must be taken and so Sherlock agrees to examine the scene.

The absence of blood at the point where the body was

found seems unusual to Holmes. The railroad cars from
the train that passed this point at the appropriate time
have been transferred to other trains and cannot be easily
inspected by Holmes now, but Lestrade assures him there
was no evidence of the crime to be found inside them.
Holmes confides to Watson that he believes West was
killed elsewhere and that his body fell from the roof of the
train. Holmes then decides to visit those who had official
access to the papers, but the first person he visits, Sir
James Walter, a distinguished public servant, is dead.
Holmes is told that Sir James was extremely disturbed
over the disappearance of the papers from his department, causing Holmes to wonder whether the death was a
suicide. Holmes next interviews West's fiancée, Violet
Westbury, who declares that West would never have
committed treason, although he had once remarked that
security for the plans was very slack. She explains that,
accompanying her to the theater on the night of his disappearance, West suddenly left her and darted into the fog;
he never returned and she walked home alone. Such a
bizarre act puzzles Holmes and Watson completely.

Back in Baker Street Holmes receives a list of important
foreign agents from Mycroft, consults a map of London,
and then goes out for the afternoon. Later Watson
receives a note from Holmes inviting Watson to join him
that evening with a collection of burglary tools. By
checking the map and train tracks, Holmes discovers that
the house of Hugo Oberstein, an important foreign
agent, overlooks the tracks at a point where trains frequently pause. Holmes and Watson then break into
Oberstein's and find bloodstains and evidence that the
body of West was passed through a window and placed
on the roof of a train. Convinced that he has solved the
mystery, Holmes ransacks the place looking for the
plans; he does not find them, for Oberstein has apparently fled, but he does discover copies of a series of adver-

tisements placed in the newspaper's personal column seemingly arranging a meeting to purchase the plans. Copying the form of these advertisements, Holmes places a spurious notice in the paper hoping to arrange an emergency meeting with Oberstein's connection. That evening, Holmes, Watson, and Lestrade wait and are visited by Valentine Walter, younger brother of Sir James. He had had duplicate keys made so he could steal the plans, but was seen and followed by West who suspected him. Confronting Oberstein and Walter at Oberstein's door, West was killed by Oberstein. The body of West was lowered onto the top of the train, and some of the plans were planted on the body to throw suspicion on West. Sir James suspected his brother had committed the crime and therefore died a broken man. Holmes has Walter write a letter to Oberstein claiming the plans omit an important detail that he would like to sell. Oberstein walks into the trap and the plans, which he had not yet sold, are reclaimed. Holmes receives an emerald tiepin from the Queen for his part in solving the crime.

The story is a bit anachronistic, for in 1895 Britain had no submarines at all; the few submarines that had been built and tested in the world at that time were largely experimental and certainly not the threatening weapons Doyle makes them out to be in this story. His own interest in submarines and his obsession with the vulnerability of England to their potential power, however, is what inspired him to create for Holmes a mystery with a touch of science fiction.

"The Adventure of the Dying Detective" (1913) is an early case, set in the second year of Watson's marriage. He is summoned to Baker Street by a worried Mrs. Hudson who tells him Holmes is gravely ill. Watson arrives to find a gaunt and listless Holmes wasted by a disease he calls "coolie disease from Sumatra." He refuses to let Watson treat him or go for other medical assistance, but asks him to stay with him for a few hours, during which time Holmes raves incoherently. Finally Holmes asks Watson to go for Culverton Smith, a resident of Sumatra visiting London, because Smith has knowledge of the disease.

Watson goes to Smith and persuades him to attend the dying Holmes. Holmes, however, asks Watson to hide behind the bed during Smith's visit, a request that Watson thinks is strange but agrees to honor because of Holmes's condition. A very unusual scene takes place when Smith arrives. He admits to commiting one murder and then explains that a small ivory box he sent Holmes contained a sharp spring which apparently infected him with the Sumatran disease. Smith is confident that he has done what others have only unsuccessfully attempted–killed Sherlock Holmes. Suddenly, however, Inspector Morton comes through the door and handcuffs Culverton Smith, and Holmes, who has been feigning illness, gets out of bed to greet the eavesdropping witness Watson.

Doyle never explains the details of this case in what seems to be a rather hastily written story. Smith has killed his nephew, Victor Savage, by infecting him with a Sumatran disease, but the reader is not told how Holmes became involved in what seemed to be a case of death by natural causes, or how Smith became aware of Holmes's investigation, or how Holmes, who explains he is always suspicious of packages he receives, linked this deadly box with Smith. Unfortunately, what Doyle has written here is what would once have constituted the second half of a Holmes adventure; he has an excellent premise for the story, but he was apparently more interested in finishing the tale than in developing his idea fully. Although it does not appear in its proper chronological place in the volume *His Last Bow*, this was the final story written before Doyle "ended" the cycle for the second time with the "final" story "His Last Bow." Its brevity and skimpy treatment perhaps reflect his growing lack of interest in the series.

"The Disappearance of Lady Frances Carfax" (1911) provides a more traditional presentation, opening with Holmes drawing some conclusions about Watson's activities on the basis of his appearance. In a somewhat atypical move, however, Holmes suggests that Watson leave the country and travel to Switzerland to look into the disappearance of Lady Frances Carfax. Lady Frances, a wealthy spinster traveling in Europe who habitually corresponds with her old friend and governess Miss Dobney, has not been heard from for over a month, although checks cleared through her bank suggest she paid up her hotel bill before vanishing. Since Lady Frances's last letter came from Lausanne, Holmes proposes that the search begin there.

At Lausanne Watson discovers that Lady Frances had intended to stay for the season, but inexplicably left on a day's notice. She had been observed talking with a bearded Englishman, and it is suggested that he had something to do with her sudden departure. Watson follows the trail to Baden, where Lady Frances decided to return to London with a missionary, Dr. Shlessinger, and his wife; she has not been heard of since she left with the Shlessingers. Watson discovers that the strange bearded man evidently followed Lady Frances from Lausanne to Baden, but his motives are unclear. Interviewing Lady Frances's ex-maid, Watson is surprised when the maid suddenly points out this mysterious man on the street. Watson charges out to confront the fellow; a struggle ensues, and Watson is rescued by a passing stranger who turns out to be Holmes in disguise. Holmes subsequently introduces Watson to the bearded man, Philip Green, an old friend of Lady Frances's, who was attempting to propose marriage to her; his proposals were repeatedly rejected. Still, he is in love with Lady Frances and has been following her to protect her rather than harm her.

Since Lady Frances was reported leaving for London with the Shlessingers three weeks before, Holmes and Watson return there, where Holmes concludes that Shlessinger is actually Henry "Holy" Peters, an Australian con man who masquerades as a missionary, and his "wife," a conspirator named Fraser. When some of Lady Frances's jewelry is pawned, Holmes concludes that she herself is either dead or being held captive. Following Fraser home from the pawnbroker's when she pawns some jewelry, they locate the house where Lady Frances may be held, but discover a coffin is also being delivered there. Holmes excitedly confronts Peters, who admits to traveling with Lady Frances but denies any knowledge of her present whereabouts; showing his revolver, Holmes demands to see the body that has been placed in the newly delivered coffin. He finds an elderly woman, a former nurse of Peters's wife. Police arrive to escort a frustrated Holmes and an angry and embarrassed Watson out of the house. The detectives then check with a nearby workhouse infirmary, which confirms that the Peterses had claimed a feeble woman as a former servant and taken her home with them a few days before. The doctor who was present at the woman's death also confirms that there was no foul play.

Holmes ponders the case overnight and the next morning rushes Watson to Peters's house. Opening the coffin they find an unconscious Lady Frances, who has been chloroformed. Her body has been placed in the unusually large coffin on top of the old woman's body; Peters had hoped to bury them together. Lady Frances is revived and survives her premature burial.

The story is a fascinating one, although it has been criticized for the curious behavior of Holmes. After sending Watson to Switzerland and then reading Watson's report from the continent that Lady Frances had left for

England three weeks previously, Holmes inexplicably turns up at Watson's side and his first words are "I rather think you had better come back with me to London by the night express." Doyle apparently wished to squeeze every ounce of suspense out of the tale, so the encounter with the mysterious Philip Green is included to surprise the reader, although there seems to be little logical reason for it. Watson's shock at discovering his assumptions have been incorrect, however, does parallel the similar shock Holmes experiences when he first discovers the wrong body in the coffin. "Such slips are common to all mortals" he later tells Watson, but Holmes is so seldom misled that readers feel as frustrated as he does, knowing that somehow he is correct but unable to prove it. His solution of the puzzle seems even more satisfying because he has to, as he says, "recognize and repair" his error (*CSH*, p.954).

"The Adventure of the Devil's Foot" (1910) finds Holmes, the victim of overwork, vacationing in an isolated cottage in Cornwall. His holiday is interrupted, however, when a bizarre death occurs. The sister and brothers of a local resident, Mortimer Tregennis, are found sitting around a card table, just as he left them the night before. The difference is that his sister is now dead, his brothers found raving maniacally; all three have a look of complete terror on their faces. Tregennis has no real clues to shed light on the occurrence beyond the fact that both he and his brother had at times experienced the sensation of being watched through the open window. Despite his vacation plans, Holmes agrees to look into the case.

At the cottage Holmes examines the grounds, talks with the housekeeper, views the body of Brenda Tregennis, and then examines the room where the death occurred. Because the cardplayers never left their places at the table, Holmes concludes that whatever happened took place immediately after Mortimer left the house. Later that afternoon, Holmes and Watson are visited by Dr. Leon Sterndale, a famous lion-hunter and explorer, who is a distant relative of the Tregennises. Sterndale claims he is anxious to help in the inquiry, but becomes upset at Holmes's questions and refuses to divulge information.

The discovery of the body of Mortimer Tregennis the next morning brings Holmes and Watson to the death scene where they discover a smoking lamp near the body. Holmes takes traces of residue from the lamp, then buys an identical model to conduct a test. Explaining to Watson he suspects that some kind of combustible poison is the cause of the deaths, he takes a quantity of the powder he has obtained from the Tregennis's lamp, places it in his own and lights it. The smoke instantly has an hallucinogenic effect on the detectives and they are barely able to stagger from the room; had they stayed they would have suffocated.

Solving the way the crime was committed, however, does not identify the criminal. Because there is no evidence that anyone was at the cottage after Mortimer Tregennis, Holmes assumes that he threw the powder in the fire upon his departure. Holmes then accuses Leon Sterndale of murdering Mortimer. Holmes has shadowed Sterndale about the village and knows that Sterndale visited Mortimer shortly before daybreak the morning of Mortimer's death. Sterndale confesses and says that he had for years loved Brenda Tregennis whom Mortimer had hoped to drive insane (along with his two brothers) in order to inherit the family estate. Mortimer used a rare poison called "devil's-foot root," which Sterndale had shown him and Mortimer had subsequently stolen. When Sterndale heard of the nature of the death he immediately recognized the cause, and used the same root on Mortimer, threatening to shoot him if he tried to leave the poison-filled room.

Holmes is sympathetic and allows Sterndale to go free, marking yet another time he has pardoned a murderer. The story also contains one of the very few premeditated murders in the cycle–Sterndale's killing of Mortimer (Mortimer's killing of his sister was actually accidental, because he had "only" planned to drive his three siblings insane with the root and she received too strong a dose). Other murders in the cycle are almost invariably crimes of passion, and although one could argue that Sterndale's crime was generated by his emotions, his actions are cool and rational; he does not kill in an angry rage like the other murderers Holmes releases. The fact that Brenda Tregennis was a secret love whom Sterndale, because of his wife, was unable to marry no doubt struck a responsive chord in the heart of the creator of Holmes, because Doyle had himself lived for ten years under a similar shadow.

"His Last Bow: The War Service of Sherlock Holmes"[5] (1917), which gives its title to the volume, was intended to be the final Holmes story, and in some ways it is, since chronologically it marks the last case in his career–August, 1914. World War I consumed Doyle's interest and energies and there was a four-year gap between the previous Holmes story ("The Adventure of the Dying Detective" [1913]) and this one. "His Last Bow" reflects in some ways Doyle's distraction. Like "The Adventure of the Dying Detective" this episode is very short; unlike any other story in the cycle so far it is told by an omniscient narrator, and not by Watson the trusty chronicler.

The use of the third-person narrator brings an unfamiliar atmosphere to the story. It begins with two German agents of the Kaiser, Von Bork and Baron Von Herling, standing on a hillside scornfully discussing the British people. Eavesdropping on such a conversation between villains would of course have been impossible in any of the other stories without a witness present to convey the information to Watson. Von Bork, posing as a wealthy country squire and sportsman, has been accepted into the highest circles of English society and has gathered a great deal of information about British defenses. Von Bork shows Von Herling his safe filled with detailed secret documents and tells him he only lacks a file on naval signals that his secret agent Altamont is bringing him that night.

Von Herling leaves and Altamont, who is Irish-American and not British, arrives in a chauffeured car with the documents. Seeing Von Bork's safe he criticizes its vulnerability and Von Bork, disagreeing, explains how it works and why it is difficult to open. Altamont then insists on his payment of five hundred pounds before turning over his package, so an irritated Von Bork writes a check and then demands the parcel, opening it to find a book entitled *Practical Handbook of Bee Culture*. Before Von Bork can object he is immediately grabbed by Altamont and chloroformed.

Altamont, the next scene reveals, is actually Holmes in disguise; his chauffeur is Watson, and Von Bork's English housekeeper is also in Holmes's employ. While the chloroformed Von Bork lies unconscious, Holmes and Watson drink a toast and then unload Von Bork's safe full of documents. Watson was summoned for his role in the drama only that evening, so he is filled in on the details of the case and Holmes explains how he infiltrated Von Bork's spy network in the guise of Altamont (Altamont was the middle name of Doyle's father). Von Bork, tied on the sofa, awakens from his chloroformed sleep and threatens Holmes, who only chides him in return. Before Von Bork is trundled off to Scotland Yard, Holmes and Watson stand together on the terrace in a quiet moment. The storm of World War I is gathering. "It will be cold and bitter" Holmes tells Watson, "and a good many of us may wither before its blast. But it's God's own wind none the less, and a cleaner, better, stronger land will lie in the sunshine when the storm has cleared" (*CSH*, p.980).

Doyle is being as propagandistic as he can with his hero-detective in this episode. The Germans are cruel, heartless, and extremely antagonistic to the British whom they scorn as "docile, simple folk." Even Von Bork's housekeeper, described as a "dear old ruddy-faced woman . . . bending over her knitting and stopping occasionally to stroke a large black cat upon a stool beside her" is characterized by him as a personification of "Britannia" with "her complete self-absorption and general air of comfortable somnolence" (*CSH*, p.974). The suggestion that the British are a slumbering people passively being manipulated by these crafty Germans reflects Doyle's own frustrated efforts to improve British defenses in the years prior to the war. The submarine and the Zeppelin were weapons Doyle correctly believed the British ignored at their peril.

The story's poignant conclusions brings the cycle to an appropriate end. There is a strong sense of change in this episode. Holmes and Von Herling travel in automobiles, not horsedrawn carriages. Holmes, a "tall, gaunt man of sixty," is of course retired and keeping bees in Sussex and has not even seen Watson for some time. "How have the years used you?" he exclaims. "You look the same blithe boy as ever." Watson replies that he feels "twenty years younger" to be reunited with his former companion and remarks "But you, Holmes—you have changed very little" (*CSH*, p.978). Holmes's book on beekeeping, what he calls "the *magnum opus* of my latter years" is completely unknown to Watson, who once kept in very close touch with his old friend. This may be, as Von Bork believes, "a utilitarian age" where "Honour is a medieval conception." Holmes's final remarks to Watson, however, as the two stand together again after over thirty years of adventures, reassure the reader that the values and chivalric

code of honor Doyle always believed in will return.
Holmes addresses Watson in these final moments as "the
one fixed point in a changing age," but obviously Watson
is not the only "fixed point." There is still Doyle himself,
looking forward to the "cleaner, better, stronger land"
that will survive (*CSH*, p.980).

The Case Book of Sherlock Holmes (1927) brings
together the last twelve stories of the cycle. The first six of
the episodes appeared at the rate of about one a year in the
period 1921–25; the last six were published in a final series
of monthly stories in 1926–27. The stories were re-
arranged by Doyle for this final volume and do not appear
in the order in which they were originally published. The
question of why Doyle returned to write Holmes stories
after "His Last Bow" is much easier to explain than was
the return of Holmes after "The Final Problem." Despite
all that he had done in the service of his country, and
despite the fame his writings had brought him, Doyle was
rather unpopular with the public at this time because of
his spiritualist crusade. Scorned and sometimes ridiculed
by the press, the one thing Doyle could do that was
always well received was write stories about Sherlock
Holmes. So he wrote more stories. Doyle was used to
challenges, so being a lonely crusader was not necessarily
overwhelming for him, but the man who twenty years
previously had been knighted as one of his country's
heroes was something of a joke after the publication of his
book *The Coming of the Fairies* in 1922. He no doubt
desired to restore some of his self-esteem and Holmes and
Watson could again be his salvation.

"The Adventure of the Illustrious Client" (1925)
begins with Watson's statement that Holmes has finally
given permission to publish the episode. The story is set
in 1902 and opens with Holmes receiving a message from
Sir James Damery, a well-known public figure. Damery
calls on Holmes and announces that Baron Adelbert

Gruner, the Austrian murderer, has become engaged to
Violet de Merville, the daughter of a famous general. Her
father is certain that Gruner, who is suspected of murdering his first wife, is up to no good; the father has attempted
to persuade his daughter to abandon this marriage, but his
daughter seems enchanted with the villain. Damery's "illustrious client," who is never named, would like Holmes
to intercede and do what Violet's father cannot.

Holmes takes on the case and visits Gruner, who
already knows about Holmes's mission. Gruner assures
Holmes that Violet is unbothered by any scandal that
might be associated with his past and is willing to let
Holmes do his best to influence her decision. Gruner
points out to Holmes that another detective who had
investigated him was beaten and crippled for life. Holmes
then contacts Kitty Winter, Gruner's former mistress
who knows that Gruner "collects women . . . as some
men collect moths or butterflies" (CSH, p.990); Gruner
keeps a record of this "collection" in a special book.
Holmes would like to get his hands on this "beastly
book," but Kitty assures him that Gruner guards it well.
She agrees to help Holmes and will do anything to have
her revenge on Gruner for what he has done to her.

Kitty Winter accompanies Holmes in his attempt to
influence Violet de Merville, but they have no luck. The
next day Holmes is attacked and beaten by two men with
sticks. Using his injuries as a cover, Holmes circulates the
news that he is near death and continues to contemplate
the case. He asks Watson to study Chinese pottery, then
gives him an alias and a rare saucer, instructing him to
pose as a collector attempting to sell the saucer to Gruner.

Watson visits Gruner's house but is exposed by the
clever Gruner who concludes he is Holmes's spy. Gruner
reaches for a gun but is interrupted by a noise and the
sight of a bandaged Holmes escaping into the garden.
Gruner's pursuit is halted, however, when Kitty Winter

materializes and throws a container of vitriol into his face, horribly disfiguring him.

In Baker Street Holmes explains that because burglary was impossible at night he needed Watson to distract Gruner while he and Kitty searched for the book. Holmes was not aware that Kitty was carrying the vitriol. The book is successfully used to persuade Violet de Merville of the truth about Gruner and the marriage is broken off. Kitty Winter is tried for her vitriol-throwing but is given a light sentence; Holmes is threatened with burglary charges, but as Watson notes, "when an object is good and a client is sufficiently illustrious, even the rigid British law becomes human and elastic" (*CSH*, p.999). The client, whose coat of arms Watson recognizes on the carriage in which Sir James leaves, was probably King Edward VII, a client illustrious enough to pull some strings on Holmes's behalf.

Although Doyle once stated that he would include this adventure among the six best Holmes stories, the tale is only a reworking of a previous episode, "The Adventure of Charles Augustus Milverton," in which a villain with a scandalous history threatens to harm a beautiful woman. In the earlier story, in fact, Holmes explains to Watson that "an illustrious client has placed her piteous case in my hands" (*CSH*, p.573). In each case, after being thwarted by a cunning and frustrating adversary, Holmes is forced to commit burglary to obtain incriminating evidence. In each case a former victim of the villain suddenly appears during the burglary and gets her revenge in a move that surprises Holmes and Watson. Each story ends with an allusion to a highly placed person whose identity must remain secret. Watson's statement that the episode "was, in some ways, the supreme moment of my friend's career" (*CSH*, p.984) seems decidedly out of place.

"The Adventure of the Blanched Soldier" (1926) marks a distinct change in the series, for it is the first of the

adventures to be written in the first person by Holmes
himself rather than Watson. James Dodd, a former soldier in the Boer War, arrives to consult Holmes about a
strange occurrence at Tuxbury Old Park, the home of
Godfrey Emsworth, one of Dodd's companions in South
Africa. Young Emsworth was wounded in the war and
the two friends were separated. Dodd's attempts to get in
touch with Godfrey after the war, however, have been
thwarted by an uncommunicative father, Colonel
Emsworth, who will not divulge the whereabouts of his
son and refuses to discuss the matter with Dodd
altogether. On his visit to the Emsworth residence, however, Dodd is told by a servant that Colonel Emsworth
knows something about Godfrey he is not telling. That
night Dodd sees the white, ghostly face of Godfrey peering through the window at him. Dodd pursues the figure
and loses it, but the next morning discovers a suspicious
gamekeeper's residence on the grounds. In it he sees Godfrey and a second man, but before he can act Colonel
Emsworth arrives to escort him off the property. Dodd
believes that for some reason Colonel Emsworth is holding his son prisoner.

Holmes travels with Dodd to visit Colonel Emsworth,
but an angry Emsworth asks them to leave. Holmes
hands him a piece of paper with a single word on it, however, and Emsworth calms down. He takes them to the
cottage to meet Godfrey who has been in isolation
because of leprosy he has contracted in South Africa;
because of the nature of the disease he has elected to live
out his life in secrecy, attended only by a surgeon, Mr.
Kent. Godfrey was unable to contain his longing to see
his old comrade, and had looked in the window and was
seen by Dodd on his visit. His skin's condition accounted
for his ghostly "blanched" appearance. Because Kent is
not an expert in tropical diseases, Holmes, foreseeing the
problem, has brought his own specialist with him. An

examination takes place and it is discovered that the illness is only a form of pseudoleprosy; he will recover.

Although Holmes complains of having to reveal some of his methods while his case is developing, Doyle actually structures this story to resemble the episodes that Watson narrates, leaving the explanation of the solution to the end. Holmes is not allowed to tell us what he is thinking or suspecting, or how he is carrying on his investigation. His engagement of a physician "present in the carriage outside the door," for example, is a detail Holmes is forced to omit from his narrative to prevent giving away the conclusion. Watson's lack of understanding, then, would seem to be a fairly necessary ingredient in the stories in the series; the alternative here, making the knowledgeable first-person narrator ignore parts of his investigation in order to preserve the suspense, seems very clumsy.

"The Adventure of the Mazarin Stone" (1921) also departs from the traditional format by employing a third-person narrator. Set at a point fairly late in Holmes's career, the story shows Watson returning to visit Holmes after a long absence. Holmes is now assisted by a young boy, Billy, who, according to Watson, "had helped a little to fill up the gap of loneliness and isolation which surrounded the saturnine figure of the great detective" (*CSH*, p.1012). Billy confides to Watson that Holmes is now working on the case of the Crown diamond, a hundred-thousand-pound burglary that has brought both the Prime Minister and the Home Secretary to Baker Street. Billy shows Watson a wax statue clad in a dressing gown that represents Holmes reading in an armchair. Holmes cautions Watson and Billy to stay clear of the statue for he expects a murder attempt that evening. He gives Watson the name of the man he suspects will make the attempt–Count Negretto Sylvius–and tells him to pass it on to Scotland Yard if Count Sylvius succeeds. Sylvius, a big-game hunter, has been seen purchasing an air-gun.

Sylvius suddenly arrives at Baker Street and Holmes dispatches Watson to Scotland Yard to bring the police (a move it would be difficult to make in Watson's narratives for the narrator needs to be present to witness the action). Holmes hides and watches Sylvius enter and notice the figure of the wax statue at the window; Sylvius silently approaches the dummy and raises his stick preparing to crush Holmes's head (he believes), when Holmes steps out of the bedroom and surprises him.

Holmes accuses Sylvius and his colleague Sam Merton of taking the Crown diamond and says he can prove it. Because his chief goal is the return of the stone, however, Holmes offers to give the pair their freedom if they return the stone. Calling Merton, a former boxer, in from the street to discuss this option with Sylvius, Holmes retires to the bedroom to play his violin while they decide. During Holmes's absence the criminals discuss how they will get the diamond out of the country and Sylvius reveals he has it with him. Merton asks to see it and when Sylvius holds it up, Holmes, who has sneaked back into the room and quietly placed himself in the chair where the wax dummy was sitting, jumps up, grabs the stone, and pulls his revolver. The police are brought up and the criminals led away. Holmes has left that "remarkable invention" the "modern gramophone" playing violin music in the next room to confuse the diamond thieves. Holmes then places the stone in the pocket of the unsuspecting Lord Cantlemere who has come to check on Holmes's progress; the befuddled peer is amazed when he discovers the missing gem in his own pocket.

"The Adventure of the Mazarin Stone" demonstrates how effectively Doyle could rework his material. The wax figure recalls the wax bust of Holmes in "The Adventure of the Empty House"; even Watson admits, "We used something of the sort once before." Doyle has also used a big-game hunter with an airgun to stalk Holmes before (Colonel Sebastian Moran, "The Adventure of the Empty House"), and had Holmes play tricks with a missing item when he returns it to its owner ("The Adventure of the Naval Treaty," "The Adventure of the Second Stain," etc.). What is interesting is how Doyle manages to make this story first-rate, given the fact that he has repeated so many of the details. Some of its freshness comes from the change of narrative technique, which in turn derives from the fact that the story was originally created as a one-act play–*The Crown Diamond*–and then rewritten by Doyle. A play does not need a first-person narrator, so Watson has virtually no function in this case; he primarily exists to allow Holmes a chance to explain the problem and then he is sent out of the way offstage to fulfill a trivial mission (Billy, after all, could be sent to bring the police).

As a theatergoer might do at a play, the reader focuses attention on a single room (or stage) and watches as the central characters pass in and out of that room. What is usually expected to be a major portion of the story–an analysis of the crime and how Holmes solved it–would require too much exposition, so that explanation is made very brief, and instead the interplay between Holmes, Sylvius, and Morton is emphasized. As might be expected, the story has a much higher percentage of dialogue than the average Holmes story does for it is essentially a series of conversations. Doyle has a good ear for dialogue, so these conversations keep us entertained even though little actually happens in the story.

In "The Adventure of the Three Gables" (1926) Holmes and Watson are sitting before the fire when a black prizefighter, Steve Dixie, bursts into the room and threatens Holmes with violence if does not stay out of a case at Harrow Weald involving Barney Stockdale, the leader of a gang to which Dixie belongs. When Dixie leaves, Holmes explains to Watson that he has received a letter from Mary Maberley at The Three Gables, Harrow Weald, asking for his help. Dixie's intervention sets Holmes's resolve even more firmly so the two of them visit The Three Gables, a somewhat small estate managed by Mrs. Maberley, whose son Douglas recently died of pneumonia in Rome. Mrs. Maberley has been approached by a real-estate agent with a client who wishes to buy her house and furniture. Mrs. Maberley first agrees to the sale, but balks when her attorney points out to her that the arrangement would forbid her from taking anything, even her personal possessions, from the house.

Mrs. Maberley's explanation of this is interrupted when Holmes suddenly opens the door and grabs a maid who has been eavesdropping. Holmes feels that the maid, who posted Mrs. Maberley's letter to him, was the one who notified Barney Stockdale that Holmes was being consulted. The maid admits her complicity, but says that Stockdale, a minor figure, is only acting on behalf of someone else.

Holmes ponders the case and concludes that something valuable has recently come into Mrs. Maberley's house—something that someone urgently wishes to acquire. Seeing the trunks and cases of Mrs. Maberley's recently deceased son, Holmes advises her to search them carefully while he tries to determine precisely who wants to buy her house and why. Holmes checks with Langdale Pike, a contact who has knowledge of underground happenings, but news of a burglary at The Three Gables interrupts the inquiry. In the robbery Mrs. Maberley was chloroformed while several men went through her deceased son's belongings. A sheet of paper that apparently came from the manuscript of a romantic novel is found on the floor, but the rest of the manuscript is missing. Holmes examines the sheet, then he and Watson return to London to the home of the wealthy Isadora Klein where the mystery is explained. Klein and Douglas Maberley had an affair, but she declined to marry him because he was poor. He then wrote a novel in which their affair was thinly disguised. The publication of this book would have damaged her socially and destroyed her forthcoming marriage to a wealthy young duke. She was willing to do anything to get her hands on the manuscript–including the purchase of the house–so she hired Stockdale and his gang to help. Once they stole the manuscript she immediately burned it. Holmes agrees to ignore her crime in return for five hundred pounds, which he plans to give to Mrs. Maberley so she can travel around the world; even he notes that he is compounding a felony in doing so.

This is not a story that has been well liked. The fundamental premise, that a woman who already has a reputation for being a romantic adventuress would attempt to buy an estate to block the publication of a novel she has never read seems a bit farfetched. The fact that Holmes (after threatening several times to call in the police) lets her go free with only a warning and accepts her check for five hundred pounds has also been criticized. His action is both illegal and unjustified by any mitigating circumstances. Finally, Holmes's venomous remarks about Steve Dixie, the black prizefighter, are viciously racist and very untypical of a man who has usually displayed compassion and concern for humanity. There is not only no justification for Holmes's comments, there is no real explanation for them either. These kinds of racial slurs do not occur anywhere else in Doyle's writing; it is not at all clear how they found their way into the mouth of a character as sophisticated and honorable as Sherlock Holmes.

"The Adventure of the Sussex Vampire" (1924) opens

with Holmes handing Watson a note he has received from a legal firm whose client, Mr. Robert Ferguson, has approached them with an inquiry about vampires. A second letter from Ferguson himself explains that a friend's wife has been acting quite strangely. The wife has twice been seen bending over the sleeping body of her infant son, apparently sucking blood from its neck. Her husband has in fact found her with blood on her face and lips.

Holmes is intrigued by what at first seemed to be a case that could not be taken seriously. He agrees to take it on and Ferguson arrives the next day, admitting straightaway that he is not acting on behalf of a "friend"; it is Mrs. Ferguson, a Peruvian he met in his importation business, whom he suspects of being a vampire. He explains that his wife refused to speak to him when he last found her with his son and accused her of foul play; she has locked herself in her room and refuses to see him. A nurse has vowed to protect the baby from future attacks, so he feels his baby is at least temporarily safe. His fifteen-year-old son by a former marriage has been struck several times by Mrs. Ferguson, however, and the boy's safety is not secure.

Holmes agrees to visit the home where these curious incidents have occurred and when he and Watson arrive one of the first things they notice is the family's spaniel, crippled (Ferguson says) by spinal meningitis. Holmes also inspects a collection of Peruvian utensils and weapons brought into the household by Mrs. Ferguson. Holmes then arranges to speak with Mrs. Ferguson who remains secluded from her husband. She says that her husband should trust her, but the vision of her rising from the baby with blood on her lips is an image he cannot erase from his mind. Holmes observes the infant, the fifteen-year-old brother (who has been crippled since a childhood fall), and the nurse, and then convenes a meeting between Ferguson and his temporarily estranged wife at which Holmes explains the mystery.

Convinced that vampirism was not a possibility, Holmes explains that he sought some other reason for the incriminating actions of Mrs. Ferguson. Her insistence that she should be trusted only further convinced him that she was not injuring the child, but attempting to save it. The Peruvian weapons and crippled spaniel persuaded Holmes that someone was trying to poison the baby with curare or some other exotic poison. Mrs. Ferguson, who recognized the problem, was attempting to suck the poison from the child when she was caught and was never given an adequate opportunity to explain her behavior. The villain in this situation is Jacky, Ferguson's older son, who as a cripple is highly jealous of his younger half-brother. Although Mrs. Ferguson was aware for some time of Jacky's dark side, she did not want to tell her husband about it because he loved the boy so and would be brokenhearted to learn of his son's cruelty.

Some readers have noted a similarity between this story and "The Adventure of Silver Blaze" in that in both stories Holmes notices crippled animals (a spaniel and sheep) that have served as experiments for a villain planning a crime. It is hard to know just how difficult this case was for Holmes to solve, because much depends on the character of young Jacky and the look of "jealousy" and "cruel hatred" that only Holmes notices on Jacky's face (CSH, p.1043). Why poison-tipped arrows were kept on the wall and how the child learned these arrows were poison-tipped—these are the mysteries Holmes does not solve.

"The Adventure of the Three Garridebs" (1925) begins with Holmes receiving a letter from a Nathan Garrideb, followed immediately by the visit of an American lawyer named John Garrideb. John Garrideb, from Kansas, explains that he was once visited by an Alexander Hamilton Garrideb, a millionaire eccentric who was interested in finding others who shared his unusual name. The wealthy

Garrideb's will, in fact, designated that if two more Garridebs were found his estate was to be divided among them—five million dollars each. John Garrideb could not find another Garrideb in the United States, but he did locate Nathan Garrideb in London who in turn also got in touch with Holmes for help.

After Garrideb leaves, Holmes tells Watson he is convinced the American was a fraud. Watson then phones Nathan Garrideb (the first telephone call in the series) and arranges a meeting with him. Nathan Garrideb proves to be an elderly gentleman with a variety of scientific interests who seldom leaves his apartment. Holmes asks a few questions, but is interrupted when John Garrideb suddenly arrives and announces he believes he has found the third man needed. He has with him an advertisement for a business owned by Howard Garrideb of Birmingham, a manufacturer of agricultural machinery. John Garrideb asks Nathan Garrideb to call on the man for him, arguing that the British native will give his fantastic story more credibility. Nathan agrees, and after John leaves Holmes asks whether he may visit the next afternoon while Nathan is traveling to Birmingham, to look over some of Garrideb's specimens. Holmes confides to Watson that the purported advertisement was a fake and the next morning he tells Watson he has identified John Garrideb as "Killer" Evans, recently released from prison where he has been serving time for murder.

At Nathan Garrideb's apartment that afternoon, Holmes and Watson hide in a dark corner and watch "John Garrideb" Evans enter and open a secret trapdoor in the floor. He disappears into the hole and Holmes and Watson pull their revolvers, but when Evans emerges he too pulls a gun and shoots Watson in the leg before Holmes can stop him. The injury is not serious, although Holmes is extremely upset to see his colleague wounded. In the cellar beneath the floor they find a counterfeiter's printing press and a large supply of counterfeit bank notes. The cache had belonged to an American counterfeiter who had lived in these rooms before Nathan Garrideb. In an argument, Evans had killed the counterfeiter after learning of the equipment and counterfeit money hidden away. When Evans was released from prison he discovered the elderly Garrideb living in these rooms, and he created the whole Garrideb scheme simply to get him out of the way for a day.

The story, of course, is a reworking of "The Red-Headed League," in which money and an outrageous premise are used to lure an individual away from a location so a crime can be committed in his absence. If we count "The Adventure of the Stockbroker's Clerk" as another repetition of the same formula, this story represents the third time Doyle used the plot, which still seems most successful in its original version.

"The Problem of Thor Bridge" (1922) begins with Holmes receiving a letter from Neil Gibson, a former United States senator, who bought an estate in England after making a fortune in gold-mining in America. His wife has been found shot to death on a lonely bridge. The chief suspect is a very attractive governess in the house, whom some believe had won Gibson's affections. A discharged revolver was found among the governess's possessions; a note in the dead woman's hand was signed by the governess, and it is believed Gibson's wife was keeping an appointment with the governess when she was murdered. Holmes is warned by Marlow Bates, the manager of Gibson's estate, that Gibson is a brutal man, "an infernal villain." When Gibson himself arrives he demonstrates he has a violent temper, but he is convinced that Grace Dunbar, the governess, is innocent; he will pay any amount of money to clear her name. After Holmes refuses to accept the case because he feels Gibson is concealing information, Gibson breaks down and re-

veals that the romance between him and his wife had
faded, and that he had told Grace Dunbar of his affection
for her. Miss Dunbar, however, was not interested in a
ménage à trois with a man who attempted to buy whatever he desired in life; she at first planned to leave the
house, then, because she could influence Gibson, agreed
to stay and attempt to reform him. His wife sensed that
something out of the ordinary was taking place and was
extremely jealous; he proposes that his wife might have
tried to kill Grace Dunbar and was in turn shot in self-
defense.

Holmes visits the scene and discovers that the murder
weapon is one of a pair of pistols, the other of which is
missing. Examining the bridge, Holmes notices a freshly
chipped spot on the lower edge of the parapet. He strikes
the ledge with his cane several times without leaving a
mark and obviously feels the chip is significant. Questioning Grace Dunbar the next morning Holmes learns
that Grace did meet Mrs. Gibson on Thor Bridge the
night she was murdered, but was asked to do so by Mrs.
Gibson. The note clutched in Mrs. Gibson's hand was
Grace's response to her invitation. Grace claims that Mrs.
Gibson was alive, but furiously angry, when she left her
on the bridge. She claims she has never seen the
incriminating pistol before.

Holmes and Watson visit Thor Bridge again, and
Holmes performs an experiment with Watson's revolver
by tying it to a stone with a length of twine and dropping
the stone off the bridge. Watson's gun chips the parapet
before it goes over the side into the water. Holmes asks
the police to drag the lake for Watson's revolver and for
the revolver used to kill Mrs. Gibson, which he assumes
was also tied to a stone that was dropped from the bridge.
Mrs. Gibson, full of jealous hatred, planted a revolver in
Grace Dunbar's wardrobe, tricked her into writing a note
saying they would meet at the bridge, then killed herself,

the weighted gun flying into the water as she fell lifeless.

This story, first published in 1922, originally appeared in two parts. Although not longer than the average Holmes story, it is appreciably longer than the average story Doyle was writing after World War I; most readers consider it the last of the truly first-rate full-dress episodes. The case presents one of Doyle's more interesting puzzles, as well as one of the very few suicides in his fiction (carefully premeditated, unlike virtually all the murders in the cycle). The story contains the familiar triangle of husband, wife, and secret paramour that so obsessed Doyle, and revolves around an action taken to achieve revenge, the motivation for most crimes in the series.

"The Adventure of the Creeping Man" (1923) opens with Holmes explaining to Watson that he would like to explore more fully the use of dogs in detective work, particularly the relationship of dogs to their masters. Specifically, Holmes is puzzled as to why Professor Presbury, a famous physiologist, has recently been attacked by his own dog. Trevor Bennett, an assistant to Presbury and fiancé of Presbury's daughter, comes to Holmes complaining of Presbury's unusual behavior. Presbury suddenly disappeared for several weeks without telling anyone; it was later discovered he had gone to Prague. Since then he has become both secretive and surly with his assistant. The elderly Presbury has been attacked twice by his dog and has been observed by Bennett crawling through the house at night on his hands and knees. Presbury's daughter Edith arrives at Baker Street and reports that she has seen her father peering in her second-floor window after apparently climbing directly up the wall of the house.

Exploiting one of Professor Presbury's increasingly more frequent attacks of amnesia, Holmes and Watson call on him, pretending that Professor Presbury has called them in. He, however, does not fall for their scheme and angrily dismisses them. Analyzing the case at the local inn, Holmes explains to Watson that Presbury's strange behavior seems to follow a pattern, with more bizarre attacks manifesting themselves every nine days. Holmes concludes that Presbury began taking some powerful drug during his mysterious trip to Prague, and has been repeating the dosage regularly ever since.

Holmes and Watson return on the ninth day of what seems to be the professor's cycle, and wait outside his house at night. As Holmes expected, Presbury comes out of the door and begins to move across the ground on his hands and feet, crouching like an animal. Amazingly, he begins to scale the ivy-covered wall of the house like an ape; returning to the ground he attracts the attention of his dog, which he agitates by bombarding it with pebbles while remaining safely outside the reach of its chain. When the angered dog breaks its chain and grabs Presbury by the throat Holmes and Watson step in and save him. After Presbury is treated by Watson and is safely under a dose of morphine, Holmes and Watson discover a letter that explains the mystery. The elderly Presbury, hoping to rejuvenate himself because of a romantic interest in a younger woman, has been injecting himself with a "serum of anthropoid" and periodically acquiring apelike characteristics. Holmes intends to warn Presbury's supplier of serum of possible criminal prosecution and assumes that will close the case.

"The Adventure of the Creeping Man" has been highly criticized for introducing the fantastic into the cycle. Whereas Holmes the rationalist clearly did not accept the existence of vampires in "The Adventure of the Sussex Vampire," we are to understand that the detective firmly believes Presbury can acquire apelike characteristics and abilities after injecting himself with the anthropoid serum. Although many stories in the cycle suggest the supernatural, Holmes's investigation always proves that there are rational and reasonable explanations for these mysteries. In this story, however, there is no "ordinary" explanation for Presbury's fantastic behavior. Presbury, exactly as he seems to, actually becomes a kind of ape-man. Such a bizarre conclusion might be acceptable in one of Doyle's science-fiction stories, many of which incorporate the fantastic or supernatural, but it seems clearly out of place in the Holmes cycle where the reader has grown used to having Holmes explain away nightmares, not reinforce them.

About the only case that can be made in Doyle's defense on this matter is that he did not see the effects of the anthropoid serum as fanciful. Although it has been asserted that this story simply imitates Robert Louis Stevenson's famous novel *The Strange Case of Dr. Jekyll and Mr. Hyde*, Doyle undoubtedly turned to real life for his inspiration. There was a good deal of interest in animal serums and animal gland transplants in the twenties. Some legitimate physicians (as well as some not so legitimate, of course) felt that the organs of goats, monkeys, and other animals could be used to restore youth, strength, and virility.

The most prominent researcher in this field was Eugen Steinach, an Austrian physiologist, who was director of the biological institute of the Academy of Sciences in Vienna. Steinach earlier taught at the University of Prague; it was in Prague, of course, the reader should not be surprised to learn, that Professor Presbury disappeared for two weeks. Steinach's experiments with injections and transplants were firmly believed in by some, and many people whom today one might think should have known better actually received his treatments. For example, the Irish poet and Nobel prizewinner William Butler Yeats had one of these Steinach operations, which he hoped would turn back the clock for him.

Although the theories of Steinach and others seem somewhat foolish today, the fact that at one time a figure as prominent as Yeats could have accepted them suggests that Doyle too might have believed that an "anthropoid serum" could have a genuine effect. What he records in his story, then, is simply a warning that the effect might be negative rather than positive. Presbury is not rejuvenated; he is reduced to an animal in what Conan Doyle, in 1923, must have believed was the demonstration of a scientific fact and was not really science-fiction at all.

"The Adventure of the Lion's Mane" (1926) is the second story in the series told by Holmes rather than Watson. ("The Adventure of the Blanched Soldier" is of course the other one.) In this story Holmes is living in retirement with his bees, and he admits that his old friend Watson has "passed almost beyond my ken" (*CSH*, p.1083). One morning, while walking on the cliff overlooking the sea, Holmes notices a neighbor, Fitzroy McPherson, staggering towards him. Falling dead at Holmes's feet, McPherson shrieks the words "the Lion's Mane" (*CSH*, p.1084). He is partially dressed and has obviously been on the beach; his back is bleeding and appears to have been beaten or flogged. While the police are summoned Holmes examines the beach, but can find no trace of McPherson's assailant. He does, however, find a note, signed "Maudie," which suggests that someone was going to meet McPherson on the beach. After questioning McPherson's family and friends Holmes has no real leads, but the death of McPherson's dog on the beach near the spot where McPherson died causes Holmes to consult his library and come closer to a solution. The sudden entrance of Ian Murdoch, another neighbor who bursts into Holmes's house with his back scourged like McPherson's, gives the case more urgency. Murdoch passes out before he is able to explain what has happened, but he has been swimming so Holmes and a neighbor rush back to the seashore. Where McPherson and Murdoch had been swimming they find a giant jellyfish, which is the murderer, and they crush it with a huge rock.

The story has been grouped among the weakest of the cycle. Critics do not understand why Holmes did not immediately suspect a jellyfish or sea creature of some type. Doyle manages to sustain some interest in this simple tale by casting suspicions on Ian Murdoch and interviewing several people close to the victim. The story records not so much a mystery but merely a curious incident; it works only if the reader is slower than Holmes in reaching what seems to be a fairly obvious conclusion.

"The Adventure of the Veiled Lodger" (1927) is another nonmystery that requires little deductive effort on the part of Holmes. Watson is summoned to Baker Street where he finds Holmes in consultation with a Mrs. Merrilow who is having problems with Mrs. Ronder, a lodger for seven years. Mrs. Ronder, who constantly wears a veil because of her mutilated face, lives a secluded life, but recently her health has begun to fail and she cries out in the night. She asked Mrs. Merrilow to bring in Holmes, because, as Mrs. Ronder says, "it would ease my mind if someone knew the truth before I died" (*CSH*, p.1096). Holmes agrees to come, and when Mrs. Merrilow leaves he finds in his notebooks the history of Mrs. Ronder.

She and her husband once owned a wild animal show and one of the animals they exhibited was a somewhat temperamental lion. One night there was a disturbance at their camp and her husband was found near the open lion cage, his skull crushed and clawed. The lion was found crouching over Mrs. Ronder and her face had been clawed and mutilated. The lion was put back in its cage and, although there are some unexplained aspects of the tragedy, it was assumed that the death and maiming were accidental.

When Holmes and Watson arrive at the home of Mrs.

Merrilow they find Mrs. Ronder, as anticipated, heavily
veiled. She tells the true story of what happened the night
of the lion attack. She had been having an affair with
Leonardo, the strong man in the show. Leonardo made a
nail-studded club that he used to kill Mr. Ronder, hoping
the wound would resemble one made by a lion's claws.
Mrs. Ronder was to open the lion cage when Leonardo
killed her husband, but when she did so, the creature,
smelling blood, attacked her instead while Leonardo fled
in terror. Leonardo then disappeared, leaving her alone to
live with the guilty knowledge of her crime; reading
about his recent accidental death has apparently brought
Mrs. Ronder the nightmares that alerted her landlady.

"The Adventure of the Veiled Lodger" is the next to
last Holmes story Doyle wrote, and it reflects the decline
in the last series of six episodes. Here, as in "The Adventure of the Lion's Mane," there is nothing for Holmes to
do, no crime to solve. He visits Mrs. Ronder, hears her
story, and the "adventure" ends. The episode does contribute to the characterization of the detective, however,
in that the reader sees him dissuading the miserable Mrs.
Ronder from committing suicide, saying to her, "Your
life is not your own." A few days later he receives in the
mail a bottle of poison and the message "I send you my
temptation," a gesture reminding us that not all of the services Holmes performs are investigatory in nature.

"The Adventure of Shoscombe Old Place" (1927) is the
last Holmes story Doyle wrote, although he did not
choose to place it last in his final collection. It opens with
the visit of Mr. John Mason, a horse trainer, who has
come to report on his employer Sir Robert Norberton.
Norberton has a horse, Shoscombe Prince, entered in the
Derby, and his entire fortune is riding on the outcome.
Even so, Sir Robert's behavior seems exceedingly bizarre.
He never sleeps and seems to have quarreled with his
widowed sister, Lady Beatrice. He has given away her pet

spaniel and she in turn no longer visits the stables as she once did regularly; apparently she is also drinking heavily. Sir Robert has been seen meeting a strange man at an old church crypt late at night; he has also evidently dug up the remains of a body there, for bits of bone have been found hidden in a corner. Moreover, pieces of charred human bone have been found in the household furnace. All of these puzzling facts convince Holmes that some investigation is necessary, so he and Watson decide to visit the area masquerading as fishermen.

On the scene Holmes and Watson stop at a local inn and ask the innkeeper some questions about the neighborhood. Then retaining their pose as fishermen, they take a walk, accompanied by the spaniel that until recently belonged to Lady Beatrice. Intercepting the carriage of Lady Beatrice on its daily drive, Holmes releases the spaniel that first runs eagerly toward its old mistress and then suddenly begins to bark and snap at the veiled passenger in the carriage, which hurriedly drives on. Holmes concludes that someone is masquerading as Lady Beatrice and taking daily drives in her carriage; he and Watson decide to visit the crypt where Sir Robert has been seen. The bones that had been found there are now missing, and Holmes assumes they were the ones found burned in the furnace. Continuing to search, Holmes begins to open a coffin he finds in the crypt, but he and Watson are interrupted by Sir Robert himself who is making a midnight visit. Holmes confronts him and demands the identity of the body he has discovered in the coffin.

Sir Robert takes them to the house and explains that his sister died of natural causes a week before. Because the estate would be affected by her death, and because he was heavily in debt, he hoped to keep the death a secret until after the Derby, which he expected to win. He removed the bones from a forgotten coffin in the crypt and placed his sister in it; as Holmes discovered, Sir Robert had an imposter ride about pretending to be Lady Beatrice.

In an important afternote Watson records that Shoscombe Prince did in fact win the Derby, then goes on to call the episode a "strange incident in a career which has now outlived its shadows and promises to end in an honoured old age" (*CSH*, p. 1112). This comment by Watson is out of place in the context of the story. The episode is set in a time in which Holmes and Watson are still living together in Baker Street, before Holmes retires to keeping bees, so Holmes's career has really not "outlived its shadows." Watson's remark actually reflects the sequence in which Doyle composed the individual episodes of the series.

There are several ways of reading the Holmes stories. William S. Baring-Gould has arranged the tales in what he feels is their proper chronological order in *The Annotated Sherlock Holmes*, and in that collection the series ends with "His Last Bow," the last case in Holmes's career. The Doubleday anthology *The Complete Sherlock Holmes*, which is the most popular and in some ways the "standard" collection, presents the stories in the order in which Doyle anthologized them, and concludes with "The Adventure of the Retired Colourman," the final story in *The Case Book of Sherlock Holmes*. The real "last story," however, is of course this one, the last one in the final series of six episodes that Doyle agreed to do in 1926–27.

It is only in the larger context of Doyle's career that Holmes's work now "promises to end." Because this was to be the final story it is clear that Doyle attempted to bring it back up to the level of the former adventures. The story has enough mystery and drama for two or three episodes, with the threatened estate, the bizarre behavior of the principals, what seems to be two sets of bones—all this set against the dramatic backdrop of the upcoming

Derby. Doyle seemed desperate to make his hero depart on a high note, so he wrote a story that combines elements of "Silver Blaze" and "The Musgrave Ritual" with a touch of Poe, throwing in a late night visit to a haunted crypt that reminds us of the story he had borrowed from successfully so often before, "The Fall of the House of Usher." Although Holmes and Watson may have found themselves in more terrifying situations than the one in which they stand in the "haunted" crypt at midnight, gazing in lantern light at the body "swathed in a sheet from head to foot, with dreadful witch-like features, all nose and chin, projecting at one end, the dim, glazed eyes staring from a discoloured and crumbling face" (*CSH*, p.1110), the episode represents a substantial improvement over the nonmysteries that form the basis of "The Adventure of the Lion's Mane" and "The Adventure of the Veiled Lodger."

"The Adventure of the Retired Colourman" (1927) begins with the visit of Josiah Amberley, a retired "colourman" who was a junior partner in a firm that manufactured paint. His problem seems to be a fairly simple one. His wife and his best friend who lives nearby have disappeared, apparently running away together and taking with them a large portion of his life's savings. He wants Holmes to find his wife and retrieve his money.

Holmes asks Watson to visit Amberley's house and see what clues might have been left behind. Watson visits with Amberley, who seems to be repainting the woodwork in a house that is otherwise crumbling in disrepair. Watson learns some more details of the disappearance of Amberley's wife but discovers no real leads. Unknown to Watson, Holmes sends a telegram to Amberley purportedly from a man who claims to have some information about the missing money. Amberley seems strangely reluctant to investigate this lead, but agrees to go with Watson to talk with the man. When they return to Baker

Street from their wild-goose chase, Holmes asks Amberley what he did with the bodies of his wife and friend. Amberley attempts to swallow a poisonous capsule but is prevented from doing so and goes off to jail.

Holmes then explains to Watson that he had sent the telegram so he could examine Amberley's house, where he discovered a hermetically sealed room with a gas pipe running into it. Concluding that the strong odor of fresh paint in an otherwise rundown house was intended to conceal something, such as the odor of gas, Holmes looked further and found part of a message written on a wall near the floor by one of Amberley's dying victims. The bodies are later found in an abandoned well by the police.

An unusual feature of this story is that Holmes suggests to the police they should look "on the body" of Amberley's friend for the pencil he used to scrawl his dying message. Since the message was not finished, the pencil should have been found in the dying man's hand by Amberley, or near the spot the man died where it had dropped unnoticed. One would scarcely expect the dying man to put away his pencil before he died when he had not finished his note. This slip was deleted when the story was reprinted and is important only in that it reflects the carelessness of Doyle in these last stories where his heart does not seem to be in his work.

It should be clear to anyone who reads *The Case Book of Sherlock Holmes* and *His Last Bow* that the volumes are much weaker than those preceding them. *His Last Bow*, for example, is a short collection, two-thirds the length of the earlier books, with the old, but previously unanthologized, episode "The Adventure of the Cardboard Box" added to fill it out. The stories in *His Last Bow* are shorter and more perfunctory than the previous adventures, even though they were written at random intervals and not under the pressure of meeting a series deadline. An even more marked decline comes in *The Case Book* where we find the episodes have become even shorter and there is more manipulation of the narrative technique with three stories not told by Watson. The real dividing point for Doyle was World War I. The loss of his son, brother, and other family members was the prime catalyst in his movement toward spiritualism.

"The Adventure of the Dying Detective" (1913) was the last of the prewar stories. There was a gap of four years until the gloomy "His Last Bow," which is, in the chronology of the adventures, the final Holmes episode. Written before the war was over, its sudden departure to the third-person narrative suggests Doyle's distraction. There was another gap of four years before the appearance of "The Adventure of the Mazarin Stone," which is, we have noted, only a reworking of an earlier play. From this point on Doyle was only putting his characters through the motions. The pattern for the series was firmly established; sometimes he saved effort by omitting or curtailing substantial obligatory introductory scenes or closing explanatory discussions. Toward the end of his final series he omitted the mystery itself, letting his readers be content with his famous characters, even when those characters had very little to do.

There is a famous sketch done by Doyle near the end of his life depicting himself as a workhorse pulling a wagon piled high with his fiction, his problems, the causes he defended.[6] When one looks at that sketch and sees again how much effort the man expended in his energetic life one cannot complain about the decline of these later Holmes adventures. Doyle wrote four novels and fifty-six stories to satisfy a public constantly demanding more Holmes. Even though he himself tried to end the series twice, he was also persuaded twice to renew the episodes of the characters for whom he no longer had a great deal of interest. One should therefore not be surprised by the

gradual decline in the Holmes cycle, but rather marvel at
the fact that Doyle could sustain its quality so successfully for the forty years he wrote the adventures.

There have been many attempts made to explain the success of the Holmes stories. Doyle created in this series
two of the most popular fictional characters of all time,
characters who are instantly recognizable worldwide,
even to those few who have not read the stories. Holmes
and Watson repeatedly have been represented, alluded to,
parodied, imitated, and caricatured in hundreds of
movies, books, stories, articles, and advertisements.
They can be seen on television, in the personages of Basil
Rathbone and Nigel Bruce, stalking the moors looking
for that infamous hound, and then, following the movie,
appearing in a commercial selling Toyotas, being two of a
small handful of literary figures such as Robinson Crusoe
or Scrooge whom any reader can identify on sight. How
did Doyle, whose other fiction is rather unmemorable,
manage to score such a complete success in this series of
tales that rival Shakespeare and Dickens in their popularity? There are several reasons.

   First, there tends to be a somewhat cultlike following
among readers of mystery fiction. Figures as diverse as
Charlie Chan, Travis McGee, Hercule Poirot, Columbo,
Miss Marple, Mike Hammer, Peter Wimsey, or Philip
Marlowe reflect the phenomenon that began with
Holmes and Watson. Fans of detective fiction like to see
detectives develop and grow in a series of stories or
novels. Because the central emphasis in the formula of
detective fiction is usually on plot, characterization
becomes secondary in the equation. Repeating a character, or allowing that character to develop gradually over a
series of stories, allows both writer and reader to devote
their attention to the central issue of the plot—the mystery. Furthermore, the repetition of the central figure or

figures provides a constant viewpoint readers can rely upon as they attempt to unravel the puzzles for themselves.

As Doyle himself discovered when writing *The Hound of the Baskervilles*, it is simply much easier to use the personalities one has already created than to invent new ones, for the new ones must be accompanied by certain explanatory background information; they need a history or "life" to be believable. Detective fiction is of course not the only kind of fiction that utilizes the series format—children's books often come in series, for example, and there are the Brigadier Gerard and Professor Challenger series of Doyle—but fans of detective fiction tend to be somewhat avid readers, and most of them who find a character they like soon read the entire series and eagerly await more of the same.[7] Since the sixty Holmes stories over a period of forty years represents one of the longest single detective series, one should not be surprised to find Holmes among the most popular of detectives. As one of the oldest detective series (the honor of creating *the* oldest must ultimately belong to Poe), it also stands to reason that Holmes is among the most popular simply because he has been around for so long.

A second factor contributing to the popularity of the Holmes cycle is the very successful pictorial treatment the stories have had nearly since their inception. Although Doyle's descriptions of the great detective and his friend are in themselves clear and memorable, if the series had continued with the type of illustrations we find in the early editions of the first novels it is safe to say that Holmes would not now be a figure visually identifiable to young and old. In what was an incredible stroke of luck, Doyle was able to secure Sidney Paget as the illustrator for most of the Holmes stories published in England. Paget clearly established the Holmesian profile that the American illustrator Frederic Dorr Steele perpetuated in

the American publications of the stories, although Steele
used as models both Paget's drawings and the American
actor who brought Holmes to life on the stage—/illiam
Gillette.

The role of Gillette in contributing to the image of
Holmes cannot be underestimated. He brought the
deerstalker hat and the curved pipe to the characterization, two props that became permanent additions to later
representations of the detective. Once this Paget-Gillette-Steel composite image was formed, Holmes became
a rather firmly fixed and clearly identifiable figure that
other illustrators did not alter, as though Holmes were a
real person who "really looked" a certain way. For twentieth-century audiences, most of whom of course never
saw Gillette, and many of whom have never seen the
drawings of Paget or Steele, the tremendously popular
series of fourteen movies starring Basil Rathbone and
Nigel Bruce established the images clearly in the minds of
millions. Although the Rathbone-Bruce series of films
has been criticized for being unfaithful to Doyle's fiction
(and it certainly is), the movies have always been popular
and have contributed a great deal to the mythic dimen-
sions of Holmes. Others since Rathbone have attempted
the role, but Rathbone's physical resemblance to the
Paget-Gillette-Steel representation has made his characterization the most popular and his face has blended with
the others into the composite image of Holmes that is
known the way the face of no other fictional character is
known. Only Dickens and Shakespeare, besides Doyle,
have had illustrators and actors contribute so successfully
to bringing their characters to life.

Thirdly, the atmosphere of the stories is a powerful factor in their popularity. The dominant image that emerges
from the cycle is one of Holmes and Watson prowling
through the foggy streets of London in a world where, in
the words of one writer, "it is always 1895." Even though

Holmes and Watson attack a number of problems on sunny spring mornings and hot August afternoons, and work in the country almost as frequently as the city, those settings tend to be overlooked as readers remember only the "classic" atmosphere of some of the episodes. Reading is a solitary activity, a withdrawn activity, and the withdrawn atmosphere of Baker Street on a foggy London night is completely compatible with one's longing for retreat as he or she settles into a comfortable chair with a volume of Doyle in hand. There is a safeness one can sense in the picture of Holmes and Watson sitting snugly before their fire browsing through their papers or books in an idle fashion while outside the elements rage. It is a very comfortable world Doyle creates: inside are warmth, safety, light, and knowledge; outside are darkness, cold, and criminal forces.

The world of Baker Street is a world that is reassuringly far less complex than the real one. Messages are sent by telegrams, which usually can be traced. (Although there is a telephone in Baker Street in some of the later stories, Holmes does not seem to like to use this newfangled form of communication.) A railroad timetable (which apparently never needs updating) can provide definitive information about long-distance travel; for short distances, of course, there is a hansom cab on every corner (cabs which can also be traced if necessary). The newspapers' "agony columns" (as Holmes refers to them) provide a kind of public bulletin board of information anyone can consult. Apparently everyone does consult these columns, for Holmes almost always gets instant responses to his advertisements and regularly discovers that the columns are being used to transmit secret and seldom encoded messages by people one might assume would choose a far less public and troublesome manner of communication. Personal security is also relatively simple in Holmes's world. A cane or stout stick is usually adequate protection; Watson's service revolver is an ultimate weapon of sorts, the absolute defense against any violence one might encounter. The very limited and contained nature of this environment makes it a safe retreat for readers because of its welcome predictability; the intricacies and uncertainties of life in the late twentieth century have no place in Doyle's simplified and well-ordered world.

Lastly, of course, the popularity of Doyle's two characters can be attributed to the personalities of the figures themselves. To say that Watson is beloved because he is loyal and devoted, or Holmes is popular because he is brilliant and fearless, however, is to miss the point. There are a number of admirable heroes in literature who have possessed any number of good qualities and not been nearly so well accepted by the public. Some of their secret lies in the interplay between the characters, the antithetical qualities they possess that cause them to complement each other. Watson is staid, for example, where Holmes is unconventional; Holmes is cerebral where Watson is physical; Watson is disciplined while Holmes indulges his many whims. We come to know these traits, these idiosyncrasies, how these characters will react to certain situations, and they themselves frequently display an awareness of their differences, giving added verisimilitude to their characterizations. Furthermore, by Watson's frquent allusions to cases that do not actually appear in the cycle (such as the infamous "Giant Rat of Sumatra"), Doyle suggests that his characters' lives extend much further than the series and thereby contributes a realistic fullness to their existence. There is the reliability of a solid friendship here, the predictability we come to expect from old companions when we have grown to know their habits nearly as well as we know our own.

The way readers relate to the personae of Holmes and Watson is also important. Watson, the narrative voice of almost all the stories, presents his case in a straightforward way. His method is the epitome of good common sense. Watson is frequently puzzled, sometimes reaches too quickly for the obvious, and often, when attempting to imitate the deductive thinking of his brilliant friend, arrives at an absolutely wrong conclusion even though he is reasoning from the same data as Holmes. Watson is human when Holmes is cold and indifferent, and readers no doubt sense in this rather practical physician the touch of humanity that makes him trustworthy. The reader can believe in these adventures because he knows that Watson reports them without exaggeration. In short, Watson reacts the way that a reader might in his shoes; one therefore identifies with his point of view.

Holmes is not perceived by Watson as an intellectual equal, and he is not seen that way by most readers either. Holmes is a kind of wizard with an endless array of tricks up his sleeve. His knowledge and skill makes him virtually invulnerable, and his presence is as reassuring as Watson's revolver, but for very different reasons. Holmes continually demonstrates that the puzzles of life are always solvable, and that they are almost always far less complex than they first appear to be. Holmes brings with him his lantern of rational thought and repeatedly flashes it into the dark corners of human existence, showing us that the shadows lurking there are not to be feared. There is a paternal quality to his actions that reinforces our confidence and reassuringly convinces us that there exists in this man what he in turn found in his friend Watson, "one fixed point in a changing age."

6

Adventure, Science Fiction, and Horror Stories

Although Sherlock Holmes will always be the most memorable fictional creation of Conan Doyle, Doyle's stories of adventure bordering upon science fiction, as typified by the Professor Challenger series, have also had a strong following and made an undeniable impact upon fiction and the twentieth-century's popularizer of fiction—film. The first story in the series—*The Lost World* (1912)—is also the most important, for it has practically created its own cinematic genre. For the hero of this novel, Professor Challenger himself, Doyle turned to his medical training at Edinburgh, and, as he did when he selected Professor Joseph Bell as the model for Holmes, created a fictional character from a real-life character he had never forgotten. This time, however, the professor Doyle selected was not the shrewdly deductive, intellectual figure he had been attracted to in the person of Bell. Professor Challenger was based on Professor William Rutherford, an outspoken, eccentric physician with a bushy beard and somewhat explosive temperament. One could scarcely imagine a figure more the opposite of the quiet aesthetic Holmes. Even though quite different from the more quiet detective, Challenger became a popular fictional figure, and *The Lost World*, which some have compared to the tales of Jules Verne (most notably *A Journey to the Center of the Earth*) and others to *Robinson Crusoe*, inspired a silent movie made during Doyle's lifetime, and countless other movie variations on the theme, including the famous *King Kong*.

There is not, of course, a giant gorilla in *The Lost World*, but the intrepid adventurers, the strange isolated plateau peopled by savages unfamiliar with the outside world, and most of all, the dinosaurs and unknown reptiles that inhabit this "lost world"–these elements of Doyle's novel, like Holmes, have taken on a life of their own.

The novel opens with a foreword "informing" the reader that a "libel suit" against the journalist E. D. Malone, the "author" or, perhaps more accurately put, the "recorder" of these adventures, has been withdrawn by Professor G. E. Challenger. Malone is, then, Challenger's "Dr. Watson," and what is a work of fiction is given the aura of truth by being ostensibly presented as a factual account. Naturally Doyle's name appears on the volume itself, so, unlike the book *Robinson Crusoe*, which was originally published with only Crusoe's name on it and not DeFoe's, there was little chance that any but the least observant reader would accept the book as fact. Still, it should be noted that an expedition was launched from the United States in 1914, sponsored by the University of Pennsylvania, with the goal of finding and exploring this "mysterious plateau" in the Amazon. As was the case with his stories of Holmes, Doyle was frequently able to find readers eager to believe in the truth of his fictional creations.

Some verisimilitude comes from Malone's opening chapter in which we are given a rather digressive discussion of his romantic attachment to Gladys Hungerton, a young attractive woman with a somewhat belligerent father. Gladys herself does not present to Malone the proper attitude–the attitude of the interested lover–for she is frank, cold, and to him at least passionless. His professions of love are turned aside by her, for, she claims, she would like a man like Stanley or Richard Burton, an explorer who "could look Death in the face and have no fear of him, a man of great deeds and strange experi-

ences."[1] The possibility of his becoming just such an
explorer and winning his lady is what prompts Malone to
seek out a heroic adventure in which he can participate.
He then, in what he describes as "the fever of . . . first
love," asks his news editor, the tough, crabby McArdle,
for an assignment with "adventure and danger" in it (*LW*,
pp.11, 13). The assignment he is instead given–exposing a
fraud (the fraud being the notable Professor George
Challenger)–promises to be an adventure only in the
sense that Challenger has a fiery temperament and a reputation for breaking the skulls of newsmen. Challenger has
recently returned from South America with stories of
seeing and shooting a pterodactyl, and with photographs–labeled "fakes" by his critics–of one of these creatures. Malone writes a letter to Challenger professing an
interest in, and an understanding of, Challenger's
theories on evolution, and arranges an interview with the
explosive zoologist himself. Challenger, who is short,
barrel-chested, with an enormous head, and the face and
beard of "an assyrian bull," sees through Malone's pre-
tenses immediately and charges at him, sending both of
them tumbling down the stairs, out of the house, and into
the gutter.

When Challenger has calmed himself, with the assistance of a passing constable, he shows Malone his evidence for believing prehistoric creatures may exist on the
South American plateau, and invites him to a lecture on
the subject that evening. At the lecture Challenger's statements are of course questioned, principally by Professor
Summerlee, a professor of comparative anatomy. Challenger proposes a trip to South America to verify his
claims and Summerlee agrees to take this journey. Two
more volunteers are chosen to be impartial observers in
what threatens to become an expedition created solely to
debunk Challenger. Lord John Roxton, a sportsman and
traveler, elects to accompany Summerlee, and of course

the journalist and narrator of the novel Edward Malone volunteers—principally because he desires to impress his beloved Gladys. So the expedition is formed and, after a brief preparation, the intrepid threesome, in Edward Malone's words, "disappears into the unknown." Upon their arrival in South America they acquire some native guides, then sit down to open Challenger's sealed instructions. The instructions turn out to be a blank sheet of paper, for Challenger, who suddenly appears on the scene, intends to lead them to their destination himself.

After an arduous journey through the jungle, they finally, despite much bickering between Challenger and Summerlee, arrive at the plateau where they find, among other things, a skeleton pierced by bamboo stems as though it has fallen from the top of the apparently unclimbable plateau. Several days of searching fail to find a way to scale the plateau's steep cliffs. Challenger solves the problem by suggesting they climb a nearby pinnacle, then cross the gap to the plateau itself by felling a tree conveniently growing atop the pinnacle.

Once on top the plateau Challenger and his comrades embark upon a series of fantastic adventures involving prehistoric animals and lost tribes of cavemen. The expedition is prevented from returning to the jungle floor by one of their guides, who pushes their tree-bridge over the edge (and is subsequently shot by Roxton, nicknamed "the Flail of the Lord" for his aggressive behavior in dealing with uncivilized natives). The manuscript record of these adventures is sent out in packets of letters that are transported by ropes across the chasm to their faithful servant Zambo, and then returned to civilization by the Indian guides. This method of telling the story through letters allows Doyle to maintain the immediacy of first-person narration that is so important to an adventure tale, and still allows him to preserve the secret of the ending. Normally a reader assumes that a first-person narrator lives through his adventures; he survives to write the story he is telling. This "packet of letters" technique only reveals that the narrator was alive at the time he recorded his narrative. The final outcome remains a secret and dramatic tension is maintained with this strategy that Doyle employed several times in his work.

In the case of *The Lost World* the tension of the adventure itself is heightened by the constant bickering between Challenger and Summerlee, and by the frustration these explorers feel at their inability to verify or prove their discoveries to the scientific establishment at home. For Challenger, of course, whose reputation as a scientist is as important as merely surviving this ordeal, the frustration is particularly keen. So when the party, after battling pterodactyls and ape-men (identified as examples of the "Missing Link") and narrowly avoiding being pitched off the plateau to be impaled upon bamboo spikes, first devises a method to return to the jungle floor, it is naturally Challenger who proposes it. Challenger's plan–floating down suspended beneath a "balloon" made from a dinosaur's stomach filled with hydrogen gas–seems so risky that the remaining explorers are eager to explore Malone's suggestion of finding a cave that will take them back to the ground. The cave is found, the explorers arrive safely back on the jungle floor, and the scene shifts to London where Challenger, at a public meeting called to announce his findings, displays a baby pterodactyl he has brought back. In the uproar that follows the creature is startled and escapes into the night, flying about London before turning southward, apparently returning to its lost world. Challenger and his friends are proclaimed heroes and are carried away by the crowd. Later, Roxton reveals he has brought back two hundred thousand pounds worth of diamonds, so all four explorers will share in this fortune. The only sour note is sounded by Malone's paramour Gladys; she has married a solicitor's clerk in

Malone's absence. The trip, which was originally under-taken by Malone to win his lady, was a complete failure from the standpoint of romance. Doyle makes clear, however, as the novel ends with Malone and Roxton con-templating a return to the plateau, that the fellowship of comrades is far more enduring and valuable than the friendship mere women can offer. The epigraph to the novel—

> I have wrought my simple plan
> If I give one hour of joy
> To the boy who's half a man,
> Or the man who's half a boy

—reflects this adventure tale's intended audience, an audi-ence of males seeking escape—escape from mothers and wives, schools and jobs, problems and responsibilities. And as a fantasy-adventure this novel succeeded in cap-turing and holding thousands of these readers under its spell. Just as important, for Conan Doyle at least, was the fact that he had created in Challenger another hero who, like Holmes, captured his readers' imagination, a hero whose exploits could be followed up in future volumes. Unfortunately, Doyle was unable to equal *The Lost World* in his future Challenger stories, probably because there were not enough lost worlds left for Challenger and his friends to explore. In a world that seemed considera-bly smaller than it had been when he was a young man in the 1870s, Conan Doyle found far fewer frontiers for his characters to conquer in 1912. Livingston was of course long dead, and by 1912 Stanley was too. Peary made it to the North Pole in 1909, and in 1911 Amundsen had reached the South Pole. Even the United States, which in 1887 was but half-settled and still a largely unexplored wilderness (and thus an appropriate setting for some of the mystery and intrigue of *A Study in Scarlet*), was by

1912, if not completely civilized, at least completely
formed into a nation that stretched from ocean to ocean.

South America was in fact one of the few places in the
world that still held the promise of adventure and discovery for Doyle, and the possibility of the unknown.
Unable to find another "lost world" as exciting as South
America, Doyle's next Challenger novel *The Poison Belt*
(1913) turned outward beyond this planet for its adventure. In *The Poison Belt*, a very short novel, we find an
only slightly calmer Challenger who has retired to a
country estate where he writes occasional letters to the
Times and putters about with his scientific interests. A
mysterious illness that breaks out in Sumatra and kills
thousands is analyzed by Challenger in a letter to the
Times. He hypothesizes (correctly of course) that the illness has no earthly source, but is the result of the planet
moving through a belt of "infinitely fine ether which
extends from star to star and pervades the whole universe."[2] One should not press Doyle too closely on just
what the exact nature of this "ether" is. He obviously
intends it to have physical properties, yet it is known
from his writings on spiritualism that Doyle believes
"ether" has spiritual powers too. It was for Doyle simply
a mysterious medium, not fully defined by the scientists
of his age, through which both radio waves and spirit
messages were transmitted. This "poisonous belt" that is
now passing across the earth is killing millions. Challenger invites Roxton, Summerlee, and Malone to his
country estate where they will presumably meet their
death together. The adventurers lock themselves into an
airtight room with a supply of oxygen, hoping to stave off
the inevitable as long as possible. The men reflect on their
lives and the nature of death until they finally resign
themselves to ending their artificially prolonged existence—and break the seal. Instead of dying as they expect,
they discover the air outside is pure. The poison belt is

"dissolving"–apparently the earth has passed through the ether band–and the crisis has ended. Not only does the dying stop, the reader finds out, amazingly enough, that there was really no dying taking place. The poison belt has not killed millions after all. It has only brought on a universal cataleptic trance. This trance, like the mysterious catalepsy Poe describes in "The Fall of the House of Usher" and "The Premature Burial," cannot be distinguished from death. Though profound, the trance is only temporary, and people who have dropped "dead" in their tracks simply pick themselves up and resume their activities once the belt passes. (Doyle does not say what happened to those unfortunate souls who were quickly and mistakenly buried.) *The Poison Belt*, like *The Lost World*, can be classified as science fiction in the tradition of Verne. With it Doyle left Challenger and his friends behind for over a decade. When he returned to the series his next novel took a very different turn.

The Land of Mist (1926), like the previous books, seeks a new unknown world. The title suggests that this time Challenger will explore some fog-enshrouded continent, perhaps another South American rain forest inhabited by mysterious beasts. Such is not the case. In this novel, except for a brief trip to Paris, no one leaves England. The mysterious "land" alluded to in the title is the land beyond the living, the land of the dead. Written at a time when Doyle was thoroughly immersed in his defense of spiritualism, *The Land of Mist* is a fictional counterpart to his two-volume work *The History of Spiritualism*. As a novel it remains an embarrassment, for readers tend to feel very much manipulated by Doyle. In *The History of Spiritualism* Doyle was at least honestly arguing his case, admitting that readers might find belief a very difficult task. In *The Land of Mist* Doyle takes characters who have come to be known and trusted, and shows them being converted to the spiritualist cause. Obviously their credibility as scientists is damaged, and the status they acquire as "intrepid adventurers" emerges somewhat tarnished.

In *The Land of Mist* Doyle begins with Malone, who is now older, presumably wiser, and apparently on the verge of marrying Challenger's daughter Enid. The novel really has no coherent plot as such; it consists primarily of a string of episodes connected only by the central issue of spiritualism. Professor Summerlee (now dead) is seemingly resurrected for a brief moment at a spiritualist church. A medium is arrested for fortune-telling by policewomen in disguise. Lord Roxton is summoned by Malone to spend the night together in a haunted house. There they discover a genuine evil presence (which turns out to be a misguided spirit) who can be talked out of his evils ways by humans who understand the spirit world better than he does. In one episode, abused children with psychic powers are led by the ghost of their mother to a new set of parents. In another episode a seance produces both a caveman–"Pithecanthropus"–who materializes and slouches beastlike around the room, and the apparently irrefutable evidence of a wax impression of a spirit's hand. All in all it is a curious collection of incidents that are presented by Doyle as amazing truths. Readers who know *The History of Spiritualism* will recognize that almost all these stories are based upon cases presented in those volumes. Professor Maupis, for example, who produces the wax impressions of spirit hands, is simply a fictional version of Dr. Geley of Paris, who performed similar experiments. (Although these wax impressions were regarded by Doyle as impossible to fake, his nemesis Houdini was able to duplicate them easily.) The "Pithecanthropus" who appears at Maupis's seance is taken from an account of another seance Doyle had read about. For readers who are still skeptics after reading the novel, Doyle included an appendix in which he "proved" his case through explanatory notes on such topics as "Clairvoyance in Spiritualistic Churches" or "Earthbound Spirits" or "Rescue Circles." These last two notes, for example, help clarify the plight of the disturbed spirit that throws Roxton and Malone from the haunted house.

One can forgive Conan Doyle for these "factual" footnotes to his fiction, for he frequently appended footnotes to his books. But it is much harder to forgive him for the fiction itself. The novel's climax comes, for example, when Professor Challenger himself is finally lured to a seance. The iron-willed Challenger is tricked into attending by Malone, who uses Challenger's strong sense of pride against him. Challenger is urged to go in order to expose and debunk the whole business as fraudulent. What happens is of course far different. Challenger is introduced to spirits who present him information that only Challenger or two long-dead patients could know. Challenger is severely shaken and emerges from the experience a chastened human being. Doyle tells us that Challenger became a "gentler, humbler and more spiritual man." Challenger realized, Doyle assures us, that "he, the champion of scientific method and truth, had in fact for many years been unscientific in his methods and a formidable obstruction to the advance of the human soul through the jungle of the unknown."[3] It is fortunate that Doyle never got around to "correcting" the scientific methods of Holmes, or to converting Holmes and Watson to spiritualism. If Doyle had lived long enough, these might have been just such a conversion for Holmes. Challenger, after all, was literally a violent advocate of rational thought and deductive logic, far more outspoken and passionate than Holmes on the subject. If Doyle could throw Challenger's convictions away and label them a mistake, it would have been a very simple matter to do the same for Holmes. (Doyle would, how-

ever, have had to bring Holmes back after his carefully
written finale "His Last Bow," and this was no doubt the
chief objection to writing a "conversion" story.) *The
Land of Mist* ends with the marriage of Malone and Enid
Challenger, an ending Doyle apparently felt gave the
book a happy ending. A world in which the "truth" of
spiritualism triumphed could be nothing less than a
happy world for Conan Doyle in 1926.

Doyle concluded his Challenger series with two
stories: "The Disintegration Machine" and "When the
World Screamed."[4] In these pieces Doyle seemingly has
rescued Challenger from his excursion into spiritualism
(at least if Challenger is a spiritualist he does not display
any signs) and restored him to his old arrogant and
obnoxious self—"a primitive cave-man in a lounge suit"
Malone calls him (*BSF*, p.167). In the first of these stories,
"The Disintegration Machine" (1929), Edward Malone
calls on Challenger for assistance in investigating a story
about a machine capable of evaporating matter. Together
they call on Theodore Nemor, inventor of the "Nemor
Disintegrator." Nemor, described as "low and repulsive"
and "a vile, crawling conspirator" (*BSF*, p.157), has just
made a deal to sell his invention to Russia (by 1929 Doyle
was already perceiving the Communists as a major threat
to world peace). Since the Russians have not actually delivered their payment yet, Nemor agrees to demonstrate his
machine to Challenger in the event the British wish to
outbid the Russian offer.

The disintegrator, because it can evaporate and then
reassemble matter, can potentially be used as a weapon
against battleships, troops, or even entire cities. Nemor
has the device rigged to a chair, and he demonstrates its
effectiveness by seating Malone in the chair, then disin-
tegrating and reassembling him. Challenger is stunned by
the demonstration. He takes his turn in the chair and also
disappears into a mist. Upon his reappearance, Chal-

lenger insists that there is some slight electrical malfunction in the machine. Disagreeing, Nemor seats himself in the chair and Challenger quickly starts the machine, evaporating Nemor into thin air.

Insisting that his move was an accident, and denying that he knows the proper setting necessary to return Nemor, Challenger suggests to Malone that they not "experiment with the unknown" (a rather unusual statement from someone who has spent his life doing so). They leave Nemor, who alone held the secret to his invention, literally in limbo. "The first duty of the law-abiding citizen is to prevent murder" says Challenger (*BSF*, pp.164–65), as he shrugs off the problem and returns to his work.

The second story, "When the World Screamed" (1929), is in fact a story about arrogance, a story about Challenger's desire to "call for attention" and become "the first man of all men whom Mother Earth had been compelled to recognize" (*BSF*, p.190). Challenger has developed the thesis that the world is literally a living creature, a huge echinus or sea urchin. According to Challenger, the earth "browses upon a circular path in the fields of space, and as it moves the ether is continually pouring through it and providing its vitality" (*BSF*, p.172). This sea-urchin earth is oblivious to the tiny men who live on its spiny surface, for they are little more to it than microbes are to us.

Challenger sinks a shaft eight miles deep into the earth's crust and penetrates its outer shell. He then hires Peerless Jones, the narrator of this tale, who is an expert in artesian drilling. Challenger's shaft, dug in secrecy with a small army of workers, has taken him down through the "epidermis," and Jones's job is to pierce the "sensory cortex" of the earth. Jones is at first skeptical when he hears Challenger's story, but when he visits Challenger's drilling site and descends the eight-mile tunnel his doubt disappears.

Jones's drill shaft is accidentally dislodged by an earth that is growing ever more restless about the hole that has uncovered its sensitive tissue. The drill point is prematurely plunged into the earth's soft "cortex" and the earth responds with a shriek heard across the English channel. All the equipment in Challenger's eight-mile shaft is blown into the air, and a geyser of "blood" and fluid erupts from the hole. The injured earth then contracts around the wound and Challenger is content to have "set the whole world screaming" even though the evidence of his work has disappeared.

The story is too fantastic to be taken very seriously and seems to be based in part on Doyle's own inability to accept certain scientific facts. Challenger, for example, refuses to believe that the center of the earth is hot, because the planet is slightly flattened at the poles and those poles are frozen; he reasons that the poles are closer to the center of the earth than any other points on the globe, and they therefore should be the warmest places. Challenger and Doyle conveniently overlook the fact that the "echinus theory" does not explain the polar ice caps either. What is most important about this story is that the plot, however improbable, reinforces the character of the egotistic Challenger. Only George Challenger the "super scientist" and "archpioneer" could have pulled off such a feat; the reader leaves him at the peak of his career.

Doyle's last book, *The Maracot Deep* (1929), also belongs to the category of adventure and science-fiction stories, and is usually thought of as being a type of "Challenger novel," even though Challenger and his friends do not appear. In place of Challenger, Roxton, Summerlee, and Malone, we have Dr. Maracot, a famous oceanographer, Cyrus Headley, an Oxford don, and Bill Scanlan, an American who speaks in what an aging Doyle evidently thought was the current American slang of the 1920s (Scanlan's language is so full of slang malapropisms he sounds like a foreigner learning the vernacular; Doyle was of course unaware how "wrong" Scanlan's slang was). *The Maracot Deep*, unlike the Challenger novels, is not a book in which the characters are defined in any depth. The reader is in fact not even given very clear physical descriptions of the three adventurers who report their story, like the characters in *The Lost World*, through a series of letters, journal entries, and dispatches that are returned to civilization and then "edited" into a coherent narrative.

This time Doyle's adventurers turn from land to sea and embark upon an exploration of the ocean at depths far greater than man has ever experienced. Maracot's hypothesis (which incredibly enough turns out to be true) is that scientific theories about water pressure increasing with depth are not true, or at least are true only in a very limited sense. Maracot reasons that delicate sea creatures are retrieved from the ocean bottom, and asserts that if water pressure really were, as Headley says, "a ton to the square inch," these creatures would be crushed. Headley's contention that pressure upon sea creatures equalizes itself and is "the same within as without" is dismissed by Maracot as "Words—mere words!"[5] Thus Maracot has constructed a diving bell or bathysphere in which the three explorers will be lowered about two-thousand feet. At that depth they observe, with searchlights, strange sea creatures that are the underwater counterparts of the dinosaurs in *The Lost World*.

One of these gigantic creatures, a monstrous crayfish, breaks their support cable with its pincers, and they fall into an underwater trench five miles deep. At this depth they discover that Maracot's theory is true; there is no more pressure than one might encounter at the bottom of a small lake. Amazingly enough, the ocean floor at a depth of five miles is not dark, but glows with a luminous phosphorescence stemming from the decaying bodies of billions of organic creatures that lie there. In *The Lost World* and *The Poison Belt* Doyle did not violate what he knew to be scientific fact. Dinosaurs did once exist and conceivably still could survive in a remote unexplored region. There are radiation belts in space and it would be possible for the earth to encounter cosmic disaster by passing through such a belt or perhaps the tail of a comet. In *The Maracot Deep*, however, Doyle pitches realism out of the window and takes his readers into the purely fantastic, somewhat as he did in "When the World Screamed."

Maracot and his party (and Doyle's readers) are startled to see a human face peering in their window just when they have resigned themselves to a slow death on the ocean floor. They are then rescued by a crew of human beings whose only protection against the water is a glasslike helmet. These people are the descendants of the inhabitants of Atlantis. They have created a city beneath the sea where, protected from the water in airtight buildings, they live much the same as people on the surface, exploring and working underwater with the assistance of their glass helmets. Why these people have chosen to remain underwater instead of simply returning to the surface is not made clear. They seem to be an advanced race—they have developed a waterproof city with its own light and oxygen-generating system, and also a kind of thought-television, which allows them to project their thoughts onto a large screen—but they apparently prefer this life of relative hardship. As if all these details did not make the novel fantastic enough, Doyle added a few more features that seem to reflect the spiritualist beliefs he then held so firmly.

Cyrus Headley, who falls in love with an Atlantean woman named Mona, discovers that she is a reincarnation of a woman who lived in Atlantis before it plunged beneath the waves. More important, he discovers that he himself is a reincarnation of Mona's lover in that life. He is a former Atlantean and had died there twelve thousand years before. The fortuitousness of Headley's being in Maracot's diving bell when the cable broke over just this spot in the Atlantic staggers the imagination. But Doyle is not through yet.

While walking about on the ocean floor, Maracot, Headley, and Scanlan discover a temple the Atlanteans avoid. In their exploration of this temple they encounter a humanoid creature who, unlike the Atlanteans, speaks perfect English and does not breathe oxygen. This creature, the Lord of the Dark Face, is a satanic figure with supernatural powers. He can appear and disappear at will, for instance, and has lived both above and below water for thousands of years. The Lord of the Dark Face threatens to destroy the Atlanteans' underwater city, but loses a battle of wills with Maracot who calls him "a prince of darkness" and commands him to return "to Hell" (*MD*, p.115). Maracot's will is stronger than that of the Lord of the Dark Face (although the reader is never told exactly why his powers surpass those of this obviously supernatural demon) and the Lord of the Dark Face, like Dorothy's wicked witch, is reduced to a puddle of ooze on the floor. This battle over evil won, the novel quickly ends with the three explorers, plus the Atlantean Mona, popping to the surface inside glass bubbles like three corks. Maracot talks of returning to Atlantis one day, but Headley, who marries Mona, muses that the ocean has given him "a precious pearl" (*MD*, p.119) and he asks no more from life.

The Maracot Deep is an incredible novel, incredibly muddled, and one wishes Doyle could have ended his writing career with a more satisfactory book. There is, one can easily see, a steady decline in the quality of his adventure stories. *The Lost World*, as its popularity over the years attests, has an originality to it that reflects the very best of Conan Doyle's talent. *The Maracot Deep*, on the other hand, is a hastily written, confusing story that unsuccessfully mixes adventure with spiritualism. The novel has been deservedly forgotten.

Besides his Professor Challenger series Doyle wrote a number of short stories that could be properly labeled science fiction, in addition to stories dealing with the supernatural and occult, stories that might be called fantasy or even horror stories in the tradition of Poe. "The Horror of the Heights" (1913), for example, resembles the Challenger stories somewhat, for it involves the exploration of a new world. This story also takes a "factual" approach and presents what purports to be the "Joyce-Armstrong Fragment," a blood-stained notebook found lying in a field with a few personal belongings. The notebook, which has some pages missing, was compiled by Mr. Joyce-Armstrong, an inventor and pilot (or, to use Doyle's term, "aeronaut"). Joyce-Armstrong investigates the mysterious deaths of several pilots who have attempted to achieve record heights–heights of around thirty thousand feet. One body was found broken and mutilated, but mutilated, Joyce-Armstrong thinks, in a manner more severe than it should be for a fall from an aircraft. Some pilots' airplanes have been found, but the bodies of the pilots are missing. One pilot returned, but died of fright shortly after landing, uttering only the word "Monstrous" before expiring.

It is Joyce-Armstrong's theory that "there are jungles of the upper air, and there are worse things than tigers which inhabit them" (*BSF*, p.108). He intends to explore these aerial "jungles" and map them. He takes his plane up to forty-one thousand feet (a height unattainable by any aircraft in 1913), where he encounters aerial monsters, some like giant jellyfish, others like "airsnakes" twenty or thirty feet long. Finally an even more threatening purplish aerial creature stalks Joyce-

Armstrong's monoplane, then attacks. He retaliates with a shotgun carried aloft with him and returns to earth to refuel, hoping to take off again and perhaps capture one of the smaller aerial creatures. The manuscript breaks off at this point except for a scribbled message by Joyce-Armstrong, apparently written aloft, stating that he is at forty-three thousand feet and is being pursued by three creatures. "God help me; it is a dreadful death to die!" is his final statement (*BSF*, p.117). Because the notebook is found and his body is not, it is presumed that Joyce-Armstrong was devoured by the aerial monsters.

In some ways the story is not as fantastic as it first seems. Because Joyce-Armstrong takes his airplane to what he describes as "the edge of the earth's envelope" (*BSF*, p.113) he becomes in effect one of the first astronauts confronting the unknown dangers of the upper atmosphere. The dangers of such flights are very real, and although today it is known one must confront subfreezing cold and cosmic rays rather than aerial snakes, it is clear that a "jungle" of hazards does face those who explore the borders of outer space. (One should remember that Doyle's story was published only ten years after the Wright brothers' first flight.) The story demonstrates Doyle's willingness to explore any possible source of adventure on, beneath, or above the planet. His eagerness to speculate on the nature of the unknown motivated and maintained his inquiry into spiritualism and, in an earlier age, would probably have turned him into a world explorer of the first order.

"The Terror of Blue John Gap" (1910) is a similar story in that it explores the possibility of a yet undiscovered life form. The story presents the diary of the late Dr. James Hardcastle, who discovers strange footprints while exploring a Roman tunnel in which a monstrous creature reputedly lives. While lost in the cavern connected to the tunnel Hardcastle also hears strange noises and smells the beast. When sheep and even people begin to disappear Hardcastle returns to the cave–Blue John Gap–with a good lantern and a hunting rifle. Confronting the beast, an enormous bearlike monster, Hardcastle is knocked unconscious after firing only one shot. He is retrieved from the cave by villagers with bloodhounds, and the cave is entirely sealed off with rocks. Hardcastle's theory is that the creature lived largely in a subterranean world, emerging through the tunnel irregularly at night to forage in the countryside. He has no further explanation for the monster's existence, and no hard evidence supporting his story at all. The creature, and others like it, may exist like underground abominable snowmen in a region that comes close to, but does not touch directly, our habitat.

"The Brazilian Cat" (1908) is a far more conventional story about a young English ne'er-do-well, Marshall King, who visits a wealthy cousin whom he hopes will bail him out of his financial difficulties. The cousin, Everard King, has spent many years in South America and has brought back to England an entire menagerie of exotic animals, among them a "Brazilian Cat" or black jaguar.

Although Everard King seems to be a jolly fellow, almost Pickwickian in his generosity, his Brazilian wife warns young Marshall to leave immediately. Because his cousin agrees to discuss the young man's financial problems, however, Marshall remains for a late-night meeting. At the conclusion of this meeting the cousins visit the room where the jaguar is kept and Everard King locks Marshall in and opens the cat's cage. A harrowing night follows in which Marshall King struggles to avoid the jaguar; the next morning he succeeds in getting it caged after being seriously clawed. His cousin returns, assumes Marshall is dead, and himself falls victim to the ferocious jaguar. Upon recovering from his wounds Marshall learns that he has inherited his uncle's estate and become "one of the richest peers in England" (*TTM*, p.106).

Everard King knew of the inheritance and, being the next in line for the estate, had attempted to kill his cousin so that he could inherit the fortune himself. No summary of the plot, however, can capture the high drama of the story—the overwhelming terror Marshall King experiences when he confronts the uncaged jaguar, and his suspenseful night along with the Brazilian cat.

"The Brown Hand" (1899) is a ghost story, although it is not a very suspenseful tale because it involves a rather friendly ghost. Dr. Hardacre, the narrator, is called to visit his uncle Sir Dominick Holden, a famous surgeon. Holden's health is shattered because of a strange series of occurrences. In India he was forced to amputate the hand of a native in order to save the man's life. In lieu of charging for the operation he kept the man's hand in his collection of specimens. The man agreed to this unusual bargain, but explained that it was important for his body to be united after death. "I shall want it [the hand] back when I am dead" is his parting remark (*BST*, pp.53–64).

Several of Dominick's specimens are destroyed in a fire and the hand is one of them. He thinks nothing about the loss until he is awakened one night by the ghost of the dead Indian who is looking for his missing hand. The Indian is an "earthbound spirit" according to Dominick, one of many held in the material world by "one dominant idea obsessing them at the hour of death." He notes that such ghosts disappear "when their wishes have been fulfilled, or in some cases, when a reasonable compromise has been effected" (*BST*, pp.55–56).

Hardacre decides that in this case a "reasonable compromise" might work so he visits a local hospital and obtains another amputated hand which the ghost accepts. The last time the ghostly Indian is seen he has two hands, the substitute hand apparently having been accepted as a kind of spirit graft. The haunting stops.

"The Leather Funnel" (1900) is concerned with both spiritualism and sadism. The unnamed narrator is visiting his friend Lionel Dacre, a collector of occult literature and bizarre objet d'art. One of his pieces is a large leather funnel that will hold about a quart of fluid and is marked with a few initials. When asked about the funnel's purpose Dacre declines to answer, but suggests an experiment. Expressing his belief in pyschometry–the power of inanimate objects to retain and project "vibrations" if these objects have been associated with highly emotional or stressful events–Dacre urges the narrator to sleep near the funnel and see whether its "associations" will convey a message to him.

The narrator agrees and has a dream in which a woman is tied down, the funnel put into her mouth and filled with water. The torture, called the "Extraordinary Question," was used in seventeenth-century France on persons accused of extremely serious crimes. Dacre has investigated this dream-vision, for he too has received these vibrations from the funnel. He believes the woman in the vision is Marie Madeleine d'Aubray, a famous murderess who poisoned her father and brothers. The scratches on the neck of the funnel have come from the teeth of this "cruel tigress." Because the torture is lingered over by Doyle, critics have noted the sadistic and even sexual overtones of this story. Although these elements are undeniably present, there is so little in Doyle's fiction that is titillating it seems far more likely that he found the inquisition depicted to be excruciatingly horrifying rather than erotic, intending it to raise goose bumps and not libidinous impulses.

It was somewhat inevitable that Doyle's interest in the occult and life after death would eventually produce some stories with Egyptian themes. One of these, "The Ring of Thoth" (1890), focuses on John Vansittart Smith, an Egyptologist who falls asleep in the Egyptian collection of the Louvre. Awakening at midnight in a darkened museum, Vansittart Smith is startled by a light moving slowly through the chambers.

The lamp is borne by a strange looking Egyptian whom Vansittart Smith had noticed in the museum earlier that day. Remaining out of sight, the Egyptologist watches as the man unlocks a mummy case, removes the mummy and unwraps it. Beneath the wrappings is the body of a beautiful young woman perfectly preserved for four thousand years. The man bends lovingly over the body talking to the mummy, and then moves to a nearby case of rings and begins going through it when he discovers Vansittart Smith. They talk briefly and then, noticing that the air has rapidly aged the exposed mummy, turning the young woman into a shriveled hag, they move from the displays to a small apartment where the Egyptian explains his actions.

His name is Sosra and he is, he claims, almost four thousand years old. As a youth he studied with Egypt's wisest priests and it was then that he created an elixir of life and injected himself with it, guaranteeing that he would live forever. He shared his secret with one other priest and wanted to grant eternal life to a young woman he loved, but she declined the elixir, arguing that it thwarted the gods. She died and Sosra was heartbroken until he learned that his priest friend had devised an antidote to the elixir and planned to take it and join the young woman in death. He did so and Sosra was left behind to live through the centuries, unable to die.

Reading of new archeological discoveries, he has come to the museum seeking the body of his lost love and, more important, the antidote to the elixir contained in the crystal ring. He now has the ring–the ring of Thoth–and, finishing his story, he escorts Vansittart Smith from the building. The Egyptologist then reads in the paper that the man's dead body was found embracing a mummy on the floor of the Louvre. The antidote in the ring of Thoth has worked.

In the story "Lot No. 249" (1892) the title refers to a mummy which has been purchased at an auction by an Oxford student (assuming that Doyle's story has at least a modicum of credibility it is interesting to notice how the value of such artifacts has changed; these relics ceased being available—at any price—early in the twentieth century). The student, Edward Bellingham, keeps the mummy in his rooms along with a collection of Egyptian paraphernalia. Another student, Abercrombie Smith (the narrator of the tale), notices Bellingham's sometimes bizarre behavior and frequently hears sounds emanating from Bellingham's rooms when they are supposedly unoccupied. Smith assumes Bellingham may be hiding a woman in his rooms, but when students who have quarreled with·Bellingham mysteriously begin to be attacked, a darker truth emerges.

Bellingham has deciphered an ancient papyrus that reveals the secret of bringing his mummy back to life. Resurrected, his mummy from Lot No. 249 stalks the Oxford countryside attacking undergraduates. Smith learns this startling fact after being chased by the mummy. He confronts Bellingham with a loaded pistol and tells him to cut the mummy into pieces, burn the pieces, and incinerate the papyrus with the powerful inscription. Bellingham protests, but has no choice for Smith promises to shoot him dead if he does not; the mummy is destroyed and peace returns to Oxford's hallowed halls.

The notion of resurrecting Egyptian mummies with mysterious invocations is as old as the Egyptians themselves, so Doyle is not introducing a new theme here, but the stories are as exciting and intriguing as any he wrote. The work of British archaeologists such as Flinders Petrie (who later was to make Howard Carter, the discoverer of

King Tut's tomb, his protégé) brought a renewed interest in Egyptology in the late nineteenth century. Doyle's stories reveal that he knew a good deal about mummies and the embalming process used by the Egyptians. The mummy in "Lot No. 249," for example, has been preserved in natron and when burned smells strongly of the resins and congealed unguents used in the ritualistic anointments, details about the mummification process that someone interested only in writing a spooky occult story might not know. Although Doyle was later to spend extended vacations in Cairo to aid his consumptive wife Louise, he had not been to Egypt at the time these stories were written, so his firsthand knowledge of mummies was limited to those returned to England by scholars such as Petrie.

Doyle's two Egyptian stories of the resurrected dead (and particularly "The Ring of Thoth") may owe something to H. Rider Haggard's very popular novel *She* (1887), in which an African princess waits through the centuries for her lost lover to return. Another possible source is the legend of Tithonus and Aurora. Tithonus was given eternal life (as was Sosra in "The Ring of Thoth") but not eternal youth; Tennyson's poem on these lovers (1883) would have been well known to Doyle. In any case the stories in turn are the probable sources for the popular 1932 Boris Karloff film *The Mummy*, and the series of film sequels it inspired. Doyle's final sentence in "Lot No. 249"–"But the wisdom of men is small, and the ways of Nature are strange, and who shall put a bound to the dark things which may be found by those who seek for them?" (*BST*, p.112),–in fact reminds one of the archetypal epigraph found at the close of any number of Universal's classic horror films of the thirties and forties, warning us what comes of exploring too far into the unknown.

Finally, one should take notice of what in some ways is

Doyle's most important story outside the Holmes series. When "Danger!" was published in 1914, World War I had not yet broken out. In an article he had published called "Great Britain and the Next War," Doyle had argued that England's insularity was both an asset and a problem. A natural fortress, Britain could also be cut off from the continent if submarines or warships blockaded the English Channel. He wanted a tunnel to France dug beneath the Channel. Such a tunnel could be defended if necessary, but it would also allow access to food and supplies in the events of a siege. A commission to study the Channel tunnel had been created by Parliament, but its progress was slow so Doyle turned to what had always been a way to arouse interest—writing fiction.

"Danger!" carries the subtitle "Being the Log of Captain John Sirius" and is told from the perspective of a foreign submarine commander; his nationality is not specified, but he himself describes his country as "one of the smallest Powers in Europe" (*BSF*, p.119). Sirius, who has only eight submarines in his command, is instructed to blockade the Channel after a colonial border dispute between his country and Britain. He recounts his exploits in retrospect, relating how in six weeks he was able to bring "proud England to her knees" with his tiny fleet.

To conquer the British, Sirius's submarines only need to submerge in the Channel and torpedo any ship that attempts passage. This they do with remarkable efficiency. Sirius disregards international law and all rules of war. His business, he claims, was "to starve the enemy any way I could." He therefore sinks ships of all nationalities and types, reasoning that "the lawyers could argue about it afterwards" (*BSF*, p.130). Such a possible breach of "proper military conduct" had worried Doyle since the Boer War, when the Boer commando troops refused to "stand and fight" in the British tradition. The Boers, like Captain Sirius, were simply concerned with winning and not with "rules."

As the weeks go by and dozens of ships are sent to the bottom (including White Star's *Olympic*, the sister ship of the ill-fated *Titanic*), grain and commodity prices rise to exorbitant heights. There are food riots among the populace and starvation is rampant. Finally the intolerable blockade ends; England capitulates and the war is over.

Fortunately for England, Sirius's country does not wish to gain more than the "adjustment" of a colonial boundary, the cause of the conflict in the first place. His fleet of submarines emerges virtually unscathed, but such a victory, he notes, will not be possible in the future. The story concludes with a story quoted from the *Times* outlining how England in the future intends to rely less on imported foodstuffs; included in the plan is the creation of Britain's own submarine fleet *and* a tunnel beneath the Channel to France.

Today, seventy years later, the Channel tunnel has still not been dug, although it is not an idea that has been abandoned either. Doyle's story proved to be amazingly accurate in several respects, of course. In World War II the island of Britain was besieged in a manner similar to the one he describes in this story, but by this time the British had some submarines of their own. As Doyle also predicted, in both World War I and II new weapons and new ethics emerged. Neither war was fought and won according to the rules of the war that preceded it. Just as the Boer War's guerrilla warfare caught the British making false assumptions about how to fight in South Africa, World War I found them largely unprepared for the machine-gun and trench warfare that resulted. Doyle's insights on these points made him a man truly ahead of his time, a man whose ideas should have commanded more respect than they, unfortunately, did.

Before turning from Doyle's adventure and science fiction stories, one point should be made. The epigraph to *The Lost World*–

> I have wrought my simple plan
> If I give one hour of joy
> To the boy who's half a man,
> Or the man who's half a boy

—is often cited as a touchstone to some of Conan Doyle's fiction as though this statement sums up or explains away his work as an exercise in a kind of mindless innocence. One should not be too eager to sweep this fiction away as unimportant.

There is, acknowledgedly, a shift of emphasis in Doyle's science-fiction and adventure stories away from what we might call "philosophy" towards what has sometimes been labeled "mere entertainment." Usually the implication is that "entertainment" in itself is a simple thing to achieve. Yet Doyle's "entertainments" represent imaginative literature in its purest sense. One must turn to figures such as Poe or Jules Verne to find fiction with the same scope, inventiveness, and creativity. This fiction carries with it an immediacy that is almost cinematic in its nature (a fact recognized even in Doyle's lifetime by an infant movie industry). If in the twentieth century, as some claim, the film medium is more powerful than print in communicating certain emotional responses, then perhaps the spontaneity and creativity of Doyle's science fiction is similarly more affecting and effective than other examples of established "cerebral" literature. That does not mean that one form of art is superior to the other. Doyle's "plan" was simple; actually carrying it out (as he did) required more talent, insight, and genius than most writers ever possess.

7

Doyle's Nonfiction Prose

Besides his numerous novels, short stories, and volumes of poetry, Arthur Conan Doyle wrote a great deal of nonfiction prose. Much of this material was published as letters and articles in magazines and newspapers and has never been collected. Some of these articles were reshaped into books and reprinted, however, and these writings, along with his large number of completely original volumes, would fill several bookshelves. Many writers, in fact, would consider that they had fulfilled productive careers if they had authored only the large number of nonfiction books Doyle wrote. Although Doyle had many interests and his eclecticism is reflected in the diverse subject matter of these books, his nonfiction prose can be divided into three general categories: histories, autobiographical accounts, and writings about spiritualism.

The most significant of his history books is *The Great Boer War* (1900), a book first published shortly after Doyle's service in South Africa (and before the war was over), and then updated over the next two years to include the later action and final conclusion of the conflict. Britain's participation in the Boer War (1899–1902) was in some ways similar to the United States' involvement in Viet Nam. The conflict took place in South Africa, a place with a climate and terrain completely alien to those who had grown up in the English countryside. As Doyle found out when he served as a medical officer, the heat and typhoid fever were foes as deadly as the Boers. While the war, which was originally expected to last only a few months, dragged on, a great deal of criticism of the army, the government, and the country's colonial policies in general began to build in the world's press. It was a particularly frustrating experience for the military, inasmuch as they were battling Boer commandos who carried on a kind of guerrilla warfare that stymied the systematic British war machine.

Doyle records the frustrations of this campaign in a comprehensive narrative that includes maps, casualty records, and extended analyses of the action. As one reads this lengthy volume (which is still regarded as a very solid history of the war), one sees that Doyle is, as always, scrupulously fair in his assessments. Boer claims to the territory had a certain justice, for in settling the country they had, according to Doyle, "travelled far, worked hard, and fought bravely." Still, the English settlers were denied any voice in government or education, even though they outnumbered the Dutch settlers. Doyle sees the conflict as morally justified then, because human rights, not simply British rights, were being violated.

Doyle's patriotism does show in the pride he feels in the fact of Empire participation. Australia, New Zealand, Canada, and other colonies sent soldiers, and Doyle never tires of reciting the names of British regiments and marveling that troops from Ireland and Scotland such as the Royal Irish Lancers or Gordon Highlanders are fighting side by side with troops from Liverpool and Lincoln and Manchester, along with elite units such as the Coldstream Guards or the Royal Horse Artillery. What he saw in South Africa was the kind of unified effort, and, to an extent, the pomp and circumstance he had idealized and fictionalized in *The White Company* and *Sir Nigel*. The fact that soldiers from all walks of life, from countries all around the world, rallied together in this effort was proof to Doyle that the Empire was more than simply a list of colonies; it was, he felt, a collective world force capable of confronting global problems and ultimately correcting them. England's ability to fashion and maintain such an Empire (which was, after all, what Napoleon attempted but never succeeded in doing), and the Empire's victory in this struggle with the Dutch, only further convinced him of the justice of the Empire's campaign. The most important lesson Doyle learned from the war, however, and the point he constantly comes back to in his history, is that the British needed to modify their conception of warfare.

The British approached the Boer War in the traditional fashion they had approached other nineteenth-century wars; the problem was that the Boer War was the first real twentieth-century war. The British, for example, brought lancers to South Africa, mounted troops armed with lances and swords. Doyle saw such troops in action and rightly concluded that "lances, swords, and revolvers have only one place–the museum" (*GBW*, p.519). Furthermore, Doyle noted, "the idea that an infantry soldier is a pikeman has never quite departed our army." The infantry soldier, though armed with a rifle, was expected "to march in step as the pikemen did, to go steadily shoulder to shoulder, to rush forward with his pike advanced." "All this," Doyle added, "is medieval and dangerous" (*GBW*, p.516).

Although Doyle felt the best thing to do with the traditional cavalry–mounted men armed with sabers (like Brigadier Gerard)–was "abolish it altogether" (*GBW*, p.519) except for ceremonial purposes, he did see a use for a mounted infantry, which could combine mobility with firepower. (The Boer commandos that proved so deadly, after all, constituted just such a mounted infantry.) Artillery units also needed to become less formal, Doyle asserted. The Boer cannon, Doyle wrote, "were as invisible as their rifles," because "the first use a Boer makes of his guns is to conceal them." On the other hand, Doyle complained, "the first use which a British major makes of his [cannon] is to expose them in a straight line with correct interspaces, each gun so near its neighbour that a lucky shell dropping between them might cripple the crews of each" (*GBW*, p.522). Proud of his army's effort, he nevertheless did not spare the criticism he hoped would improve its performance in a later war.

All of these individual lessons of the Boer War convinced Doyle that the notion of a foreign power conquering Britain through an invasion was nonsense. Such a threat was a very real possibility in the Napoleonic era, but Doyle became convinced that modern warfare–the kind of·guerrilla warfare the Boers waged–would make England as simple to defend as South Africa had been for the Boers. Invading "a country of hedgerows" filled with hiding soldiers armed with rifles was, in Doyle's opinion, "always a desperate operation, [and] has now become an impossible one" (*GBW*, p.514). Even though some of these insights would later prove to be incorrect, as France found out in World War I, Doyle was amazingly perceptive in his plans for reform. *The Great Boer War* proved that Doyle was enough of a historian to learn from the past and not remain committed to concepts that had outlived their usefulness. Valor, courage, bravery, duty, honor–these values he felt were universal, but winning was also important. The British, as Doyle saw firsthand, came close enough to losing in South Africa that some reform seemed necessary; that reform, he felt, was to be ignored at his country's peril, and he further believed it was his duty as a patriot to apprise his fellow citizens of this truth.

Although Doyle had a genuine interest in the Boer War in which he actually participated, it was World War I that generated his greatest amount of prose. Two short books about it, *The German War* (1914) and *A Visit to Three Fronts* (1916), were principally composed of articles he had written for newspapers and then collected into brief volumes.

In them one sees his traditional patriotism and pride in the British spirit mixed with a willingness to adopt new ideas and a scrupulous desire to be fair in his assessments. In *A Visit to Three Fronts*, for example, he records his admiration for the innovations he finds on the French and Italian fronts. He finds that the French issue chevron emblems to soldiers who are wounded (what today would be the equivalent of the American "Purple Heart"), a policy he thinks the British should adopt. He also discovers that the Italians have developed and long used ways of coping with the barbed wire that the British are only beginning to explore. Doyle is not such a chauvinist that he cannot praise these foreign armies for their insights. It is in *A Visit to Three Fronts* that Doyle also records that while visiting the trenches he was asked by a French general if Sherlock Holmes was a soldier in the English army. Doyle notes that he replied in French that Holmes was "too old for service"[2]; the incident caused him to reflect on the matter, however, and ultimately stimulated him to write the short story "His Last Bow," which was originally subtitled "The War Service of Sherlock Holmes" (1917).

Conan Doyle's major work on World War I is his six-volume work *The British Campaign in France and Flanders* (1916–20), his longest single project. The first volume appeared in November, 1916, and the series advanced at a rapid rate, with Doyle completing five more volumes in just over three years. Although the first volume sold very well, going through three printings in two months, each succeeding volume drew less attention and sales fell off proportionately.

In the first volume, devoted to the year 1914 exclusively, Doyle attempts to explain the causes of the war. He uses the occasion to criticize his countrymen for their lack of foresight, and once again brings up his pet complaints about submarines and a Channel tunnel. His general opinion of Germany is very low. He partially blames Nietzche for the war, contending that Nietzche "inoculated the German spirit with a most mischievous philosophy."[3] Essentially he sees Germany as an "upstart" or "newcomer," a nation with no culture, no superiority in "spiritual and intellectual matters," no colonies to help sustain its emerging economic strength. War with such an upstart country seemed nearly inevitable to Doyle, who felt that countries such as Britain and France, with had built up their Empires over "three centuries," could not help but become Germany's rivals and ultimately the civilizations it wanted to conquer.

Doyle's series does not cover the entire war, but only the battle on the western front. As such, it is an exhaustive record compiled from newspaper accounts, letters, and interviews, as well as Doyle's frequent visits to the battlefields. Doyle crams a massive amount of detail into his six volumes; there are dozens of maps, numerous lists of troops involved in each engagement, and hundreds of references to the specific actions and fates of individual soldiers (enlisted men as well as officers). Conan Doyle was obviously totally involved in the drama as it unfolded, and it takes a persistent reader to follow all the twists and turns and not wish for a more concise summary that does not include what is at times literally an hour-by-hour record.

It is very significant that Doyle does conclude his lengthy history (as he did his history of the Boer War) with a series of lessons that can be learned from the struggle. The enormity of the "Great War" was both exhausting and appalling to Conan Doyle. The loss of life on all sides (which he computes at seven million dead), as well as the intense personal loss of his son, brother, and other members of his immediate family, was so devastating he could not analyze the war's impact rationally. He concludes his work somewhat dazed by the carnage, and "with the deep conviction that the final results of this great convulsion are meant to be spiritual rather than material." Reaffirming his faith that the world is evolving according to a distinct plan rather than by accident, he claims it is in "mould[ing] the hearts and spirits of men" that we will find "the explanation and justification of all that we have endured" (*BC*, VI, 305). When he finished *The British Campaign in France and Flanders* Doyle was no longer interested in writing political or social histories; the physical world of soldiers and governments had stunned and disappointed him. He was now looking "through" the external physical drama of political events such as the Great War to what he perceived as the spiritual forces causing these events. He then turned almost exclusively to the study of these forces and the recording of his own memoirs.

Several of Doyle's autobiographical volumes, such as *The Wanderings of a Spiritualist* (1921), *Our American Adventure* (1923), and *Our Second American Adventure* (1924), are little more than travel diaries recording his experiences while lecturing publicly on behalf of spiritualism. His principal autobiography, *Memoirs and Adventures* (1924), is not as interesting or informative for his readers as one might suspect. Like many autobiographies it is skewed by the writer's own interests and perceptions at the time it was written. In Doyle's case the great force in his life in 1924 was spiritualism, so the book tends to emphasize the points in his conversion to that philosophy, and passes over quickly some other things we might be more interested in today, such as his attitude about Sherlock Holmes.

In 1924 World War I was also still very much on

Doyle's mind, so six of the book's thirty-two chapters are devoted to an analysis of the war.[4] Doyle's general interest in military operations tends to dominate the volume, with a whole chapter given over to an Egyptian "frontier adventure" of little consequence in which Doyle became entangled in 1896, and another four chapters devoted to his involvement in the Boer War. A far more sensitive involvement–his involvement with Jean Leckie, which had lasted for many years without his wife's knowledge–is not mentioned. He describes his marriage to Jean in a few sentences, explaining only that she was someone "whom I had known for years, and who was a dear friend of my mother and sister" (*MA*, p.258). Doyle tells the truth about Jean Leckie; he just does not tell all of it.

What Doyle is refreshingly honest about in *Memories and Adventures* is his writing. He is able to say that *The Doings of Raffles Haw* (1892) is "not a very notable achievement" (*MA*, p.112), and that *The Parasite* (1894) and *Beyond the City* (1892) are "on a very inferior plane" (*MA*, p.117). His assessment of *The Firm of Girdlestone* (1890), one of his very first books, is astonishingly blunt: "Save for occasional patches it is a worthless book, and, like the first book of everyone else, unless he is a great original genius, it was too reminiscent of others" (*MA*, p.89). The works of fiction that Doyle is most proud of might be seen as somewhat unusual selections, for in spite of the fame that popular characters such as Holmes, Challenger, or Gerard brought to him, Doyle seems to have been particularly proud of *The Refugees* (1893), *The Great Shadow* (1892), which he calls "a booklet . . . I should put near the front of my work for merit" (*MA*, p.117), and *Sir Nigel* (1906), which he feels represented his "high-water mark in literature" (*MA*, p.251), even though the book was not a critical success at the time of its publication. These historical novels are not what has made Doyle's reputation survive, of course, but even he was aware that his popular writings were entertainments and not first-rate "literature" as it was coming to be defined.

The single work Doyle seems to have been most proud of was *The War in South Africa–Its Cause and Conduct*, a paperbound pamphlet of about 160 pages. Characterized by him as "an appeal to the world's opinion" (*MA*, p.221), this defense of British policy was originally financed by private subscriptions and all profits then turned back into the enterprise. When the publication figures soared to hundreds of thousands of copies (the English and American editions alone amounted to 400,000 copies), the pamphlet was translated into twenty languages and sold throughout Europe. *The War in South Africa* was seen by Doyle as a publishing (and patriotic) coup–and it was. He, as a private citizen, was able to draw international attention to Britain's foreign policy in a way the government itself was unable to do. Doyle's work on the production and distribution of this pamphlet was a typically selfless gesture on his part, a gesture that truly did influence the world's opinion of Britain's role in South Africa. It was principally because of this pamphlet and his extraordinary effort on behalf of his country that he was eventually knighted by King Edward VII.

Finally the reader comes to Doyle's most controversial writing–his books on spiritualism. To understand his fascination with spiritualism is not easy. His conversion to this philosophy–or "religion"–apparently came in the autumn of 1916 when he received a "spirit message" from his dead brother-in-law Malcolm Leckie. The message was transmitted through Doyle's maid Lily Loder-Symonds, who had practiced automatic writing and influenced Doyle's wife Jean to be sympathetic towards spiritualism. Doyle himself had long been simply that–sympathetic towards spiritualism–but because he felt this new spirit message contained information only Malcolm Leckie could have known, he became convinced that the message was absolutely valid and that spiritualism was fact and not fancy. He first became a disciple and then rapidly emerged as the movement's most prominent and famous spokesman. Always a prolific writer, he quickly began to churn out books explaining and defending his newfound truth.

One of Doyle's first spiritualist books, *The Vital Message* (1919), asserts that there was an "inner reason" for World War I, arguing "it was needful to shake mankind loose from gossip and pink teas, and sword-worship, and Saturday night drunks, and self-seeking politics and theological quibbles–to wake them up."[5] Because of the war (which he calls "the most frightful calamity that has ever befallen the world"), Doyle feels religion needs to be simplified and purified "by the facts of spirit communion and the clear knowledge of what lies beyond the exit-door of death" (*VM*, pp.12–13). Two "great readjustments" are necessary, according to Doyle.

First, the Bible should be "placed on the shelf of the scholar, and removed from the desk of the teacher [of religion]" because "it has no connection with modern conceptions of religion" (*VM*, p.14). Secondly, Doyle argues that there has been too much emphasis placed on the death of Christ, and not enough attention paid to His life. It is the teachings of the living Christ Doyle values and not man's interpretations of His resurrection. Despite the fact that he finds these readjustments "needful," Doyle does not believe they will ever come to pass and therefore they are not "vital" to an enlightened understanding of life.

What is vital is the acceptance of spiritualism as fact. Doyle gives a thumbnail history of the "science," and then describes at length what life on the "other side" is like. "The sullen husband, the flighty wife, is no longer there to plague the innocent spouse. All is sweet and peaceful," he assures the reader. "Happy circles live in pleasant homesteads with every amenity of beauty and of music. . . . There are no poor and no rich" (*VM*, p.95). Those who have died in childhood grow to maturity, but then stop, for "age, which is produced chiefly by the mechanical presence of lime in our arteries, disappears" (*VM*, p.93).

Finally Doyle compares spiritualistic phenomena with events described in the New Testament and concludes that a great many of the miracles described there reflect spiritualistic principles. The disciples of Christ, for example, were chosen not for their intelligence, Doyle reasons, but for their psychic powers. The most powerful psychics in this circle, he argues, were Peter and the brothers John and James. "These were the three," Doyle assures us, "who were summoned when an ideal atmosphere was needed [to perform miracles]" (*VM*, p.124). Doyle concludes that Christ practiced automatic writing on several occasions, serving, like a medium, as a channel for "those great forces which were under His control" (*VM*, p.126). According to Doyle, then, nineteenth-century spiritualists such as D. D. Home, who claimed to be able to levitate himself, simply possessed powers similar to those of Christ, who levitated himself and Peter over water. Such an interpretation of Christ's activities, Doyle reasons, "would be in strict accord with the most modern psychic knowledge, and which, far from supplanting Christianity, would show the surprising accuracy of some of the details handed down to us" (*VM*, p.130). Churches need to recognize that the religion they are teaching is dead, Doyle argues, and that they will gain new strength only if they turn to the religious "truths" that spiritualism provides. The book concludes with appendices containing statements on ectoplasm, automatic writing, spirit photography, and clairvoyance. Doyle feels the evidence he supplies is conclusive; modern readers will be somewhat less enthusiastic about it.

Another book that is equally interesting (and disappointing) is *Pheneas Speaks* (1927), which was characterized by a statement on the cover of the first edition as "A Striking Message from the Hereafter." It consists of a number of spirit messages delivered to Doyle, his wife, and their children between 1921 and 1926. The first third of the book reports the communications of various spirits—those of Doyle's dead son Kingsley and his late brother Innes, for example—all of which tell of the wonders of the "other side" in a rather vague rambling way. The remainder of the book presents the message of Pheneas, an "Arabian" who lived "thousands of years ago," but has since converted to Christianity.[6]

Pheneas travels about the globe visiting spiritual "trouble spots"; Doyle frequently points to seismic activity in these locations as evidence of Pheneas's visits (even though the earthquakes usually take place one to two years after Pheneas has left). Pheneas's commentaries are frequently very vague and general: "There will be a sign which you will at once understand, and you will never have one moment's uncertainty after that. Your whole soul will know that it is just right and beautiful when it comes. There will be no points to cross over. It will seem a continuation, it will be so clear" (*PS*, p. 182). He can also be very specific and practical, however—"I wonder if a Dictaphone would not be desirable to save you writing" (*PS*, p. 189)—or solemnly prophetic—"Houdini is doomed, doomed, doomed. He will not be allowed to stand in the way of God's progress" (*PS*, p. 126). (Houdini, of course, was notorious for exposing spiritualist fraud.)

Doyle concludes his volume of transcribed messages with "A Last Word" in which he attempts to align the teachings of Pheneas with established religious doctrine and asks "agnostic critics" "whether the script bears out their oft repeated assertion that nothing but rubbish comes through [in spiritual messages]" (*PS*, p.197). Sadly, most readers would have to say the book's transcriptions do indeed bear out that assertion.

But there is worse. *The Coming of the Fairies* (1922) is clearly the nadir of Doyle's nonfictional works and is a book that brought him a good deal of ridicule and embarrassment.

In 1917, two sisters, Elsie and Frances Wright, used their father's camera to photograph some fairies and elves whom they claimed were their frequent playmates. The photographs and an account of the incidents were published in 1920 and a great deal of controversy ensued. Doyle reviewed the case carefully, and then entered the fray on behalf of the fairies. Asserting that "the matter is not one which can be readily dismissed," Doyle writes "I have convinced myself that there is overwhelming evidence for the fairies."[7] When it comes to stories of the fairy horses some fairies have been seen riding, however, he feels compelled to add "I have by no means been able to assure myself of these adjuncts" (*CF*, p.159).

Besides the photographs taken by the Wright girls (which look blatantly fraudulent), Doyle includes in his book some other fairy photographs he has been sent, along with numerous accounts of fairy sightings. To give this fanciful collection the dignity Doyle assumes it should have, he includes a "scientific" explanation for the fairy phenomenon. Complaining that "Victorian science would have left the world hard and clean and bare, like a landscape in the moon" (*CF*, p.125), Doyle speculates that the world's fairies could exist outside the spectrum of light that is visible to us. According to Doyle:

We see objects within the limits which make up our colour spectrum, with infinite vibrations, unused by us, on either side of them. If we could conceive a race of beings which were con-

structed in material which threw out shorter or longer vibrations, they would be invisible unless we could tune ourselves up
or tone them down. It is exactly that power of tuning up and
adapting itself to other vibrations which constitutes a clair-
voyant, and there is nothing scientifically impossible, so far as I
can see, in some people seeing that which is invisible to others. If
the objects are indeed there, and if the inventive power of the
human brain is turned upon the problem, it is likely that some
sort of psychic spectacles, inconceivable to us at the moment,
will be invented, and that we shall all be able to adapt ourselves
to the new conditions. If high-tension electricity can be converted by a mechanical contrivance into a lower tension, keyed
to other uses, then it is hard to see why something analogous
might not occur with the vibrations of ether and the waves of
light. (*CF*, p.14)

It is clear here that Doyle, who did possess a medical
degree after all, is trying to deal rationally with a very
ethereal subject, but is in waters that are over his head.
Photography was a relative mystery to him, and he dismissed as insignificant the fact that Elsie Wright worked
several months for a photographer, because he did not
feel she could have acquired the knowledge necessary to
fake a plate. (Ironically, Doyle notes that one of Elsie's
jobs was "spotting," that is, retouching negatives or
printed photographs.) One immediately senses from his
volume that he regards photography as being an
extremely complicated and technical procedure, something a teenager could not possibly understand.

The truth is, however, Elsie's fairy photographs were
"genuine" and not faked by manipulation of negatives or
prints. As one looks at them closely one can see that they
seem to be of two distinct types, either using cardboard
two-dimensional drawings of fairies or three-dimen-
sional fairy dolls to convey their very amateurish effects.
In fact, in a 1983 interview filmed for British television,
an aging Elsie Wright finally admitted the photographs

were faked, saying she and her sister had attached paper cutouts to bushes with hatpins and then photographed each other with these cutouts. This possibility was pointed out at the time of the photographs' publication by critics who felt some of the fairies were identical to fairies seen in printed advertisements for a particular nightlight.

It is very hard to explain why Doyle would have been taken in by these rather crude photographs. By the time his book was published he had viewed a movie version of his novel *The Lost World*, which employed far more sophisticated special effects to create the illusion of the dinosaurs in that novel. And yet he did not seem to see the parallel between the two cases; Holmes would have been aghast.

In the fairy episode, which probably more than any single incident in his life destroyed the notion that he was a man to be taken seriously, Doyle was as always too trusting. Why did he believe in fairies? Because he could not believe that these two apparently simple country girls would lie. The fact that they seemed uninterested and even tired of the attention their photographs brought was sufficient proof to him that their story was true. In defense of his position he cited the axiom he repeatedly used when mediums were discovered to be faking their spiritualistic effects: "the ancient argument that because conjurers on their own prepared plates or stages can produce certain results, therefore similar results obtained by untrained people under natural conditions are also false, is surely discounted by the intelligent public" (*CF*, pp. v–vi). The "intelligent public" did not agree with Doyle on this point, however, and the joke was widely circulated that Arthur Conan Doyle led the applause when J. M. Barrie's Peter Pan asked all those in the audience who believed in fairies to clap their hands and revive the expiring Tinker Bell.

Not all of Doyle's spiritualist writing suggests that he had totally lost touch with reality. His two-volume work *The History of Spiritualism* (1926), for example, is for the most part a very interesting work, and although few modern readers will agree with Doyle's assertion that the spiritualist movement is "the most important in the history of the world since the Christ episode,"[8] they will find the volumes a sincere attempt to document the history of one of the more curious phenomena of the last hundred years. Beginning with Swedenborg and touching upon the stories of the Shakers, the Fox sisters, Daniel Douglas Home, and the Davenport brothers (among others), Doyle's history records in a fairly neutral fashion the careers of the most prominent spiritualists and mediums.

After he brings his history up to date in the second volume he then turns to discussions of spiritualist phenomena such as "Spirit Photography," "Voice Mediumship and Moulds [of spirit hands]," and "Ectoplasm," rounding out the volume with an analysis of how spiritualism teaches us of the afterlife. These chapters at times border on the bizarre, but it is fascinating to read of what Conan Doyle and his fellow spiritualists took seriously. Ectoplasm, for instance, a substance that, like fairies, no longer seems to exist in this world, is described as a

streaky, viscious stuff hanging like icicles from the [medium's] chin, dripping down on to the body, and forming a white apron over the front, or projecting in shapeless lumps from the orifices of the face. When touched, or when undue light came upon it, it writhed back into the body as swiftly and stealthily as the tentacles of a hidden octopus. If it was seized and pinched the medium cried aloud. It would protrude through clothes and vanish again, leaving hardly any trace upon them. (*HS*, II, p.109)

Amazing stuff. But Doyle can testify to the elasticity of ectoplasm because he himself had touched it during a sitting of the female medium Eva C.:

> Upon that occasion this strange variable substance appeared as a streak of material six inches long, not unlike a section of the umbilical cord, embedded in the cloth of the dress in the region of the lower stomach. It was visible in good light, and the author was permitted to squeeze it between his fingers, when it gave the impression of a living substance, thrilling and shrinking under his touch. (*HS*, II, pp. 122–23)

The image of Doyle almost erotically fondling Eva C.'s ectoplasmic extension would be humorous if it were not for the underlying pathos of it all. It is quite disturbing to read of Sir Arthur Conan Doyle, D.L., L.L.D., M.D., reduced to this condition. "There was no possibility of deception upon this occasion" (*HS*, II, p. 123), he confidently asserts, and one winces to read such a statement, knowing that Holmes would have boldly exposed such a fraud in one grand sweep.

How can one explain Doyle's sustained interest and belief in the spiritualist movement? What seems so far-fetched today was accepted, even crusaded for, by a rational man (indeed, millions of rational men and women), in spite of what was at times considerable public ridicule and scorn. The "proofs" that Doyle found completely convincing sixty years ago seem painfully inadequate today, yet Doyle apparently did not notice how flimsy and ludicrous his evidence was. One could conclude, of course, that Conan Doyle was a fool, or that he had become senile and simply a doddering old man in his sixties, out of touch with life. Such a view, however, would not be consistent with his total work. Although his fiction decreased sharply in quantity in his later years, this was principally because he was devoting so much of his effort to the spiritualist cause. It can honestly be said that there was some falling off in the quality of his later fiction. The last Holmes stories, for example, are among his weakest. But this in itself does not indicate that his mind was weakening. One must remember that Doyle had been writing about Holmes and Watson for nearly forty years. Some decline in quality was to be expected; indeed, it would have been surprising if the quality of the stories had not fallen off.

Still, although he was old and tired, Conan Doyle's powers were diminished but he had not taken leave of his senses entirely. He was essentially the same man who created Holmes, the world's model deductive thinker, but he had become a man who sat in darkened rooms watching glowing objects floating about and engaging in meaningless exchanges with disembodied voices. To understand this paradox we must try to recreate as best we can the zeitgeist, the spirit of the times or world picture Doyle and others shared in the first quarter of this century.

There are a number of things viewed today quite differently from the way Conan Doyle viewed them. Most important of these is World War I. For Doyle, of course, it was not World War I, it was the "Great War," and the notion that such conflicts would someday have to be numbered was beyond his conception. In *The History of Spiritualism* Doyle devotes an entire chapter to "Spiritualism and the War" (again, there would have been no question of which war he meant). In this chapter and throughout his spiritualist writings he makes it clear that the Great War was prophesied, that it was part of a divine plan, an armageddon that was to cleanse and purify the world before the emergence of a utopian state.

The sense that an important cosmic change is just about to happen permeates Doyle's spiritualist writings, and World War I, which seemed to have gone far beyond what the world had previously conceived of as a military struggle, was the surest proof that something fundamental in the universe was changing. The duration of that conflict, the numbers of countries and forces involved, the terrible loss of life on all sides, these seemed absolute proof that the apocalypse was at hand. The fact that the ultimate revelation did not come with the passing years noticeably decreased the influence of spiritualism after 1930.

Secondly, the great loss of life in World War I brought death directly into thousands of British households in a way it had never come before. The Battle of the Somme, for example, claimed over a million lives; it is often said, with little exaggeration, that a whole generation of British youth was lost in the conflict with Germany. Conan Doyle himself lost his son, his brother, two brothers-in-law, two nephews, and many friends in the combat. The grief felt by the bereaved families was intense. Unwilling to accept the sudden loss of so many loved ones, the survivors sought any solace they could find.

Religion was helpful, but spiritualism was even better—for it brought all these souls back to life. Suddenly Conan Doyle could talk with his son and brother again, could converse with spirits who assured him that death was not the end and that the "other side" was beautiful. Anyone who has experienced the death of a close friend or relative knows how great the longing is for that particular death to be magically "undone" somehow. Spiritualism was able to work the necessary magic for the grieving Doyle and his family.

Thirdly, one must understand that Conan Doyle lived at a unique moment in history. Although he was born a Victorian, he lived to become a citizen of the twentieth century. His life spanned a period of years in which he could read the latest novels of George Eliot, and the latest novels of Scott Fitzgerald. He could have sat on the lap of Charles Dickens had the Great Inimitable's path ever

crossed his (it did not), and later bounced on his own knee
a boisterous baby Norman Mailer (fortunately for both
this did not occur either). Although technology is reshap-
ing our world daily, it is still difficult for us to grasp the
changes Conan Doyle lived through. The many develop-
ments that we take for granted today—movies,
automobiles, the telephone, radio—were near miracles to
someone who grew up listening to war stories at the knees
of those who had fought Napoleon.

One can see in Doyle's explanations of spirit communications repeated attempts to link the phenomenon with
the amazing scientific discoveries around him. The world
seemed on the edge of discovering something even more
fantastic than the wonders that were beginning to appear.
Radio transmissions, like the Great War, seemed to be
proof that they were standing on the brink of a marvelous
breakthrough. There is much pseudoscientific jargon in
his spiritualist writing, talk of "ether," "vibrations," and
"electrical forces." In *Pheneas Speaks* the spirits say,
"When you make a wireless here [on earth] you have to
put up a pole, aerials, etc. It is the same with us" (*PS*,
p.167). The spirits speak of "receiving stations" on the
other side and repeatedly compare their messages to
"electrical transmissions." One senses that by fine-tuning
some electrical device it might be possible to pick up
transmissions from heaven itself without ever leaving
one's fireside.

What we should realize though, is that before the
development of radio there were no "spirit transmissions" of this type, because transmitting voices of any
kind through the air was not a possibility. In the
nineteenth century, the time of the telegraph, spirits com-
municated principally through "rapping," that is, messages were transmitted in code through knocking sounds,
a system very similar to telegraphic communication.
After radio was introduced there were more actual voice

transmissions, and rappings were no longer used very much by the spirits. This very curious change in the nature of the spirit messages suggests that the "miracle" of radio helped revitalize the "miracle" of spirit communications. Rather than seeing this as a change inspired by human technology, however, Doyle would no doubt contend that the spirits abandoned the raps and became more sophisticated because man was closer to the millenium. (Ironically, some of this new technology that seemed so marvelous to Doyle helped create spirit communication in a very literal way; loudspeakers were hidden in seance rooms and many "spirit transmissions" were actually coming from microphones nearby.)

Doyle's scientific and pseudoscientific explanations of spiritualism represent an attempt to codify metaphorically the unknown in terms of known technology, technology Doyle only partly understood. Later in the century another generation would react to the uncertainty of a new technology—atomic energy—by also creating a mythology out of pseudoscience. The flying saucer sightings that peaked in the fifties and sixties have been attributed by several psychologists to anxieties over the possibility of a nuclear holocaust. The saucers, piloted by superior beings, were frequently said to be powered by "magnetic lines of force," an energy source known to those who read science fiction but not to physicists, an energy source only slightly more credible than the "ether transmissions" in which Doyle believed. Such stories may seem no more plausible sixty years from now than Doyle's appear today.

Finally, the spiritualist movement was a reaction to the materialism of the Victorian age. Doyle himself says in *The History of Spiritualism* that without spiritualism mankind is "destined to descend lower and lower into a purely utilitarian and selfish view of the universe." He goes on to say, "the typical materialistic state was pre-war

Germany, but every other modern state is of the same type if not of the same degree" (*HS*, II, 247). The materialism and greed of the Victorians that Dickens was attacking as far back as 1843 in *A Christmas Carol* (and was still railing against in 1865 in *Our Mutual Friend*) had led to the decadent fin de siècle world of Wilde, Swinburne, and Beardsley, a world of sensual pleasures and erotic pursuits. When the materialistic age of massive furniture and gingerbread-covered houses gave way to the dissolution at the end of the century, even those eminent Victorians who had relished their overstuffed chairs and shelves of bric-a-brac became a bit nervous. It was easy for the aging Doyle to feel that the middle-class Victorian love of possessions had led to some kind of an Edwardian Sodom and Gomorrah, which the Great War would purge with a smashing Calvinistic fury.

Shortly after Doyle died the great depression of the thirties made most of the world lose interest in the evils of materialism. The thirties also brought a corresponding rapid loss of interest in spiritualism, putting a great many mediums out of work and diminishing greatly the audience for the kind of books Doyle wrote in his last years.

8

Conclusion

When we attempt to place a final evaluation on the work of Sir Arthur Conan Doyle we must pause. Obviously in Holmes and Watson he has created two of the most popular and famous characters in literature, characters that are truly immortal in the same sense that Hamlet, Don Quixote, Tom Jones, and Tiny Tim are immortal. But after we make that statement we must also acknowledge that Conan Doyle's work belongs to a tradition that has largely gone out of style in literary study today. Doyle and other writers of his era who sought primarily to entertain–authors such as H. Rider Haggard, Edgar Rice Burroughs, H. G. Wells, and Robert Louis Stevenson– have been displaced by the tradition of cerebral "serious" literature that began with writers such as George Eliot, George Meredith, and, most important, Henry James.

Doyle is not "studied" today because there is no subtext there to study. One does not usually finish a Holmes story and ask what it "means," for the story that is presented overtly is the meaning; there is essentially no covert theme to be teased out of the characters and the action. *Moby-Dick* is a novel about a whale that is really not simply a whale; *The Hound of the Baskervilles*, which is in many ways Doyle's most "literary" novel, is about a dog that in the end is really just a dog after all. And although we can see in *The Hound of the Baskervilles* a touch of naturalism, a hint of symbolism, the suggestion of a philosophical message, most critics today would relegate the novel to the category of "subliterature," because it merely entertains and does not broaden our understanding of the human condition.

But the lack of a philosophical subtext in the fiction of Conan Doyle does not mean that Doyle has no philosophy to give us. His message is somewhat easier to see in the collected body of his work than it is in any one selected story or novel. He is opposed to pettiness, greed, lying, meanness of temper and low character. He values courage, chivalry, truth, valor, honor, and loyalty. Most of all we see in him, as we see in his fictional characters, what it means to have principles and to remain loyal to these principles–no matter what. What raises Holmes, Watson, Gerard, Challenger, Sir Nigel Loring, and Doyle himself above the masses is our assurance that these men will remain true to their convictions; they will not be compromised.

Conan Doyle was not merely an author who was so fascinated with chivalry that he wrote novels about noble knights; he dedicated his life to the principles of loyalty and patriotism that he portrayed in his books until he himself, like Sir Nigel Loring, was literally knighted for the extraordinary selflessness of his actions. He righted injustice (in the cases of Edalji, Slater, and others), he served his country loyally (in the Boer War), and he faithfully stood his ground in the face of great public scorn (in his later spiritualist years). He never compromised his principles and died convinced that even his most controversial stands would one day be vindicated. Such a life, and this body of work asserting the values of that life, must have some worth for us today.

At the close of "The Last Adventure of the Brigadier" Gerard comments on the value and purpose of his stories. He asks those who have read his history to "Treasure it in your minds, and pass it on to your children," justifying this by saying "the memory of a great age is the most precious treasure that a nation can possess" (*AG*, p.297). Given the fact that Arthur Conan Doyle embodied the finest qualities of his era, that he represented the highest ideals of his age, if we accept Gerard's assumption we need no further justification for studying Doyle's work and preserving his memory.

Notes

1. Doyle's Life

1. G.M. Young, *Victorian England: Portrait of an Age* (Oxford: Oxford Univ. Press, 1936), p.77.
2. Holograph letter reproduced in Adrian Conan Doyle and P. Weil-Nordon, eds., *Sir Arthur Conan Doyle, Centenary 1859–1959* (London: John Murray, 1959), p. 52.

2. Historical Fiction

1. Arthur Conan Doyle, *The White Company* (London: Smith, Elder, 1892), pp. 124–25. Hereafter cited as *WC*.
2. ———, *Sir Nigel* (New York: McClure, Phillips, 1906), p. 340. Hereafter cited as *SN*.
3. ———, *Rodney Stone* (New York: D. Appleton, 1896), p. 168. Hereafter cited as *RS*.
4. ———, *The Great Shadow* (London and Bristol: Arrowsmith/Simpkin Marshall, 1892), p. 140. Hereafter cited as *GS*.
5. Pierre Nordon, *Conan Doyle* (London: John Murray, 1966), p. 327.
6. Arthur Conan Doyle, *The Exploits of Brigadier Gerard* (New York: D. Appleton, 1896), pp. 133–34. Hereafter cited as *EBG*.
7. ———. *Adventures of Gerard* (New York: McClure, Phillips, 1903), p. 39. Hereafter cited as *AG*.

3. Sherlock Holmes: 1887–1894

1. There have been hundreds of reprints of the Holmes stories, but the most accessible modern collection of the complete Holmes cycle is the two-volume Doubleday anthology (preface by Christopher Morley) first issued in 1930 and reprinted sev-

eral times in slightly different forms. All references will be to *The Complete Sherlock Holmes*, 2 Vols. (Garden City, New York: Doubleday and Co., 1960). Hereafter cited as *CSH*.

2. Edgar Allan Poe, "The Fall of the House of Usher," in *Selected Writings of Edgar Allan Poe*, ed. David Galloway (Harmondsworth: Penguin Books, 1967), p. 157.

3. All the stories in this series were designated "adventures" when reprinted. "The Five Orange Pips," for example, became "The Adventure of the Five Orange Pips." Conversely, the "adventures" in the second series of stories lost this designation when they were collected. "The Adventure of Silver Blaze" became simply "Silver Blaze." Although some stories have slightly different titles in their various reprintings (i.e., "The Adventure of the Reigate Squire" was also published as "The Reigate Puzzle" and "The Reigate Squires"), I will refer to the stories by their first published titles except in unusual cases.

4. English editions of "The Musgrave Ritual" include an additional couplet at this point. For a note on this textual variation see William S. Baring-Gould, *The Annotated Sherlock Holmes* (New York: Clarkson N. Potter, 1967), I, 132.

4. Holmes Redux: 1901–1904

1. Fans of the cycle disagree on the exact dating of the story. It seems to be 1889 according to Holmes's remarks, but this, like many dates in the series, is disputed. Doyle was not consistent, or even very careful, in the chronology of the individual cases.

2. Poe, p. 138.

3. Arthur Conan Doyle, *Memories and Adventures*, 2nd ed. (London: John Murray, 1930), p. 116.

4. Charles Higham, *The Adventures of Conan Doyle* (New York: Norton, 1976), p. 182.

5. His Last Bows: 1908–1927

1. Ronald Burt De Waal, *The World Bibliography of Sherlock Holmes and Dr. Watson* (New York: Bramhall House, 1974), p. 173.

2. Trevor Hall's article "The Documents in the Case" explores

the publishing history of this story. See *Sherlock Holmes: Ten Literary Studies* (New York: St. Martin's Press, 1969), pp. 109–22.

3. See H. W. Bell, "On the Variant Readings of 'The Resident Patient,'" in *Sherlock Holmes and Dr. Watson* (London: Constable and Co., 1932), p. 40–45.

4. Baring-Gould's collection of the stories, *The Annotated Sherlock Holmes*, reprints a third version of "The Adventure of the Resident Patient" which follows neither the original *Strand* version nor the version found in *The Memoirs*.

5. The story was later subtitled "An Epilogue of Sherlock Holmes."

6. See Pierre Nordon, *Conan Doyle*, p. 199.

7. There is admittedly a problem here that smacks of the chicken and the egg. Do mystery lovers read Doyle because they like a fiction series, or did they come to prefer the fiction series because Doyle gave them one? Because Doyle did not invent the concept of a single detective appearing in a series of cases, one could assume that readers were conditioned before Holmes and Watson came along.

6. Adventure, Science Fiction and Horror Stories

1. Arthur Conan Doyle, *The Lost World* (New York: A. L. Burt, 1925), p. 7. Hereafter cited as *LW*.

2. ———, *The Poison Belt* (New York: Hodder and Stoughton, 1913), p. 11.

3. ———, *The Land of Mist* (New York: A. L. Burt, 1926), p. 275.

4. Much of Doyle's short fiction (including these two final Challenger stories), although anthologized in his lifetime, has not been reprinted frequently. The short stories discussed in the remainder of this chapter, published between 1889 and 1929 in a number of collections, are readily available to modern readers in several reprints. See Charles G. Waugh and Martin H. Greenberg, eds., *The Best Science Fiction of Arthur Conan Doyle* (Carbondale, Ill.: Southern Illinois Univ. Press, 1981), hereafter cited as *BSF*; E. F. Bleiler, ed., *The Best Supernatural Tales of Arthur Conan Doyle* (New York: Dover, 1979), hereafter

cited as *BST*; and Nina Conan Doyle Harwood, Intro., *Tales of Terror and Mystery* (Garden City, New York: Doubleday, 1977), hereafter cited as *TTM*.

5. Arthur Conan Doyle, *The Maracot Deep*, Intro. John Dickson Carr (New York: W. W. Norton, 1968), p. 9. Hereafter cited as *MD*.

7. Doyle's Nonfiction Prose

1. Arthur Conan Doyle, *The Great Boer War* (London: Smith, Elder, 1900), p. 31. Hereafter cited as *GBW*.

2. ———, *A Visit to Three Fronts* (New York: Doran, 1916), p. 85.

3. ———, *The British Campaign in France and Flanders*, 6 Vols. (London: Hodder and Stoughton, 1916–20), I, 8. Hereafter cited as *BC*.

4. The second edition omits one chapter contained in the 1924 version. Hereafter cited as *MA*.

5. ———, *The Vital Message* (New York: Doran, 1919), p. 15. Hereafter cited as *VM*.

6. ———, *Pheneas Speaks* (New York: Doran, 1927), p. 67. Hereafter cited as *PS*.

7. ——— *The Coming of the Fairies* (New York: Doran, 1922), p. 159. Hereafter cited as *CF*.

8. ———, *The History of Spiritualism*, 2 Vols. (New York: Doran, 1926), p. vii. Hereafter cited as *HS*.

Bibliography

1. Works by Arthur Conan Doyle

(Only principal works are listed. There are a number of plays, pamphlets, collections, and editions not identified.)

A Study in Scarlet. London and New York: Ward and Lock, 1888.

Micah Clarke. London: Longmans, Green, 1889.

The Mystery of Cloomber. London: Ward and Downey, 1889.

Mysteries and Adventures. London: Walter Scott, 1889. Reissued under the titles *The Gully of Bluemansdyke* and *My Friend the Murderer*.

The Captain of the Polestar and Other Tales. London: Longmans, Green, 1890.

The Firm of Girdlestone. London: Chatto and Windus, 1890.

The Sign of Four. London: Spencer Blackett, 1890.

The White Company. London: Smith, Elder, 1891.

The Adventures of Sherlock Holmes. London: George Newnes, 1892.

The Doings of Raffles Haw. London: Cassell, 1892.

The Great Shadow and *Beyond the City*. Bristol and London: Arrowsmith/Simpkin, Marshall, 1892.

The Refugees. London: Longmans, Green, 1893.

An Actor's Duel, and *The Winning Shot*. London: John Dicks, 1894.

The Memoirs of Sherlock Holmes. London: George Newnes, 1894.

The Parasite. London: A. Constable, 1894.

Round the Red Lamp, Being Facts and Fancies of Medical Life. London: Methuen, 1894.

The Stark Munro Letters. London: Longmans, Green, 1895.

The Exploits of Brigadier Gerard. London: George Newnes, 1896.

Rodney Stone. London: Smith, Elder, 1896.

Uncle Bernac: A Memory of the Empire. London: Smith, Elder, 1897.

Songs of Action. London: Smith, Elder, 1898.

The Tragedy of the Korosko. London: Smith, Elder, 1898.

A Duet with an Occasional Chorus. London: Grant Richards, 1899.

The Great Boer War. London: Smith, Elder, 1900.

The Green Flag and Other Stories of War and Sport. London: Smith, Elder, 1900.

The Hound of the Baskervilles. London: George Newnes, 1902.

The War in South Africa–Its Cause and Conduct. London: Smith, Elder, 1902.

The Adventures of Gerard. London: George Newnes, 1903.

The Return of Sherlock Holmes. London: George Newnes, 1905.

Sir Nigel. London: Smith, Elder, 1906.

The Croxley Master: A Great Tale of the Prize Ring. London: McClure, Phillips, 1907.

Through the Magic Door. London: Smith, Elder, 1907.

Round the Fire Stories. London: Smith, Elder, 1908.

The Crime of the Congo. London: Hutchinson, 1909.

The Last Galley: Impressions and Tales. London: Smith, Elder, 1911.

Songs of the Road. London: Smith, Elder, 1911.

The Case for Oscar Slater. London: Hodder and Stoughton, 1912.

The Lost World. London: Hodder and Stoughton, 1912.

The Poison Belt. London: Hodder and Stoughton, 1913.

The German War. London: Hodder and Stoughton, 1914.

Great Britain and the Next War. Boston: Small, Maynard, 1914.

The Valley of Fear. London: Smith, Elder, 1915.

The British Campaign in France and Flanders. 6 vols. London: Hodder and Stoughton, 1916–20.

A Visit to Three Fronts. London: Hodder and Stoughton, 1916.

His Last Bow. London: John Murray, 1917.

Danger! and Other Stories. London: John Murray, 1918.

The New Revelation. London: Hodder and Stoughton, 1918.

The Guards Came Through and Other Poems. London: John Murray, 1919.

The Vital Message. London: Hodder and Stoughton, 1919.

The Wanderings of a Spiritualist. London: Hodder and Stoughton, 1921.

The Case for Spirit Photography. London: Hutchinson, 1922.

The Coming of the Fairies. London: Hodder and Stoughton, 1922.

The Poems of Arthur Conan Doyle. London: John Murray, 1922.

Tales of the Ring and Camp. London: John Murray, 1922.

Tales of Pirates and Blue Water. London: John Murray, 1922.

Tales of Terror and Mystery. London: John Murray, 1922.

Tales of Twilight and the Unseen. London: John Murray, 1922.

Tales of Adventure and Medical Life. London: John Murray, 1922.

Tales of Long Ago. London: John Murray, 1922.

Our American Adventure. London: Hodder and Stoughton, 1923.

Three of Them. London: John Murray, 1923.

Memories and Adventures. London: Hodder and Stoughton, 1924.

Our Second American Adventure. London: Hodder and Stoughton, 1924.

The History of Spiritualism. London: Cassell, 1926.

The Land of Mist. London: Hutchinson, 1926.

The Case-Book of Sherlock Holmes. London: John Murray, 1927.

Pheneas Speaks. London: The Psychic Press and Simpkin, Marshall, 1927.

The Maracot Deep. London: John Murray, 1929.

Our African Winter. London: John Murray, 1929.

The Edge of the Unknown. London: John Murray, 1930.

The Field Bazaar: A Sherlock Holmes Pastiche. Summit, N. J.: Pamphlet House, 1947.

2. Works About Arthur Conan Doyle

(Those who wish to read more about Doyle, and particularly those who wish to read more about Holmes and Watson, have a world of materials to review. A 1974 bibliography, for example, lists over 6000 entries. Some of the most important and interesting works are listed here.

Baker, Michael. *The Doyle Diary*. New York and London: Paddington Press, 1978.

Baring-Gould, William S. *The Annotated Sherlock Holmes*. New York: Clarkson N. Potter, 1967.

————. *Sherlock Holmes of Baker Street: A Life of the World's First Consulting Detective*. New York: Clarkson N. Potter, 1962.

Bell, H. W. *Sherlock Holmes and Dr. Watson: The Chronology of their Adventures*. London: Constable, 1932.

Brend, Gavin. *My Dear Holmes, A Study in Sherlock*. London: Allen and Unwin, 1951.

Brown, Ivor. *Conan Doyle*. London: Hamish Hamilton, 1972.

Carr, John Dickson. *The Life of Sir Arthur Conan Doyle*. London: John Murray, 1949.

Christopher, Milbourne. *Houdini: The Untold Story*. New York: Crowell, 1969.

De Waal, Ronald Burt. *The World Bibliography of Sherlock Holmes and Dr. Watson*. New York: Bramhall House, 1974.

Doyle, Adrian Conan and P. Weil-Nordon, eds. *Sir Arthur Conan Doyle, Centenary 1859–1959*. London: John Murray, 1959.

Ernst, B. M. L. and H. Carrington. *Houdini and Conan Doyle: The Story of a Strange Friendship*. New York: Albert and Charles Boni, 1932.

Green, Richard Lancelyn and John Michael Gibson. *A Bibliography of A. Conan Doyle*. Oxford: Clarendon Press, 1983.

Hall, Trevor. *Sherlock Holmes: Ten Literary Studies*. New York: St. Martin's Press, 1969.

Hardwick, Michael and Mollie Hardwick. *The Sherlock Holmes Companion*. London: John Murray, 1962.

————. *The Man Who Was Sherlock Holmes*. London: John

Murray, 1964.

Harrison, Michael. *In the Footsteps of Sherlock Holmes.* London: Cassell, 1958.

———. *The London of Sherlock Holmes.* New York: Drake, 1972.

Higham, Charles. *The Adventures of Conan Doyle.* New York: W. W. Norton, 1976.

Klinefelter, Walter. *Sherlock Holmes in Portrait and Profile.* Syracuse, N. Y.: Syracuse University Press, 1963.

Lamond, John. *Arthur Conan Doyle: A Memoir.* London: John Murray, 1931.

Locke, Harold. *A Bibliographical Catalogue of the Writings of Sir Arthur Conan Doyle.* Tunbridge Wells: D. Webster, 1928.

Nordon, Pierre. *Conan Doyle.* Trans. Frances Partridge. London: John Murray, 1966.

Pearson, Hesketh. *Conan Doyle: His Life and Art.* London: Metheuen, 1943.

Rosenberg, Samuel. *Naked is the Best Disguise.* Indianapolis and New York: Bobbs-Merrill, 1974.

Smith, E. W., ed. *Profile by Gaslight.* New York: Simon and Schuster, 1944.

Starrett, Vincent. *The Private Life of Sherlock Holmes.* New York: Macmillan, 1933.

Warrack, Guy. *Sherlock Holmes and Music.* London: Faber and Faber, 1947.

Index